Building Community in Buildings

The Design and Culture of Dynamic Workplaces

Jana M. Kemp and Ken Baker

Westport, Connecticut
London

Library of Congress Cataloging-in-Publication Data

Kemp, Jana M.
    Building community in buildings : the design and culture of dynamic workplaces / Jana M. Kemp
and Ken Baker.
        p. cm.
    Includes bibliographical references and index.
    ISBN 0–275–99220–9 (alk. paper)
1. Office layout. 2. Work environment. 3. Office buildings. 4. Buildings—Environmental
engineering. 5. Labor productivity. I. Baker, Ken, 1952– II. Title.
HF5547.2.K45 2007
306.3'6—dc22 2006025917

British Library Cataloguing in Publication Data is available.

Library of Congress Catalog Card Number: 2006025917
ISBN: 0–275–99220–9

First published in 2007

Praeger Publishers, 88 Post Road West, Westport, CT 06881
An imprint of Greenwood Publishing Group, Inc.
www.praeger.com

Printed in the United States of America

The paper used in this book complies with the
Permanent Paper Standard issued by the National
Information Standards Organization (Z39.48–1984).

10 9 8 7 6 5 4 3 2 1

Contents

Preface: Where
the Conversation Started

AFTER A DOZEN years of working on the premises that buildings without people do not matter and that people working in buildings need community in a very basic human way, I decided it was time to bring the discussion public. As a result of the fall 2001 interviews with security guards who had worked in the New York City World Trade Towers, I started thinking again about the need for community in our workplaces. What if each company's internal community was so strong that when the security guard said leave, everyone would leave? What if the cross-company community in each tower had been stronger and an agreed-upon plan for evacuation decision making had been in place for the entire building complex?

And this line of thinking and questioning reminded me of working at several corporate headquarter buildings during the 1980s in Minnesota. The difference in the buildings I worked in made it clear to me that long, flat, one-, two-, or three-story buildings created a greater sense of community than tall, narrow, six-story or more buildings. Here is why: People who walk through other work areas have more of an opportunity to get acquainted with each other, to share ideas, and to collaboratively solve problems. People working in two-story buildings are more likely to take the stairs. Some people working in towers walk the stairwell bowels of the building rarely seeing others. More often, people working in towers take the elevator and stare vacantly ahead or at their feet rarely talking to each other. People riding elevators rarely network because the tight physical space creates such a sense of intimacy that they are afraid of interacting with each other. Thus the need to focus on the buildings *and* on the people in order to create a sense of community in which people can

- work well together,
- communicate effectively in crisis,
- creatively problem solve and complete daily work,
- feel inspired to contribute and to achieve more, and
- feel safe and comfortable enough to get to know each other and to collaborate more.

In 2004, wanting to bring the building and people discussion together, I approached Ken Baker whom I had known for about a decade. I asked Ken whether his work in energy, buildings, and work environments included the joint building and people discussion and as I recall, he said "not as often as it should." So began the book you are about to explore.

As Ken and I wrote and managed this project, we discovered that if we had had to trade office spaces, it would have impaired our individual and collective writing productivity. Here is why: I work by seeing things and pictures and paper spread out on flat surfaces—my desk, the conference table, the floor of my office, and sometimes even the floor of my living room. Then with organized thoughts I approach the computer and assimilate and write. Ken on the other hand prefers order and has been visibly unsettled when visiting my office when my brain, if you will indulge the image, is out all over the place in full view.

Back to the World Trade Towers, while we will never know the answers to the World Trade Towers questions, the questions beget others—questions such as the one that is the premise of this book and those that you will find throughout the book. The main premise of this book is that "buildings without people don't matter." The question that follows then is, "What kinds of buildings most inspire creativity and productivity and protect safety and health for the people who work in them?" This is the discussion that follows.

Jana M. Kemp
May 2006

I was born and raised in a small community in rural Nebraska. Our home was small, about 1,600 square feet, but comfortably provided my parents, two brothers, four sisters, and myself with the shelter and space we needed to enjoy a healthy life. Seriously, it was comfortable. Most families I knew lived as we did, in the same size and type of spaces. Even the then common Palladian-style farmhouses that dotted the countryside, as large as they seemed, would be considered a small home today.

Old in 1957, the two-story home I grew up in had six rooms, four of which were bedrooms. The middle of three bedrooms in the upstairs, where all of us kids slept, was also the access to the other two rooms. After leaving my crib and my parents' bedroom sometime around two years of age, I shared the middle upstairs room with my brother. My four sisters enjoyed a small privacy in their rooms with doors but even then they were seldom closed.

In such a small space, sharing and organization were important. We did not have room to spare for errant piles of clothes, papers, or personal items. By today's standards I suppose our belongings were few. I had an oak dresser with a mirror where most of my clothes were kept except for a few nicer shirts and slacks that were hung in a single wardrobe shared by the entire family.

My sense of space and community has grown out of my life experiences as has yours. To this day, I like organization and am somewhere just short of detesting what I consider as clutter. My mind goes all fuzzy when encountered with stacks of papers. I do not mind the piles that accumulate in other people's homes or workspace; as long as I am not expected to work there it is fine by me. But my mind solves problems more easily when the drawing board is clean and the desktop is organized.

Having previously performed facilitation work with my coauthor, Jana Kemp, I know that her working style is highly effective. The first time I co-facilitated a group meeting with her I learned a lot. Her ability to change a process in motion to fit the changing need of the group turned what would have been failure into success. If facilitating alone, I would have faltered because I do not believe I would have been able to bring several hours of clutter developed by the group into focus. Jana could and did. She could detect the patterns in what I perceived was chaos.

So it is good to keep in mind the value of our differences and to honor different working styles as we look to make building spaces more productive. Pairing work skills allows us to see another perspective and take advantage of ideas we would not have caught onto by ourselves. Like Jana, I am interested in the kinds of spaces in our buildings—community, public, and private—that can help us to interact with creativity. We are both interested in the kind of spaces that provide us sustenance and inspire us to get our work done with efficiency and effectiveness, day after day.

Since 1980 my work has been in energy efficiency and integrated design. The first business I created in 1982, Integrated Living Designs, grew out of my understanding of principles of architectural design and psychology. During undergraduate work in psychology and ethnology I was most impressed with the concept of Gestalt that was manifest through psychologist Fritz Perls. The Gestalt, in part, proclaims the whole of something is greater than the sum of its parts. To me, in 1982, this concept fit perfectly with the need to design building systems that responded to people and environment in larger ways than current thinking considered.

Buildings to me are one of the keys to our cultural awareness and practices. Done right, spaces can expand our ability to think and process. Designed poorly, buildings and spaces take from our heart; they literally bleed our energy. Our ability to design and build to reflect and respond to the changing natural environment just seems like a healthier alternative than designing and building an unaware box. It is no coincidence that we are most productive when most healthy.

Ken Baker
May 2006

Acknowledgments

CONTRIBUTORS AND NETWORKERS—Thanks to these building, community, and culture contributors, and the people who have championed, networked, and contributed to this book; you have the book before you.

- AMI Semiconductor, Terri Timberman and Christine King
- Hewlett Packard, Denise Kohtz
- The Longaberger Company, Bonny Fowler and Rose Anzalone
- Northwest Energy Efficiency Alliance and their Better Bricks program
- Pfizer Research and Development, Kevin Wilkins, Michael Mirabito, David Greunke, and Sean Nugent
- Portneuf Medical Center's Cal Notham, Crista Madsen, and especially John Watts, Director of Facility Construction, and Gary Adams, Davis Partnership Architects, for taking time to talk with us about hospital design.
- St. Luke's Children's Hospital, Dr. Jerry Hirschfeld
- Union Pacific, Charlie Clark
- University of Idaho, Living Learning Centers, Michael Griffel
- And: Ernest Lombard, Kevin Graham, Deni Hoehne, Tom Bender, Mary Murray, Robert Vande Merwe, Stan Wakefield, Shauna Wilson, Mike Kaltenecker, Kevin McGowan, Elizabeth Criner, Brad Giles, Mark Olsen, Trish Terranova, Kathi Denton
- Researchers and specialists—without their help, we would be without footnotes and photographs.
- Kevin Van Den Wymenlenberg, Director of the University of Idaho Integrated Design Lab, either provided or coordinated many of the photos used throughout the book. He also assisted with much of the

technical research for the book. We are very grateful to Kevin's invaluable assistance.

- Thanks to those in the building community trenches that daily work toward change in our buildings: Judith Heerwagan, Judith Heerwagen and Associates; Gail Brager, University of California Berkley's Center for the Built Environment; R.J. de Dear; Vivian Loftness, FAIA, Professor of Architecture, Carnegie Mellon University; Carnegie Mellon University Center for Building Performance and Diagnostics; Adrian Leaman and Bill Bordass and the Usable Buildings Trust.
- John Black, Information Architecture in Moscow, Idaho, was our graphic artist and photo layout specialist. As always, John produced superior work.
- Janis Petersen, for coaching on index creation.
- A special thank you to Eric Korte of Laughing Dog Productions, for Ken's cover photograph, and to Peg Owens and Dan Allers who captured Jana's author head shot photograph.
- Project Champion—the man who brought this project to published form! —Nick Philipson—Editor Extraordinaire at Praeger Publishing.

Coauthors:

- Ken has been a dream to work with. Our individual writing time, Ken's photographs, and our collaborative efforts have produced something greater and better than I could have achieved on my own. THANKS.

                                                                    Jana Kemp
- This book was crafted at Jana's suggestion. I can't imagine working on a first book with anyone else. Jana's inspiration guided this process, and I am deeply grateful for the opportunity that she created—to write a book. Thank you.

                                                                    Ken Baker

Introduction: Where
the Conversation Is Going

WE EXPLORE A systematic approach to workplace productivity through the marriage of people and space. The marriage of people to the buildings in which they work is for better or worse, for sicker or poorer. Buildings and the communities within buildings can foster a culture for productivity, health, and creativity. Or they can diminish the well-being of an organization and the individuals within. Consider that in the 1950s the average North American spent approximately 50 percent of his or her time in buildings. A North American child born today will spend 90 percent of his or her life inside. Because of this indoor migration, community culture exists as a result of and in relationship to buildings. *Building Community in Buildings* takes us on a fascinating journey through workplaces large and small, old and new, traditional and contemporary, to explore the dynamic relationships between people and the buildings in which they work. We will integrate insights from corporate culture and organizational behavior on the one hand and architecture, construction, and design on the other to provide a unique perspective on working in buildings in the twenty-first century. We also will explore the degree to which people can influence and be influenced by the physical spaces in which work is conducted. The book includes feature photos, case examples, provocative questions, and an occupant survey so that you can identify strengths and weaknesses in your own organization.

A variety of studies reinforce the positive effects of a healthy workforce on productivity and bottom-line business results. A large factor that can affect this productivity includes the community or culture within the work environment—in particular, the physical space in which people work. Building spaces and the correlated lighting and ventilation systems, views, floor plans (e.g., offices, cubicles, meeting spaces), decorative design, and other physical elements have a profound effect on the work and the development of the individual and subsequent culture.

Building Community in Buildings is divided into three parts of conversation: The Science of Healthy Buildings, The Art of Creating Culture in Towers, and The Science and Art of Increased Productivity in Buildings. The first two parts introduce conversations that are woven together in the third. The Science and Art of Increased Productivity in Buildings marries the conversations and provides conversation checklists and tools that help you ensure a healthy and productive building is built or rebuilt for the people who will work there.

PART I: THE SCIENCE OF HEALTHY BUILDINGS

This part focuses on the history of workplace design in the context of change in architectural materials and environmental design features, the use of electricity, the environmental movement, and architectural sensibilities. A base is formed for the relationship between people and buildings and the natural environment connection, the need for building occupants to have relationship and control with the building, and the precepts of health and productivity.

Chapter 1: A Century of Change

It has been well documented that the twentieth century was one of change, from rural to urban settings and from an agrarian-driven economy to the industrial and information ages and now, some would say, to the service economy or even the molecular economy. Because of changes in energy resources and the availability of cheap electricity, workers went from buildings that were designed for natural ventilation and natural lighting to a mass production of buildings in the 1950s that stood, and to a large part still stand, in defiance of natural systems. In contrast to renowned U.S. architect Louis Sullivan's philosophy that "form follows function," buildings from the mid 1900s on could be built with what was considered a more modern "functional" approach where people and the natural environment were separated for 8 to 10 hours a day while business and production were being pursued. This chapter compares the infrastructure of buildings at the beginning of the twentieth century to those at the beginning of the twenty-first century.

Chapter 2: People, Buildings, and the Natural Environment Connection

Look at any of the old Carnegie libraries and you will see a great example of form that responded to function. The high arched windows allowed light to penetrate into building interiors for reading. Operable windows allowed occupants to control ventilation and cooling. Many of these lessons are now being reviewed and revitalized in the current green building renaissance. This chapter also will look at building trends during the golden age of energy, the downward slide into energy dependency, and the impacts on office workers; in particular, it considers a positive going-forward approach that considers the natural environment-people connection and how it affects physical, intellectual, and social health, and bottom-line economics. A new design term is introduced, human responsive design, that will help building designers and owners, managers and human resource professionals identify those strategies that will affect health and productivity.

PART II: THE ART OF CREATING CULTURE IN TOWERS

This part explores the development of community and organizational culture in relation to place and space. Strategies from major corporations, residential communities, and small businesses are presented so that any organization can focus on conscientious creation of community and culture in their workplaces and towers.

Chapter 3: Workplace Lessons from Working and Living in Towers

Once a building passes the two-story mark, people start getting onto elevators and stop walking past others, which means that the human connection is lost and the potential for creativity is diminished. Unless structures for human interaction are built into each day, people and buildings become barriers to each other. The discussion will include examples from Fortune 500 companies and other best places to work as well as stories and lessons from residential communities—such as nursing homes, apartments, and planned neighborhoods—and from social enterprises—such as churches, libraries, and neighborhood gyms.

Chapter 4: Turn of the Twenty-first-Century Workplace Communities

From working at all times of the day and night to working in virtual teams spread out all over the globe, our world of work has brought new challenges. Beyond the physical dimensions of our workspaces, organizations are now created around "communities of interest": like-minded people who seek each other out, regardless of the physical boundaries. This chapter looks at the ways in which social community and physical place interact, how distal work occurs, and how online communities form. Discussions of organizational design, such as docking stations and video conferencing, also can be found here.

PART III: THE SCIENCE AND ART OF INCREASED PRODUCTIVITY IN BUILDINGS

This part weaves together the elements and discussions of the first two parts, making recommendations for the creation of more productive workspaces.

Chapter 5: Building Mindfulness and the Humanization of Buildings

Mindfulness is the practice of being present, focused, meditative, and connected. This chapter will look at how a "mindful" orientation on the part of the office worker can increase productivity and efficiency and add value to the work culture. The chapter makes the case for building spaces that make human-scale connections possible. Consider, for example, play spaces, gardens, coffee bars, lounging areas, and other design elements that encourage spontaneous, informal interaction, as well as offices and meeting rooms designed to promote privacy.

Chapter 6: The Productivity Variables of Buildings and People

What are the productivity variables within building types? What is the impact of the shape and configuration of the building on the work force and how does this differ for the work and learning styles of employees? We know that an engaged and motivated work force makes money; this chapter presents several case studies that show the successful application of human responsive design in combination with human resource development and discusses six productivity variables—health, safety and security, comfort and control, community, rewards, and creativity and morale—and how they are affected by building design.

Chapter 7: How to Build Buildings for Productive People

A marriage is most functional when both partners bring something to the relationship—not just one time, but again and again. The building and physical space also play a role in the relationship. If people are to spend a third of their working lives in union with space and people, what can be done to ensure that there is ongoing growth and satisfaction? This chapter explores the roles that business owners, leaders, and managers can employ to create positive, productive, and profitable workplaces that promote both individual and organizational well-being. It also offers practical solutions to the issues highlighted throughout the book's chapters.

CONTINUING THE CONVERSATION—WORK ENVIRONMENT COMMUNITIES AND SOME DEFINING TERMS

Conversations, just as buildings, require firm and agreed-upon foundations before successful structural, cultural, community, and individual working relationships can be built. In the conversations explored in *Building Community in Buildings*, the key terms are building, build, community, and culture.

Just as an architect or engineer needs to know what is wanted in a building, he also needs to know what is not to be incorporated. The definitions that follow are drawn from *Merriam-Webster's Collegiate Dictionary*, tenth edition, and are expanded upon as relevant to this book.

Building—Noun

A building is a place. It may be a single room, a few large rooms with cubicles, dozens of rooms, or thousands of rooms and spaces configured into a tower. For the purpose of this book, buildings are those structures where people are the main occupants or users as they go about the daily activities of work. According to *Merriam-Webster's*, a building is

1. "Usually a roofed and walled structure built for permanent use." This is the base definition for building that will be used in this book.
2. "The art or business of assembling materials into a structure." For instance, the building and construction trades.

Build—Verb

The act of building comes from the verb build. The actions associated with building buildings, building community, expanding and maintaining culture can all be discussed in such phrases as "we are focused on building a workplace community that allows us to be more innovative and productive."

According to *Merriam-Webster's*, to build is to

1. "Form by ordering and uniting materials by gradual means into a composite whole." This mindful, organized, and gradual approach to accomplish a complete unit or a complete set of behaviors and interactions is where the chapter discussions that follow will lead.
2. "Cause to be constructed." This definition carries the implication that actions are occurring in a manner that allows something to be

constructed, to be completed for use. This definition will apply to the conversations ahead as well.

3. "Develop according to a systematic plan by a definite process or on a particular base." This definition applies to the discussion of the entire book and especially Chapters 6 and 7 where we will bring together the questions you may ask internally and ask of all potential vendors, architects, engineers, and landscape architects working on your buildings.

4. "Increase, enlarge. For instance, to 'build your profits.'" Indeed, this book is equally about building healthy workplaces, productivity, creativity, and all around well-being so that profitability and continuity for the organization are ensured.

In its verb form, building is the ongoing act of forming, causing, and developing an enlarged, composite whole. The discussion in this book is about the uniting of materials and of people's needs in such a way that a better-than-ever construction of buildings occurs for the greatest productivity, creativity, and health of the people working, visiting, and transacting business in the buildings.

Community—Noun

What community do you live in? What is your sense of community where you work? Do your children have a sense of community where you live? These are common questions in weekly conversation. What is less commonly discussed is one of the key questions of this book: "What is the sense of community you and your fellow employees have in your workplace, and how is that community grown and refined?"

Merriam-Webster's defines community as "1. a unified body of individuals as: a. a state, commonwealth, b. the people with common interests living in a particular area, the area itself, c. an interacting population of various kinds of individuals in a common location, d. a group of people with a common characteristic or interest living together within a larger society, e. a group linked by a common policy, f. a body of persons or nations having a common history of common social, economic and political interests, g. a body of persons of common and especially professional interest scattered through a larger society."

Community in *Building Community in Buildings* is collectively the definitions found in 1.b, 1.c, 1.d, and 1.e above. A community is a group of people in one workplace or working for one organization in multiple locations. A community also is made up of people who have shared interests within their organization of employment and may include people who work in like professions yet work for different companies. The explanation in 1.e, "a group linked by a common policy," by definition makes everyone working for the same company or organization a part of a community whether or not it is acknowledged, recognized, or appreciated.

The other definitions for community that apply to the discussions of this book are "3.a. joint ownership or participation, b. common character: likeness, c. social activity: fellowship, d. a social state or condition." Of these definitions, 3.a is most relevant because along with the key question about what someone's sense of community in their workplace is, is the two-pronged question of "What ownership do you feel for that community and how do you participate in your workplace community?"

Sometimes people use the word community and culture interchangeably. In this book, each word carries its own meaning. Community will be used to mean the group of people within a business, corporation, agency or association that is charged to work together in the creation of work products or process.

Culture

In the conversations of *Building Community in Buildings*, the term culture is used as a noun. Culture will be used to mean the work force attributes assigned or developed as a result of working in community.

Merriam-Webster's lists six definition groups for "culture." Interestingly, the definition most applicable in this book's conversation is the fifth definition, where culture is defined as "5.a. the integrated pattern of human knowledge, belief, and behavior that depends upon man's capacity for learning and transmitting knowledge to succeeding generations." In this case, to succeeding employees who will work for an organization in the generations of the organization's life.

"5.b. the customary beliefs, social forms, and material traits of a racial, religious, or social group." Every company and organization can be considered both a workplace and a social group. As such every organization has unwritten—and many companies have written—beliefs, values, and social norms that guide the decision making and behavior of the organization and the individuals in it. The next definition states this again in a different way.

"5.c. the set of shared attitudes, values, goals and practices that characterizes a company or corporation." Think of the organizations that are known for "innovation," "problem solving," "having fun," and "being the best." These well-known characterizations are often a part of both the employee workplace culture and the branding used in marketing a company. The focus here is on workplace culture.

Here is one more definition that may be helpful. When writing her first book, Jana discovered that the word meeting was first used in the 1300s to describe a fox hunt. Think "track meet" which we still use today. In other words, a meeting is a coming together for a clear purpose. The purpose may be social, activity, or task related. So, every time a meeting is held, a community of sorts is formed. That community formed in a meeting may last for the length of the meeting, the length of a project, or for months and years.

The main concern of all this defining is that conversations require agreed-upon foundations before successful structural, cultural, individual, community, and working relationships can be built. Definitions for a book matter in the way that blueprints matter for a building. The end goal for this book's existence is for it to serve as a conversation starter that helps individuals, executives, managers, owners, team managers, architects, engineers, building managers, project foremen, and anyone wanting to be engaged in the conversation to be able to successfully communicate and interact with each other in order to effectively build community in buildings.

CONCLUSION

Drawing on over three calendar decades of our attention, observation, and mindfulness about people and their relationships, interactions, and culture as they work in buildings, this book brings the architectural discussions and the human working behavior discussions that until now have largely been independently discussed with only paragraphs, or a chapter referring one to the other. As early as 1995, Jana asked her clients, "Are your meeting rooms dead or alive?" The response was that progress was being made in company meeting rooms across the country and yet the meetings happening were still largely seen as being a waste of time and even deadening. What follows is an article adapted from her *Better Meetings for Everyone Newsletter* and republished in several training and development newsletters and magazines over a two-year period. It begins with this question: "Have you ever felt like the participants in a *Farside* cartoon where the walls of the meeting room are decorated with spikes that close in on participants as the meeting wears on?"

Rooms that give you this feeling of being trapped are dead rooms. Alive meeting rooms on the other hand, make you feel comfortable and ready to interact to accomplish work as soon as you enter. Picture for a minute the living room in your home. What is in it? Why did you decide to include the items in the room? What environment did you create to make your family, friends, and guests feel welcome and alive? Just like the living rooms in our homes, companies can consciously design rooms that encourage guests to engage in accomplishing the purposes that brought people into the meeting rooms in the first place. Why do people meet and come to work in buildings? To solve problems, generate ideas, share information, instruct, address moments of crisis, update each other, sell ideas, ask for help, and more.

With meeting purposes like these, what environment would encourage accomplishment of meeting room guests? Probably an environment similar to your living room. One that invites people to talk, to listen, to share ideas, to ask questions, to tell stories, and to leave the room feeling like they would really like to stay longer, or at the very least like to visit again.

With these thoughts in mind, what would the "alive" meeting room environment look like? Following is the beginning of a list to help you assess your meeting rooms and remodel them into living meeting rooms. See Chapter 7 of this book for more checklists. Include the items on the Alive Room list to create an environment where people can work together to accomplish their meeting purposes, clean up after themselves, and leave the room looking forward to the next meeting or the next day of work.

Dead Room—things to avoid:

- White walls
- No windows
- Light that is patchy, too dim, all on or all off without variable dimming options
- Visual equipment and tools not in the room or not even available
- Folding chairs
- Granite tables or any table too heavy to move so the room can be versatile
- No places to deposit trash or to recycle

Alive Room—things to incorporate:

- Walls with color, texture, pictures, posters, whiteboards
- Windows—or pictures of the outdoors
- Lighting that is evenly bright throughout the room, is controllable in parts, and has a dimmer switch so that you can still have the lights on while you are showing slides, overheads, or computer images
- Visual equipment that is available: flip charts, markers, whiteboards, overhead projectors, computers, screens
- Ergonomic chairs—contoured, upholstered seat and back, adjustable seat height and backrests, lumbar support, five-star base for stability, and dual-wheel self-braking casters for easy movement
- Sturdy, yet lightweight tables that can be moved by one person
- Trash cans large enough for the amount of trash generated in the room during one day and recycling centers for paper, beverage cans, and cardboard

Building Community in Buildings is about the integrated discussions of people working productively and healthfully in buildings that meet human needs. In fact, while working on the early stages of the book outline, Jana and Ken discovered that the acronym HRD tied to both bodies of work exemplifying the married discussions. Human resource development (HRD) has long been the phrase used to describe a focus on improving workplace human behavior, skills, knowledge, attitudes, and abilities so that increased productivity and problem solving and improved team and customer relations, as well as increased bottom-lines, follow. Human responsive design (HRD) is a process of building design and subsequent actions that provides for considerations of passive strategies for lighting, ventilation, and air-conditioning and provides an element of occupant control of these strategies within the interior building environment. Together, human resources development and human responsive design create the HRD^2 acronym.

This book is designed to be an interactive reference for readers and everyone you work with when building communities in buildings. You are wholeheartedly invited to take action to increase your and your employees' health, sense of belonging, and productivity within your workspace to bring positive change to your building environment and culture. If you are a building owner or manager of people within an office space, this book will help you to understand and successfully apply a set of actions that will change worker health and productivity. For individuals, this book offers an opportunity to have a participatory voice in the physical layout and control of your space. At the very least, it offers everyone the opportunity to develop and practice a mindful approach to work, thus reaping greater satisfaction from your day-to-day and moment-to-moment activities in buildings.

Part I: The Science of Healthy Buildings

THIS SECTION FOCUSES on the history of workplaces in the context of change in architectural materials and environmental design features, the use of electricity, the environmental movement, and architectural sensibilities. A base for the relationship between people and buildings, the need for building occupants to have a relationship with and control of the building, and the precepts of health and productivity are established.

1 / A Century of Change

ALMOST ANYWHERE YOU sit these days, whether in an airport, a coffee shop, your office, or workspace, you can see the evolution from what was to what is. The older you are the more pronounced the changes possibly seem. The world and society have shifted. Thirty and forty years ago most of the world's middle class worked in factories and industrial jobs, and our workmates lived in our neighborhoods. We knew them at work and we knew their spouses and children and pets all by name. Children walked to the same schools together and played together at home and on teams at school. We shared neighborhood-centric values because we lived them shoulder-to-shoulder in our neighborhoods. We understood what our ancestors and theirs understood intrinsically: that building community together made the whole of the human experience better.

During the twentieth century, the populace in transitional economies such as Western Europe and the United States moved from field and factory work into office environments that expanded in the 1950s and on through the end of the century. Population density and land values shifted over the century, concentrating people and real estate value into cities and towers. Towers became places of both office-oriented work and year-round living. *Building Community in Buildings* is about the exploration of the dynamic relationship between people and the buildings they work in and the community that gets created in these buildings. In workplace buildings and towers, people want and need soulful connections to themselves and others as well as to their work. People want group space and individual space, accessible and healthy space, and space that supports thinking, being present, and being focused on and productive with the work at hand.

At the start of the twenty-first century, people walk about perpetually in headsets, earpieces, and cones of silence not interacting with their immediate community members. In fact, these zones of self-imposed solitude are impeding the formation of community that formed organically when we stood next to each other in line at the post office, sat next to each other waiting to get on a plane, or jostled along together on the commuting bus or train system from home into work and back. Community-building interactions are also increasingly limited at grocery stores and gas stations where now, rather than interacting directly with a cashier we use a self-checkout machine that only requires human interaction when the machine is malfunctioning. In all of our places of work, machinery interferes with our ability to connect with other human beings. Computers at work allow us to e-mail the person in the next cubicle workspace without getting up to talk, generate ideas, think, or problem solve together in live time.

A community forms only when people interact, share ideas, solve problems, and converse with each other. In other words, community is made of the human connections, face-to-face or over distance, that convey common interests, goals, achievements, and even common hopes and dreams. The United States has largely exported industrial jobs and is now more office based in its work endeavors. Professional technical jobs such as plumbing, auto repair, electrical, and construction remain tied to locations as do hands-on craftsmanship oriented jobs. These are the jobs that we will not wait for someone in a distant location to complete. Additionally, all of the jobs that are location dependent require workplaces with the right tools, equipment, and built environments that meet the needs of the people working there.

So, very simply, we reiterate the premises for *Building Community in Buildings*. First, when in community, we are most creative and most productive. Community provides a structure from which human relationships are built—and ultimately our work productivity is too. Another way to say this is that when work truly comes from the community, the community takes responsibility for the work.

If an office manager can support the development of a healthy community among the working staff, good work products will be an outcome. Productivity will go up. Second, the building space plays a major role in the type and quality of community we can develop in our work environments with our co-workers. We believe that on a very basic level we each long to run through the savannah in pursuit of the day's meal and in the evening to sit in close circles around the community fire telling our tribesmen stories of the hunt. In essence, the more connected our buildings are with the outdoors and the changing climatic activity, the healthier and more energetic human beings feel, and the more people will connect with one another.

Third, building systems have a direct impact on the development of the community in buildings. Building mechanical systems, lighting, windows, color schemes and textures, furnishings, and layout all play a role in our acceptance of space and our ultimate physiological and psychological comfort within that space. The more that the building operates as a whole and the more systems are designed and built to interact, the easier it will be for building occupants to integrate healthfully and productively into the building.

EVOLUTIONS IN PEOPLE'S USE OF BUILDINGS

The evolution of building materials is as varied as the climates, geology, and geography of the sites of the built structures. However, there is one constant material that has been utilized worldwide since the transition of nomadic Cro-Magnon man to agrarian society—earth. In 1982 when Ken wrote his masters thesis in architecture, he was surprised to find that a full 90 percent of the world's population continued to live in some form of earthen structure. Consider that brick, mud, daub, rammed earth, adobe are all construction methods that use soil as the primary ingredient.

Other natural based materials continue to be utilized as well. Thatch, made from native vegetation such as reeds, grasses, palm fronds, bamboo, and straw, is still being utilized—since the Middle Ages—and is still used for roofing around the world. In fact, depending on the vegetation used, a good thatch roof can last 60 to 80 years if properly maintained. Wood and stone are other examples of materials that are native to most world geographies and their use and complexity of use evolved with the needs of particular cultures.

Originally, built structures served as shelter for living in inclement weather and for sleeping. Then, permanent building structures arrived on the landscape to provide shelter, housing, and occasionally places to work. Most work was accomplished outside in daylight hours. Not long after, grand buildings for worship and built theater structures for entertainment were painstakingly built. Some of the first indoor workplaces (4000 B.C. to 800 B.C.) include monasteries, city centers and halls of government, and tradespaces such as blacksmithing and spinning that needed a roof to work in all seasons. Some of the world's greatest and best-known architecture was built long before electricity. This same architecture was built around communities— communities of entertainment, worship, and occasionally workplaces and education.

Take the Coliseum of Rome. It brought communities from city and country locations together in a new community of entertainment and celebration. Today, sports stadiums from Munich, Germany, to Sydney, Australia, and from the Indianapolis Speedway built in 1909 in Indiana (which seats

250,000 people) to the Shanghai International Circuit racetrack built in 2004 in Shanghai, China, bring people together in communities. These spectator communities last for a few hours, or a few hours of every event if you sit with the same people game after game or race after race. In ancient times as well as today, the structure, timing, rules of play, and known players, gladiators, riders, and drivers create a sense of order for people whose daily lives may be very stressful, chaotic, and uncertain.

Consider too the amazing places of worship from around the world that still inspire awe and hopefulness in our lives. Notable and recognized houses of worship, which are also places of work and study, include Notre Dame in Paris, France; Canterbury Cathedral in England; Dome of the Rock mosque in Jerusalem built in 691–692; Hagia Sophia Church in Istanbul (originally Constantinople), Turkey, built in 537 with minarets added in 1453 when Hagia Sophia became a mosque; and the Sistine Chapel built between 1475 and 1483 in Vatican City, Italy. Buildings built hundreds and even thousands of years ago are still standing.

And what of our buildings today? How long do you think they are built to last: 100 years, 80, 50? If you have ever sat in on a design committee meeting for a new building you may know the answer is more likely 30 years. It is true. Many new buildings are designed to last for only 30 years! That means that within one person's lifetime, a building would have to be replaced two or three more times, or more likely undergo a major remodel including the replacement of mechanical, electrical and control systems; and possibly windows, roof systems, siding, flooring, and so on. Even many public buildings, such as libraries, school, and university buildings, are designed and built to last for only 30 years. Does this not seem like an incredible waste? This is our new disposable building mentality where initial costs win over the more appropriate long-term view of life-cycle cost analysis.

But when one considers the life-cycle costs of operating and maintaining a building, it just makes good sense to buy the best quality materials and systems available. It also makes sense to use nonmechanical strategies such as daylighting and natural ventilation for lighting, heating, and cooling because they become part of the building's structure (for example light shelves, overhangs, operable windows, thermal mass) and are not as subject to failure due to age and use; and they are not subject to replacement because the technology of the system or product has improved. Data gathered by Carnegie Mellon University supports that the initial design and construction represents only 2 percent of a new office building's 30-year life-cycle cost, while ongoing operation and maintenance represents 6 percent.[1] There is every reason to consider life-cycle costing for your building, whether it is a new design or whether you are considering a remodel, because it is the only way to fully understand the choices you are making.

While touring a U.S. Air Force base, Jana discovered that personnel housing is built on a 50-year model. In other words, the housing must last 50 years before being replaced. The Presidio complex, which was first used for military purposes in 1776 under the Spanish flag, is in San Francisco, California. Over the years it has been used as a military post, a park, and even as a business park complex. In 1994 the Presidio became part of the Golden Gate National Recreation Area, and in the twenty-first century, businesses such as Lucasfilm set up their offices and world headquarters in the Park. The point is that a great site typically endures as a great site for buildings and human community building.

Purpose Makes the Difference

An indoor climbing wall is safe in any weather as compared to a naturally occurring outdoor rock face. Purpose and design is the difference: one is man-made for recreation, and mankind, for his enjoyment, appropriates the other. Another way of discussing that purpose and design make the difference is that the same materials make prisons as make cathedrals. People desire to use buildings in different ways: sometimes to inspire and other times to punish; sometimes to glorify and other times to demean. Take for instance the building material of concrete. Romans started using cement in buildings and paving over 2000 years ago. Now, a prison, a memorial, a cathedral, a courthouse, a home, a building or a school can all be built from concrete. Modern cement materials include a transparent concrete created by Aron Losonczi, a Hungarian architect. Losonczi mixes fiber optic glass and concrete for a product he calls Litracon (for more information, visit www.litracon.hu). As strong as regular concrete, Litracon can be used for walls, floors, or sculptures.

Twentieth-Century Transitions

The accomplishment of work moved largely indoors during the industrial revolution. Of course, fields in agricultural and landscaping will always have portions of their industries in outdoor work environments. Once the trades and guild work moved indoors, however, manufacturing sprung up in buildings, and office work in support of manufacturing grew indoors too. Furthermore, with the advent of electric candles and light bulbs, work could occur indoors in rooms without windows all day and all night. Beginning in the late 1800s in large urban areas, the ability to work all 24 hours a day existed, but the culture did not move to the 24-hours-a-day/7-days-a-week known as the "24/7" pursuit of productivity until the 1980s and 1990s. From indoor education and office work, workplaces have moved to include indoor exploratory, research, and creative work. By the 1930s, people were working more hours year round because of electricity: production plants and offices could be lit consistently 24 hours a day 7 days a week. Back then, the drive to run a business all hours of every day was actually less than the super-connected cell-phone-attached world of today.

While many think that the baby boomer generation originated the focus on healthy buildings, it really began centuries ago when issues of personal hygiene clearly were creating unhealthy living environments. Workers in buildings at the end of the 1800s began taking notice of health—healthy air, healthy and productive people, navigable stairwells for wheelchairs, and natural lighting that allowed detail work to be done indoors.

Today, most mature market economies have outsourced blue-collar jobs to countries or regions where labor is cheap by comparison (emerging or transitional economies) and products can be manufactured in greater quantities for less cost. Our living environment, neighborhoods, and communities have changed as a result of this shift from industrial to information economies. In just over two generations, much of the world has gone from neighborhoods and communities where we all knew each other to urban subdivisions that are in many ways culturally sterile with fences keeping us cloistered at home and cubicle walls dividing us at work with limited options of community space. In an information economy, we are all too busy catching up with our day-to-day work priorities to take time to know families that are two or three houses away. Yet we secretly crave the security of community, for ourselves and for our children.

For many, perhaps even most of us in mature market economies, communities no longer emerge from the neighborhood. Community manifests itself not in the front yard while out talking with neighbors, but in the buildings where we daily work. And more, community is created in the after-hours buildings where we exercise, socialize, and play. The office building has become our new neighborhood. The winding pathways surrounding our cubicles have become the streetways we most frequently walk. The relationships and the sense of community we build at work can provide a necessary social structure and support system that keep us healthy and give our lives value.

Change in the Workplace Environment

During the last 100 years, building architecture has changed considerably. Materials and resources that were used for building construction in 1900, for example, were more locally based because our systems for transportation and delivery were not yet mature enough to move large quantities of materials. Localized quarries for mining stone were common where stone was available and it was uncommon for stone to be shipped long distances except for use in high-profile buildings. Even rural areas with small populations could support brick-making operations, and many of the public buildings—such as libraries, city and county buildings, and schools—were constructed of either brick or stone.

When available, wood was used for both public and private buildings. Wood holds up well when structure and joints are connected well and when moisture and insects are kept at bay. In the Eastern United States, immigrants from Europe built timber frame buildings that, 300 to 400 years later, continue to provide function and service. Beautiful old framed buildings such as the wood and brick Maryland Statehouse in Annapolis, Maryland, attests to longevity of wood in structures. Unfortunately, as subsequent generations (the American pioneers) moved westward, many of the timber frame methodologies lost some of the detailing that made them lasting structures, as can be attested by looking at the many dilapidated and sagging barns sitting in western farm yards.

High-rise buildings, those exceeding 12 stories, first appeared in the 1880s but were rare outside of the most populated cities until about the mid-twentieth century. Though architecturally significant, they were and currently are a minority of the total commercial building stock. For the purpose of this book, the materials that comprise skyscrapers and their building systems will not be the focus. Instead the focus is on the built workplace environment and how we can create communities in these workplace buildings. What is presented here is the story of human migration into buildings as workspace environments. The subsequent evolution from natural systems of heating, cooling, and lighting, to electric and fuel-based systems has a consequent impact on building culture and on business development.

THE EVOLUTION OF BUILDING SYSTEMS

Building Examples from the Early Twentieth Century

While researching the changes in architecture over the past century, Jana and Ken looked to two historical buildings for reference: The National Building Museum, in Washington, D.C., and the Idaho State Capitol building. Both are representative of U.S. public-building period architecture and both were designed to utilize strategies for lighting and ventilation that predated total reliance on electricity.

The National Building Museum

This 1880s building, originally designed to house the U.S. Pension Bureau, is now the National Building Museum of U.S. architecture.[2] Created by an act

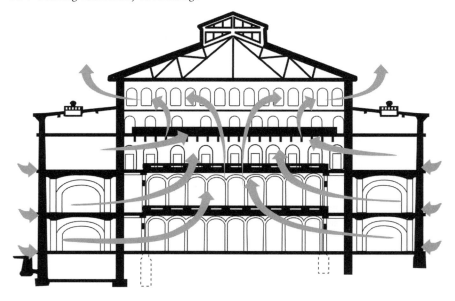

Figure 1.1 Airflow patterns in the National Building Museum (graphic reproduction by John Black Design).

of Congress in 1980, its sole purpose is to celebrate the American building culture. Jana had occasion to visit the Washington, D.C., building during 2005. She returned with a story that is fascinating and closely aligned with our intent to acquaint the reader with nonmechanical design strategies for building lighting and ventilation.

The National Building Museum was designed and engineered by Montgomery C. Meigs, a civil engineer and former Quartermaster General for the U.S. Army. The General enjoyed a long and quite distinguished career in military and public service. The National Building Museum (pensioner's building) was his finest and final building design.

The Italian renaissance design has many classic Greek architectural features such as Corinthian columns that support the great interior hall and a terra-cotta frieze that wraps the building's exterior. Thick brick walls support the 159-ft. height of the building and also provide a cooling mass for the building's interior space. Windows are numerous throughout the exterior façade, as are air vents, and skylights in the roof provide both natural light and natural ventilation and cool air to wash the building's interior. A description on the National Building Museum web site indicates that this strategy "allows the Great Hall to function as a reservoir of light and air."

Two strategies were used for building ventilation. All offices were without doors and open to the 15-story great central hall. Air would enter through office windows and be drawn convectively into the hall and up and out the top story windows. Also, on the office level, three bricks under each window were eliminated to allow air to enter behind each room's radiator, warming winter air as it entered the occupied space. The natural air distribution system worked very well. It was documented that the entire air volume of the building could be replaced with outside air in about two minutes under the right conditions. Without electricity, machinery, or fans, the building's design kept air flowing and people's health at an all-time high level of well-being.

It is interesting to note that the natural lighting and airflow were intentional. Meigs sought to design and build an environment that would be healthful for the occupants with office spaces surrounding the exterior building perimeter so that light and air were available to all workspaces. This was in direct contrast to office environments of the day that are described as being "dark stuffy rooms, lit by gaslight if at all, were reached by long, dark corridors with no sources of ventilation."[3] The building was almost fully occupied by 1886. In that year's annual report, Meigs noted that the building's systems for ventilation and light had reduced sickness among employees by 8,622 days.

The Idaho State Capitol Building

As a first-term state legislator, Jana made another exciting building discovery in 2005. The Idaho State Capitol building, begun in 1905 and completed between 1912 and 1920, incorporated a number of strategies to make it adaptive to the natural environment and to provide occupants with a healthy workspace.[4]

Native sandstone was mined within three miles of the building site, and although marbles for wainscoting and hardwoods for flooring were imported, the bulk of the structural materials included in the building were local based. Architect J.E. Tourtellotte wanted the building to integrate as much as possible with the natural surroundings and so the colors of the exterior sandstone were chosen to closely match the surrounding high desert landscape. Original floors in the Senate and House were made of cork, a product that today is making a comeback because of its durability, nontoxicity, and sustainable qualities.

Although building designer Tourtellotte took great pride in the application of fully mechanical heating, and ventilation of the building and in the use of electric lighting to literally flood the interior and exterior space during nondaylight hours, he also recognized the health benefits of natural lighting and ventilation. Tourtellotte, in a short 1913 essay on the Capitol project, describes the natural lighting of the building to be "...nearer perfect...than any building of its kind perhaps in the world." The people on the Capitol Commission in 1905 visited capitols from Ohio to Georgia to Colorado in an effort to guide the Idaho Capitol building's design. One particular comment of the group was that the Georgia statehouse had poor lighting that "dampened the Capitol's architectural strengths."

In Idaho, skylights were used to illuminate the fourth floor rotunda and a concentric circle of windows lighted the Capitol's dome during daylight hours. Perhaps the most innovative strategy is the light wells that brought daylight from the fourth story to the basement level of the building. There are four light and air shafts in the center interior of the building, two on the east and two on the west side of the Capitol's rotunda. The shafts were used for natural ventilation of the building and each floor level had windows that opened to the internal shaft, thus driving a nonmechanical convective ventilation system. By the time of the 1999 renovation, these shafts had been put to use carrying electrical conduits, telecommunication cables, and ductwork between floors. Electricity usurped natural light. Fortunately, they are being restored to their original use as recommended by the 2000 Idaho Capitol Commission.

Buildings Create Environment

As architects Meigs and Tourtellotte seemed well aware, the built environment affects our perceptions of our world, affects our ability to pursue work and pleasure, and has the power to give us health or illness. Famous concert halls such as the I.M. Pei designed Morton H. Meyerson Symphony Center in Dallas, Texas, and the Sydney Opera House in Australia come to mind here because of their ability to move and reverberate, echo and amplify sound. Heating, ventilating, and air-conditioning (HVAC) systems supply ventilation air and temperature control; windows, doors, walls, wall coverings, and furniture affect the quality of air we breathe in a building. That is important to us because humans breathe, teams breathe, and organizational cultures breathe. Siemens Corporation in one of its 2003 advertisements led with this headline: "A building is no longer just a place you do business. It's a silent partner." This is true because the air we breathe, the floors we walk, the cubicles we navigate are silent and yet clearly affect the well-being of workers.

Sick buildings create sick people. Some reports indicate that asthma cases increased by 75 percent in the 25-year period after 1980. Each year, more and more children are affected by breathing disorders and asthma. The American Lung Association reported in 2005 that "asthma is the most common chronic disorder in childhood," and that "it currently affects 6.2 million children under 18 years." It has become almost epidemic with 1 out of 10 American children suffering from asthma. We do not conclusively know the full contribution of buildings to asthma in children but studies have shown that moisture and mold in classrooms correlate with elevated levels of asthma. In fact a small inquiry on the National Library of Medicine and National Institutes of Health web site generated 87 professional citations that show a relationship to building air quality and lung disorders.[5]

Sick buildings can affect health quickly. For instance, while writing this book, on two consecutive Fridays, Jana was at client sites. The first Friday, after an elevator ride up four floors, she sat down for a client meeting and began coughing to the point of asking for water to drink. Now, there was no problem with her health when she entered the six-year-old building. Something that was in the circulating air caused the coughing attack. The following Friday, in a 100-year-old stone office building basement for a meeting, another coughing attack occurred. This time, the employees of the building said "yes, this old building seems to have an effect on people." How healthy are your buildings?

The U.S. Environmental Health Center lists the following as contributing factors of SBS (sick building syndrome):

- Chemical contaminants from outdoor sources: Outdoor air that enters a building can also be a source of indoor pollution. Pollutants from motor vehicle exhausts, plumbing vents, and building exhausts (bathrooms and kitchens) can enter the building through poorly located air intake vents, windows, and other openings. Combustion byproducts can also enter a building from a nearby garage.
- Chemical contaminants from indoor sources: Most indoor air pollution comes from sources inside the building. For example, adhesives, upholstery, carpeting, copy machines, manufactured wood products, cleaning agents and pesticides may emit volatile organic compounds (VOCs) including formaldehyde. Research shows that some VOCs can cause chronic and acute health effects at high concentrations, and some are known carcinogens. Low to moderate levels of multiple VOCs may also produce acute reactions in some individuals. Environmental tobacco smoke and combustion products from stoves, fireplaces, and unvented space heaters all can put chemical contaminants into the air. VOCs also can come from synthetic fragrances in personal care products or in cleaning and maintenance products.
- Biological contaminants: Biological contaminants include pollen, bacteria, viruses, and molds. These contaminants can breed in stagnant water that has accumulated in humidifiers, drain pans, and ducts, or where water has collected on ceiling tiles, insulation, or carpet. Biological contaminants can cause fever, chills, cough, chest tightness, muscle aches, and allergic reactions. One indoor air bacterium, Legionella, has caused both Pontiac fever and Legionnaire's disease.
- Inadequate ventilation: In the 1970s the oil embargo led building designers to make buildings more airtight, with less outdoor air

ventilation, in order to improve energy efficiency. These reduced ventilation rates have been found to be, in many cases, inadequate to maintain the health and comfort of building occupants.

SBS is not a new issue. Off and on over the last hundred years, architects and building owners have considered the effects of buildings on the health and productivity of building occupants.

WORLD WAR II—LARGEST TRAINING EFFORT EVER

World War II brought the largest training effort in modern history. Men were at war and women moved en masse into the workforce. Military and workforce training happened at a pace unseen in the past. Electricity, communication technology, aircraft changes, and bomb availability changed the pacing and the results of battles and of the overall war. While military training was in full swing, entire U.S. bases were built for training purposes and some were torn down within three years. Private sector training was at an all time high volume and carried high urgency. The jobs vacated by men at war were being filled with women and men that had not held manufacturing and industrial jobs before. "Rosie the Riveter" was born in this era. Nearly everyone was being trained and prepared to do new jobs. The culture of work was forever changed in this era.

Once the war was over, military personnel returned to jobs filled by others. In order to create more jobs and in an effort to create jobs for everyone now prepared to work and used to working, one could say that large-scale office work was born to support manufacturing work and to provide jobs. More than half a century of men and women working side by side in both indoor and outdoor workplaces has changed workspace dramatically. For instance, at the Idaho Capitol and others around the world, more women in the workplace meant a need for more women's rest rooms on each floor of a building.

The volume of desk work during these decades also created new workspace demands for light, ergonomic furniture, and healthy air circulation. At the same time, people's use of workplaces were changing, and Abraham Maslow was hypothesizing about how people are motivated and behaving to make decisions, both on their own and in relation to others.

1940s Maslow's Hierarchy and How It Relates to Buildings

Originally published in 1943 by Abraham Maslow in a paper titled "A Theory of Human Motivation," Maslow's Hierarchy is based on several propositions. Maslow's 13 human motivation conclusions included that evolving human needs appear only after the prior satisfaction of any more basic needs having been met, which means that until the need for food is met, a need to be liked will not get attention. Maslow also believed that "motivation theory should be human centered rather than animal centered" which is akin to the discussion of this book: buildings should be human centered rather than built-structure centered. Maslow said that behavior is nearly always motivated from biological, cultural, and situation-specific factors, which Jana and Ken agree with from the standpoint that buildings built without consideration for the company culture, the human interactions with and within the space, and the site, climate, and demographic needs of the building leave the people working in the building unmotivated and even uninspired to work.

This middle-of-the-century article continues to play a part in psychology, human resource development, and training, as well as self-development and counseling discussions. Maslow's Hierarchy remains relevant because it presents a memorable model for recognizing our own and others' motivating forces. Thousands if not millions of renderings have been created over the years to illustrate Maslow's Hierarchy of Needs. The model has been applied to personal life, to managing people, to selling products based on people's needs, and to dozens of self-development and team-development scenarios. Maslow's Hierarchy also applies to people as they interact with and in buildings, and to what people want, need, and expect from buildings depending on where they personally are on the Hierarchy's continuum. Maslow indicated that the five motivating domains can affect current decision making and focus. The model also recognizes that the human organism, when it is dominated by a certain need, can have its whole philosophy of the future change. So for example, if our workplace cultures and buildings threaten a sense of personal safety then productivity goes down.

Maslow's Hierarchy is comprised of five domains of concern that influence the motivation and therefore the decision making of human beings.

1. Physiological—food, water, sleep, physical activity

When we are hungry or tired we cannot think well. When we are not well rested we tend to behave with impatience, intolerance, or even temper-filled fits. Until physiological needs are met, other needs and desires remain in the background or do not even have a chance to surface in consciousness.

The ways a building meets this domain of needs can include cafeteria space, water fountains, rest rooms, lighting that does not produce eye strain, and space for taking walks.

2. Safety—security, order, discipline

When we feel caged in and prevented from an outlet for physical activity we tend to feel edgy and agitated. When faced with or threatened with bodily harm, all attention is focused on getting to safety. Preferences for some kind of undisrupted routine or rhythm fall here in the safety concern too.

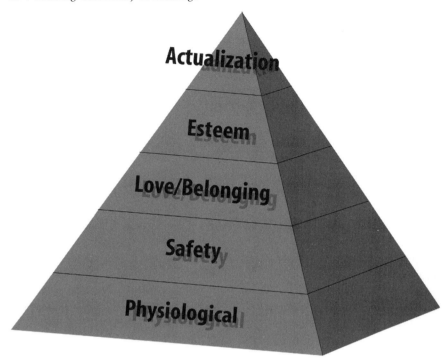

Figure 1.2 Abraham Maslow's Hierarchy of Needs.

Preferring a sense of stability and familiarity over constant change and unfamiliarity is a part of the safety domain.

A built environment can meet this domain of needs by having clear exits, having pathways for exiting the building, and offering access to a security service. The culture of an organization can threaten a sense of security through its constant demands for change and its level of workplace noise rather than creating a sense of safety through encouraging repeatable routines and stable work teams and work processes.

3. Belonging—affection, to love and be loved, to belong

This domain's focus is on feeling a part of a group, feeling loved, and feeling affection toward and from others. The belonging-oriented needs related to having friends, a significant other, a spouse, children, and even having co-workers with whom you can relate. Once the first two domains of need are met, people begin feeling motivated to fit in, to belong, to be loved, and to express love or kindness to others.

Buildings can address the need for belonging by providing clear community gathering spaces in lobbies, in cafeterias, in meeting rooms, and in teamwork areas.

4. Esteem—recognition, appreciation, self-respect and respect for others, confidence

The esteem domain is characterized by "having a need or desire for a stable, firmly based usually high evaluation of self, for self-respect, or self-esteem, for the esteem of others, a desire for independence and freedom, as well as having confidence in the face of the world." When esteem needs are thwarted or unmet, the result is a "feeling of inferiority, of weakness and of helplessness."

Esteem needs are less building based and more people and company-culture based. For instance, recognition of individual and team accomplishments is part of meeting esteem needs. Saying "thank you" for work accomplished, for efforts made, and for teamwork is a part of speaking to esteem needs. This discussion will be explored more in Chapter 4.

5. Self-actualization—meeting your potential and becoming whom you want to be, independently of anyone or anything else; Maslow said "What a man *can* be, he *must* be."

Again, this is based on the people and company culture interactions that support a person "being what he or she is capable of and passionate about." When an organization stands in the way of a person achieving his potential, the person tends to leave the organization by quitting and leaving for another job or by mentally disengaging and staying on the job in your company.

While hundreds of versions of the pyramid exist, suffice it to say that the rungs on the ladder stay the same. In fact, while writing this book, Jana stumbled across someone who had Maslow's pyramid hanging in his office space. Out of curiosity she asked about it. Here is the response given: "I've got so many stressful, life-changing things going on right now that I posted that to remind myself that amid all these changes I still have to take care of myself, still need to eat right, to exercise, and to take care of my health. Otherwise, I'll hole up in my home-office computer room and distract myself with games hour after hour."

BUILDINGS OF THE MID-TWENTIETH TO EARLY TWENTY-FIRST CENTURY

Interestingly and perhaps unfortunately, we can group 55 years of buildings together and talk system design, or the lack thereof, as though they were one building. Yes, technologies changed over that time period, and the materials and processes for construction have changed considerably. And yes, you can readily see differences between buildings built in 1955 from those built in 2005—glass façades were dominant in office buildings during the last half of the twentieth century. But by looking beyond the surface technologies into the underlying strategies that were use for circulating air, for lighting interior and exterior spaces; when you look at how the buildings responded to the site or needs of the community; and when you look to how responsive they were in providing the occupant with a healthy, comfortable, and controllable space, you will find striking similarities. These buildings were designed and built to serve as conditioned boxes, separating people from the environment so that business could be conducted in at best, a neutral setting. One glue that bound these buildings together was cheap power.

Looking worldwide, to the so-called mature market economies, we see that there were literally thousands of buildings that were designed and constructed between 1950 and 2005. They certainly were not all energy hogs and many of the designs did consider needs of the occupants, though the underlying trend in construction of the past fifty-five years was to provide low-cost workspace for an expanding office work force. Energy was relatively cheap and easy to come by so energy efficiency was not a top goal for most commercial building owners and developers. Even the 1972 oil embargo and subsequent gas price increases did not have significant impact on the design of buildings from an energy efficiency perspective.

In fact, the real movement toward energy efficiency in buildings has yet to come; looking at U.S. energy prices we can begin to see why. Data on the U.S. government Energy Information Administration web site[6] verifies that the average price for commercial end-user electricity from 1993 through 2004 increased from 7.74 to 8.16 cents a kilowatt hour (1000 watt hours)—just over a five percent increase in twelve years. That is less than half a penny of an increase on average across the United States. During that same time period, electric utility revenue for commercial buildings went up from 61.5 to 100 billion dollars—an increase of over 38 percent. For the most part, the utility companies were not making profits from large markups on the commodity but from the increase in use, that is more buildings using greater amounts of energy. For a building owner, there is hardly incentive to invest in efficiency when returns are so low.

The future should look different. North American electric use from 2002 to 2025 is projected to increase by 36 percent. Prices of tomorrow will make today's rates seem exceedingly low. But the real story lies with the transitional economies. China used only 1,457 billion kilowatt hours in 2002, but by 2026 they are posed to be using 4,260 billion kilowatt hours of electricity (equivalent to every man, woman, and child in the world using 0.655 billion kilowatt hours per year), an increase that represents more energy than is currently used each year by all the existing buildings in the world. In fact, transitional economies including Asia, Africa, the Middle East, and South America will soon use the bulk of the world's energy resources, out-stripping the total use of North America, Japan, Western Europe, Mexico, and Australia/New Zealand.[7] What will be the impact of buildings on energy use? In mature economies of the world, buildings currently account for over half of the energy resources used; worldwide (all countries) about one-third of total energy consumption can be accounted for in buildings.[8] If the transitioning world continues to utilize the same technologies and strategies that have been used throughout the developed world over the last half century, worldwide energy use attributed to buildings could reach the 40 to 50 percent mark!

There are a couple of additional points to be considered from this data. First, commercial buildings are mainly users of electricity and not so much direct users of fossil fuels. Energy in commercial buildings is mainly used for cooling, lighting, and equipment. Colder climate buildings do directly use fossil fuels such as natural gas for heating, but by and far a commercial building's largest load is electric in nature. Second, though commercial buildings use mainly electricity, the bulk of this electrical power—68 percent in the United States—is generated through burning fossil fuels. According to the U.S. Energy Information Administration emissions generated from energy consumption for electricity production in 2004 was 2,444,443 thousand metric tons of carbon dioxide, 10,307 thousand metric tons of sulfur dioxide, and 3,951 thousand metric tons of nitrogen oxides. Over half of these global warming and ozone depleting gases can be directly attributed to buildings. Buildings seem to be contributing to our quality of life and our health from the inside and the outside.[9]

Let us consider the physical attributes of office buildings of the past half century. Their exterior skins were mostly glass. Because we were not trying to heat the building there was less need for insulated walls so large glazing walls became the norm. This was a lower cost construction method because, though glazing costs more per square foot than concrete masonry blocks, for example, the labor costs for finishing a masonry wall make it a more expensive option than for a glazed wall. In Chapter 2 you will learn about the benefits of glazing for views and daylighting. A fully glazed building envelope does provide wonderful view potential, but it also acts as a huge heat collection device for the sun's radiant energy and allows direct sunlight to penetrate the interior causing discomfort due to increased temperatures and glare.

Heating, ventilation, and air-conditioning systems, especially on the cooling side, were necessarily large for these buildings. Mechanical systems were relied upon by the building operators and the office workers to overcome the discomfort of high heat gain through windows; and interior blind systems were commonly used to cut glare and ultimately the positive benefits of natural light and views. Rooftop units for cooling were many times so large and/or numerous that their operation combined with the large flows of air through the duct systems provided a constant level of background noise that effectively handicapped the office workers' ability to focus and to communicate with fellow workers.

Workers who sat by windows were frequently too hot and needed higher flows of cooled air to provide for their comfort, while working in the interior building core and out of direct contact with sun penetration suffered discomfort due to cold conditions; and almost every office worker in the building's core had their 1000 watt electric space heater plugged in and turned to high. In an attempt to keep everyone comfortable, building operators had to ensure that building systems provided simultaneous heating and cooling. But this was okay because energy was cheap.

FROM GOOD TO BAD AND BACK TO GOOD

But cheap energy did not stop all sectors from trying to reduce their fuel and electric costs. Late nineteenth and early twentieth century schools in North America were built with large expanses of tall windows, inviting natural light and ventilation to flood classroom spaces. During the late 1960s and through the 1980s school districts decided that by physically framing in and insulating all or portions of these windows they could save energy.

This school was built during the first decade of the 1900s when daylighting was a major contributor to classroom light levels. The tall windows are typical of that era and were designed to provide deep penetration of natural light into the classroom interior. At some point during the last forty years the upper glazed area of the windows were framed in and insulation was added to decrease heat loss.

No one was thinking about trade-offs between energy loss and the need for good light distribution and airflow. In fact, boarding over windows, which was a standard treatment for energy efficiency, followed a growing trend, beginning in the late 1950s and continuing through 2006, that saw windows as an unnecessary part of classroom design. As electric lighting became the norm, natural lighting became less used.

Performance data of college students' reaction to light as presented by H. Richard Blackwell in 1959 tended to show that higher and more consistent levels of electrical illumination were most conducive to learning.[10] However Blackwell's testing procedures seemed set up to follow late 1950s behavioral analysis condition-response theories such as were developed by B.F. Skinner in the study of operant conditioning of rats. This is to say they were not studies of students in their natural environ—the classroom. Blackwell's studies were followed by reports in the 1960s maintaining that there was no positive evidence for windows in schools, and a National Bureau of Standards report in 1974 further stating that the data was inconclusive in identifying positive elements of windows in classrooms. So school districts and architects felt it

Photo 1.1 Window energy efficiency measures (Ken Baker).

was okay to build school buildings with large expanses of concrete walls intersected sparsely with windows. These buildings look conspicuously like prisons from the outside and make one wonder about the subtle messages we have given several generations of students.

Studies by Dr. Judith Heerwagen, beginning in 1986, began to break this windowless design paradigm.[11] Heerwagen was able to demonstrate that lack of visual stimulus (views) and variability in lighting (daylighting) made classrooms boring places in which to work and learn. The price of boredom was further proved in 1999 with the publication of the Heschong Mahone Group study for the California Board of Energy Efficiency that showed math and reading test scores to be 20 and 26 percent higher, respectively, in classrooms with natural daylighting, and that larger window areas also facilitated faster learning.[12]

1980s and 1990s—The Rise of Malls

By the time the last two decades of the twentieth century arrived, the world of work was moving from being driven by brawn and Maslow's first three domains of motivation to being driven by the brain and all five domains of motivation. Workplaces demanded brainwork and turned into cubicle mazes meant for individuals to get work done. Workplaces continue to range from manufacturing and offices to field work and into virtual-technology-based

Photo 1.2 Daylighting—blending old and new. St. Joseph's Elementary school in Boise, Idaho, is an example of an early 1900s building with windows restored to full daylighting benefit. In contrast to the school shown in Photo 1.1, these windows are being used per original design, for bringing natural light into the classroom. Note the photo of the interior classroom space and the addition of a set of skylights to the back of the classroom. This is a recently added feature (designed by InSight Architecture, Boise, Idaho) and shows how modern and old design can integrate with great compatibility and purpose (Ken Baker).

work. Then there was the services sector with restaurants, hotels, and shopping malls also being places of work.

Centuries ago, outdoor market bazaars were both workplaces with wares being sold and places for people to fill their Maslow domains needs one through three of food, security, and belonging. Coliseums used to gather and entertain people were also places of work because the people doing the entertaining were working, just as entertainers in venues today are working. As early as the 1960s, indoor shopping malls, as they are known today, came onto the scene. Food courts, furniture, jewelry, clothing—all the things of old-time marketplace bazaars—plus retail extravaganzas and events designed to draw people to the malls for entertainment, eating, and shopping. From the shopping crazes in Dubai to the acres of indoor retail space in American malls, these workplaces are communities unto themselves. As a place of and for community, shopping malls model many of the domains of Maslow's Hierarchy.

For example, the $650 million Mall of America in Bloomington, Minnesota, built by the Germazian brothers in 1992 is a community unto itself and a creator of community for those who come to visit, shop, and dine. Each of the three floors is about one half mile to walk; thus, walking all three floors nets a total of one and one-half miles (Maslow's domain two: security in the freedom to roam). Depending on the season, there are 11,000 to 13,000 employees in the Mall of America. The number of employees alone is larger than the population of many cities. Then depending on the day, add another 8,000 to 20,000 people who are the guests, shoppers, diners, students in classrooms, amusement riders, and movie goers in the building. Security personnel number more than 120 with more than 130 security cameras to monitor (Maslow's domain two, security, is clearly a focus). More than half of the cities in America have fewer than 120 police officers working to keep citizens safe—and here, in one place, there are enough security officers to police several cities.

Mall of America events such as Lego building contests, talent contests, theme parties, movie premieres, and constant birthday parties add to a sense of community that invites participation and creates a reason to come to the Mall of America. Camp Snoopy is the amusement park, replete with rides, in the central court of the mall. In fact, the indoor amusement park approach taken by the Germazian brothers has been used in malls from Lisbon, Portugal, to Durban, South Africa. The 4.2-million-square-foot Mall of America is located on the site that once was home to the Minnesota Twins's outdoor baseball and the Vikings's football stadium (Metropolitan Stadium). One community gathering place has literally been built on top of the site of another. It is estimated that the Mall of America workplace and shopping place contributes more that $1.8 billion in economic impact to Minnesota annually. The mall includes more than 520 stores, 20 sit-down restaurants, 30 fast food restaurants, 36 specialty food stores, and 14 movie screens. Again, this one workplace is bigger than many towns around the world. To accommodate all of the workers and visitors, there are more than 12,550 parking spaces as well as bus and rail service to the mall. To get a sense of its size, the total square footage of the stores is 4.3 square miles and seven Yankee Stadiums can fit inside the Mall of America.

All of our ancestors experienced community during hunts, harvests, camp fire circles, and home-building projects. Today, we tend to build community at work, in our neighborhoods, during our exercise and entertainment time, as well as during shopping trips in search of great buys. Building outdoor space inside is accomplished at the Mall of America with the park-like atmosphere and landscaping of Camp Snoopy and other places that Ken has experienced.

For instance, in early 2000, Ken and his wife Judy were visiting Las Vegas, Nevada, when they experienced an indoor space that so realistically created outdoor space that it invited sitting and staying for a while. The new Paris casino and hotel had opened only two months prior to their trip. They decided to take a walking tour through the building:

Entering from the Boulevard side, just north of the Eiffel Tower replica, we stepped into the casino. Like most Vegas casinos it was filled with people, slot machines and other gambling machines, gambling tables, hundreds if not thousands of signs, multihued lights, and of course nonstop noise. Casinos, especially the popular ones on the Vegas Strip, are busy places with hundreds of simultaneous activities. And I find them difficult to physically navigate as there is rarely a direct route through the gaming areas. After about five minutes of wandering, my senses are usually over-whelmed and I'm looking for an escape route to a quieter place.

In the Paris Casino, the ceiling is very high and we could see what seemed to be a street on the other side of the gaming area so we headed that way. It really was a street, a replica of a Parisian alley that wound its way by shops and restaurants, fountains and statuary. It was much quieter than the casino and really made for quite a pleasant walk. The ceiling was very high and vaulted and looked like a bright blue sky with scattered clouds. The lighting on the ceiling was such that you could imagine that the sun was just beyond the top of the buildings that silhouetted the skyline.

We found ourselves relaxing into the stroll and decided to stop and have lunch in a French restaurant fronting the little street. When the head waiter asked us where we would like to sit, in unison we said, "Outside please." It took about 2 seconds for us to look at each other and begin laughing. We had become so caught up in the space that our minds became convinced that we were actually walking in the outdoors.

Certainly climate was not an aspect of this experience. But it could have been. In another section of the same building an aspect of climate is most convincingly and cleverly brought to the building interior. Next door to the Paris Resort is a Vegas shopping area called Desert Passage. It has a décor and feel very similar to the Paris Resort, with a faux street and skyline above winding along the way through shops and restaurants.

Somewhere in the middle of the Desert Passage mall an approximately 15 ft. by 30 ft. water garden bisects the street. The shallow pool is full of coins from wish makers and is nondistinct at first look. While near the pool, my wife and I stopped at a shoe store adjacent to the pool area. While browsing in the store, I began to hear what sounded like thunder, at first distant and then closer and louder. I also caught flashes of light in the periphery of my eyes. I then looked "outside" and could see people gathering around the pool and so took Judy's arm and strolled out to the poolside.

The faux sky flashed with lighting and thunder followed soon after. A few scattered drops of rain begin falling into the pool, an unsteady drip, drip, drip. The lightning grew more fierce and the thunder more cacophonous. The rain came down in earnest and was soon literally pounding down onto the pool. You could feel the humidity level rise and the air surrounding the space became cool. It was a wonderful human-made experience of a thunderstorm. I frequently work in Las

Vegas and have gone back to experience the storm several times. It storms every hour and there's always a good crowd of people willing to wait for the next event.

Speaking of traveling, when business travelers fly on an airplane, the promise of community can be seen from the sky. The structure of the community unfolds as roads, travel patterns, school yards, subdivisions, city centers, parks, and pathways distinguish themselves from the air. The density of a landscape far below the plane communicates the likelihood of workplaces and community centers. Picture an online map search with satellite images showing any city in the world. The centers of work stand out because of the density of built structures. The parks and schools often stand out because of play fields and grass. From the plane, the outdoor space humans long to be in is visible and for a time, at least in thought, the plane and our indoor workspaces are forgotten.

In any case, the three examples of creating outdoor spaces indoors present tangible cases for making the outdoor connection in an indoor setting that aims to create a sense of safety, pleasure, and community belonging (Maslow's domains two and three). Although it may feel dishonest, Ken does not believe it is as long as we are not striving to permanently replace the natural with the faux. In the three stories just related, the experiences came from buildings that are in essence theme parks. Consider too the outdoor experiences recreated in indoor spaces such as athletic clubs for exercising, climbing walls in retail stores and in special gyms, and even professional sporting events that were once largely outdoors with bleachers but are now played nearly exclusively indoors. Everyone expects novel experiences from theme parks; but could and should we apply ideas like these to our typical office building? Yes. In Chapter 5, you will discover more about the reasons why, the strategies, and the benefits for the building community.

BUILDING EXAMPLES FROM THE TWENTY-FIRST CENTURY

Buildings That Respond

With cheap power quickly becoming something of the past, and building occupants becoming more educated about the effects of the built environment upon health and productivity, there is good reason for building owners and managers to consider a new approach to design and construction. The green building trend or movement (which will be more fully described in the next chapter) has given us hope. Architecture is entering a twenty-first-century renaissance where system design strategies that are supported by life-cycle costs are taking precedence over first cost strategies. It is happening slowly but buildings are beginning to change.

Photo 1.3 Banner Bank building, HDR Architects, Boise, Idaho. Developed by Gary Christensen of Christensen Development, the Banner Bank was given the highest rating—Platinum—through the U.S. Green Building Council's Leadership in Energy and Environmental Design Standard (Ken Baker).

Fortunately, there are many wonderful examples of that change. Buildings that are designed to be human responsive are emerging as the new trend in architecture. This is hopefully an evolving trend as it is based on the bottom line with identifiable payback for many of the high performance measures these buildings feature. Materials and systems that are more attuned to the vernacular of a region, that are designed to work in alliance with the climate, and that reflect the societal and cultural needs of the broader community (the building occupants and users) have gained at least a foothold into our design and construction culture.

The Banner Bank building in Boise, Idaho, typifies this new architecture. The building is designed to use captured rainwater from the roof and adjacent streets for toilet flushing; it has an underfloor air distribution system for cooling and heating, giving occupants some control over airflow and temperature in their personal spaces; and natural daylighting is used to light much of the interior space.

We have yet to see if this new architecture will continue as a trend—finding favor among some but not all building owners—or evolve into a clear system of architecture that truly pushes the boundaries of what is possible. The next chapter will explore some exciting possibilities.

CONCLUSION

Building community in buildings and in towers begins with the process of building construction itself. *Fortune* magazine pursued such a conversation in its January 26, 2004, issue in a story about what is to be done with the World Trade Center site. The story depicts the struggles and fights over erecting a building that meets the needs of commemoration, of good use of real estate, of replacement of lost office and retail space, and of revenue flow for the land owners. When a construction project begins on shaky interpersonal ground, can the finished project reflect the grandeur of vision that is meant to inspire, calm, and generate positive actions? No. The discussion that underpins a construction project can make or break the results of the project. If all we focus on is the beauty of a building, then the lighting, heating, cooling, and usefulness of the built space can end up being overlooked. A building that fosters and encourages community takes into account all of the elements of the built space, from the landscaping to the colors of the bathroom tiles and everything in between our feet and our seats and that passes under and through our fingers in order for us to accomplish work each day.

2 / People, Buildings, and the Natural Environment Connection

THE TURN OF the twentieth century was a time just prior to the large-scale use of electricity. Out of necessity, many of the buildings between 1900 and the 1950s were responsive to the need for natural strategies for lighting, heating, cooling, and ventilation. The people who worked in these buildings were in relationship with both the building and the prevailing climatic conditions. Building occupants were expected to dress appropriately for the daily and seasonal changes in climate—dressing warmer for cold weather and cooler during warmer weather thus offsetting some of the effect that climate placed on the buildings' interior conditions.

Fortunately for us, we do not need a time machine in order to look at the climate responsive strategies that were incorporated into buildings 100 years ago. With a little effort we can locate examples of these buildings today, such as the National Building Museum and Idaho State Capitol buildings highlighted in Chapter 1 and the Carnegie Library that will be presented later in this chapter. Though some have been altered with new systems for heating cooling and lighting, or expanded upon with additions, a handful stand intact in most communities. Fortunately, it is difficult to deconstruct the good ones, as many are also aesthetically pleasing and representative of both period and historical architectural styles, with design elements ranging from Grecian to Elizabethan to Tudor to Federalist.

THE BUILDING AS ENVIRONMENT

These buildings are important because they represent our history and thus give us insight into our societal roots. Many, though not all, were built solidly with native stone or brick and will endure for years, perhaps centuries, if maintained. The design concepts represented in the best of these buildings, such as the two highlighted in Chapter 1, set a firm base for comparison to buildings of the 1940s through the early 1990s—an era when electricity and oil were viewed as cheap and unlimited. The large share of the buildings constructed during that fifty-year period celebrated cheap power by defying the need for external and internal environmental considerations in their design and construction. Because buildings were heated and cooled on demand, people no longer needed to be concerned with climate-driven day-long dress, at least not from a thermal standpoint. Temperature stabilization became reliant on a building's heating and cooling systems, and comfort became an ultimate responsibility of the building's manager. Of course if you ask any building manager they will tell you that about 90 percent of occupants complain about temperature.

Drawing on the wisdom of early environment-focused builders and on the best use of energy resources, in the late 1990s the green building movement appeared. Green building brought some fresh if not always new perspective on a more environmental and human focused architecture. The green building movement has gained incredible momentum since the beginning of this century and is now experiencing rapid growth—as of December 2005, more than 2200 new buildings in the United States and Canada were registered with the U.S. Green Building Council (USGBC)[1] indicating intent for being certified as a green building. Green buildings typically address issues surrounding the building site, water and energy efficiency, use of more localized materials, and human health and comfort.

Globally, green building programs like the United Kingdom's BREEM (Building Research Establishment Environmental Assessment Method) have done much to change our approach to architecture. For example, it has become more common for both governmental and corporate clients, such as the U.S. National Park Service and Herman Miller Company, to insist on green architecture setting the challenge for architects to respond with appropriate integrated strategies and technologies.

Yet there is still an immense amount of change needed in our built environment—changes that go beyond our current approach toward more action. In the U.S., the green building movement is still only capturing about 5 percent of the new construction market. Wasteful practices continue to be the status quo and occupant discomfort the norm. On the waste side, in 2005, residential and commercial buildings consumed over 72 percent of

U.S. electrical resources. That is about one-fourth of the current electrical use of the remainder of the world. Buildings contributed to the depletion of natural resources and air and watershed pollution, including 39 percent of atmospheric carbon dioxide that drives global warming, and accounted for 24 percent of the waste mass in our landfills.[2]

From the perspective of humans, buildings provide the basic shelter within which we participate in work, play, and rest. As society is beginning to understand, the spaces we occupy have a major influence on all aspects of our lives. Consider this: As a population, North Americans spend over 90 percent of their lives in buildings. That which buildings offer us, both good and bad, has influence over who we are becoming and directly impacts our quality of life.

So here is the thesis of this chapter: A building that provides for the intrinsic need for humans to relate to the available natural environment will fulfill a function as basic as providing shelter from the summer sun or winter rain. Most of the buildings you see on your way to work, and probably the one you enter each day, would fail to meet this standard of providing space where humans can relate to the natural environment. We the people suffer as workers in these sterile environs, and our work suffers too as you will see when we talk about productivity in this chapter and in Chapter 6.

Edward O. Wilson in his acclaimed book *Biophilia* points to the urge for humans to connect with the natural environment. He treats it as an elemental need and suggests that when given an opportunity, people "...will walk into nature, to explore, hunt and garden," and that we "...prefer entities that are complicated, growing and sufficiently unpredictable to be interesting."[3] The human resource development field concurs with Wilson's human responsive design approach because the more complicated and chaos-filled a person's life is, the more there exists a need for predictable, safe, interesting, and controllable environments.

Most of us cannot leave our buildings and be surrounded by forest or savanna or desert or, unfortunately, even a small garden. Unless there is a park nearby we may not be able to take a walk in the woods. A building in the middle of an urban area sits within an environment where topography, vegetation, available sunlight, winds, temperature, and humidity have been altered from the conditions of decades or centuries past. In fact, the microclimate, the very localized climate of the space that your building occupies, can change with the construction of a new neighboring building or with the planting of trees.

Still, the sun, wind, and humidity surround us and are available for tempering the indoor environment and affecting our senses, our health and comfort, and our subsequent productivity. Because of this recognition of how the environment affects our well-being, a new model of architecture is slowly but surely emerging. A model that takes good ideas from the past and through innovation and creativity makes them better, as you will see in the Hood River County Library example later in this chapter.

In the past few years the terms "integrated design," "climate responsive design," and "green buildings" have offered models for architectural design and have quickly entered into the vocabulary of building owners and design teams. Now, twenty-first-century strategies, processes, and materials are helping us to more fully express green design. We believe, and sincerely hope, that in the future design teams will hear a clear message from their clients: the health, well-being, and productivity of the building occupants are a primary design goal for the building's design. The driver for this directive may be self-serving: Happy and healthy workers are the most productive and therefore most profitable for the organization. This goal is most directly achieved through facilitating occupant interaction with features of the natural environment that surround and are built into the building. This new architecture is a practice in human responsive design.

BEYOND ENVIRONMENT—THE GOLDEN AGE OF ENERGY

Buildings and Energy

In his 1982 book, *The Next Economy*,[4] Paul Hawken notes that the availability of electricity in the early 1900s gave each North American access to a lifestyle that previously would have required 100 servants. By the 1940s the availability of cheap power, rural electrification, and a war-driven economy expanded the type of work and processes that could be performed in buildings. In the West, cheap power helped to fuel a march of unprecedented growth and expansion. Not until the oil embargo of the 1970s would we find that power was not unlimited as many once thought.

In the United States, the energy produced and consumed was in balance through the late 1950s. Since that time, imports to the United States in the form of natural gas from Canada and oil from the Middle-East, South America and other markets have increased each year so that by the year 2000 imports exceeded 29 quadrillion Btu, or 27 percent of total United States use.[5]

United States Department of Energy data show a 49 percent improvement in energy use from 1949 to 2000. That seems like good news until you look deeper into the numbers. In the United States there are three broad sectors where energy is used: transportation, industry, and buildings. Most of this increase in efficiency came from the industrial sector and was driven by the need to reduce bottom-line production costs. But as industry increases efficiency—and outsources production to other countries—buildings continue to grab a larger slice of the energy pie. On the whole, many new buildings are more efficient than their predecessors of only a decade ago. However, worldwide we continue to build at a rapid rate so the total percentage of commercial building energy use continues to increase.

As of 2005, commercial buildings used 35 percent of the electricity sold in the United States, about one-sixth of the world's total consumption of electrical energy. By 2025 that number is expected to go up to 40 percent. This is noteworthy to our future discussion about people and buildings and the return to active use of natural light to illuminate workplaces. A full 72 percent of energy used in commercial buildings is electrical energy, and much of this —40 to 50 percent—is used for lighting, and about 50 percent of that is unnecessary and thus wasted energy because natural light can be used instead. One more point to consider: Unless they sit in a very cold climate, most commercial buildings need to cool year around. About 42 percent of this cooling load is in response to the heat generated by lighting.[6]

So, we see a large magnitude of direct and indirect energy consumption as an outcome of electric lighting. Is that such a big deal? Do we not need light to see and to work? Certainly we need light, and good light. Especially for aging baby boomers who have lost an ability to focus on close up reading, fine detail, and computer work. But consider two things: First, as we indicated above, we tend to overlight our buildings by about 50 percent. A lot more than even baby boomers need. Second, electric lighting technology has advanced to a point of being able to provide great lighting on our work surfaces using about half the power that was used just a few years ago. In other words, luminaries today offer more output for less input.

It is conceivable that with good lighting design we could reduce electric lighting by 50 percent or more and the subsequent need for cooling the building by another 20 percent. Now we are looking at some very real energy savings in the building and all it takes is a small application of design and logic to get there. Proper design of the lighting system can come from the growing field of lighting specialists with knowledge of the readily available lighting technologies that are able to produce appropriate lighting output with fewer watts than did older technologies, thus reducing the output of wasted heat that needs to be cooled for occupant comfort. The logic can come from modeling the building. Software is available that predicts a building's energy use, or assists the designer in understanding building energy load, and is based on documentation of a building's physical attributes such as the R-value of walls, ceilings, and floors, the efficiency of windows, orientation to the sun, building mass, and lighting wattages. With this data the software can help the design engineer understand building system interaction, e.g., lighting and cooling, and aid in selecting the best type and size of heating and cooling equipment.

Furthermore, new off-the-shelf lighting technologies can render colors much truer than previously, offer new and smarter control strategies for our use, and, when partnered with natural daylighting, can save tremendous amounts of energy and thus dollars. The potential for integration of electric lighting and daylighting will be explored further in the discussion on human responsive design.

Impact of Buildings on People

Though there are notable exceptions, post World War II buildings were reflections of the move from the industrial age to the information economy in much of the world. Alvin Toffler identified this impending transition well in his book *The Third Wave.* By the late 1940s the transfer of manufacturing to Asia was only beginning, but by 1980 only about 9 percent of U.S. workers were directly involved in manufacturing.[7] In the large industrialized cities of the world, business practices changed and a full crop of office buildings were needed to house a growing American and European corporate and information culture.

Even though the United States began outsourcing manufacturing, industrial processes continued to increase until the advent of the 1970s oil embargo raised fuel prices cutting into corporate profits. The years between 1950 and 1973 were known as the golden age of industrialism in the United States with productivity gains of 3 to 4 percent annually.[8] By the mid 1950s, more than 50 percent[9] of the U.S. work force were office workers. By 2000 a full 73 percent of working Americans spent their workdays in an office environment. As manufacturing waned and office work became more of the norm, worker needs and issues changed. When subjected to extended periods in a confined space, the spread of illnesses began to have more and more of an impact on the health of the business. Indoor air quality is a primary concern with a full half of the office workers in the United States—34 percent of office workers have stated that poor indoor air quality has kept them from coming to work.[10] This is reason enough to look at passive ventilation strategies (airflow that is powered through nonmechanical means such as the opening of a window) that ensure good air exchange throughout the building.

In addition to the indoor air quality effect on productivity, worker concerns range from thermal comfort (too hot or too cold), ergonomic comfort, light quality, office layout, and office noise to the growing stress of commuting, parking, and making it to the office. Both interior and exterior building spaces have a direct but complex set of impacts on productivity.

Many if not most of the buildings from the so-called golden era of cheap energy magnified these office worker concerns. Because they were built in reliance on mechanical systems to provide air, light, humidity, and temperature, mechanical operation, maintenance, and system integration became keys to building effectiveness. Building managers became responsible for ensuring that everyone remained comfortable in their workspaces. Moreover, these managers had to rely on what was generally poor documentation of building system operation, piecing together systems and controls that were not designed to be integrated. Large heating, ventilation, and air-conditioning systems became more and more complex and smaller systems were not generally integrated into a full-building air-conditioning strategy.

During the past few years, the Carnegie Mellon Institute has compiled research and literature on buildings and human productivity.[11] One of their observations from these thousand papers is that there are good buildings and bad buildings and that the building occupant knows the difference between a good and a bad indoor environment. When asked, most any office worker will tell you that a bad building has features such as poor indoor air quality, inadequate or too much lighting, glare, no view, noise from mechanical systems and other sources, little space for privacy, and is laid out poorly. A good office space is pretty much the opposite with views, operable windows, electric lighting that can be controlled at the desk, daylighting, good ventilation, and so on. Research data from the Carnegie Mellon Building Investment Decision Support (BIDS) program indicates that worker productivity in a good building is about 20 percent higher than productivity in a bad building. That is big!

If this statistic excites you, consider relating this story to your building manager. They may not share your amazement but simply shrug and say, "of course, that's an easy percentage to believe." Your building manager can most likely, in quick order, count off half a dozen complaints that are voiced daily by your fellow workers. People are always complaining about being too hot or too cold or that the air is stagnant or the lighting too bright or too dim. Such is the nature of a typical day of building occupant complaints in a typical building.

So, is productivity an issue of comfort? If only we could help our employees to be more comfortable then would they be more productive? Although comfort seemingly comes to the top—there is good research to show that it is certainly an *indicator* of productivity—it is not the *key* indicator. It becomes clearer why comfort is not our top goal when you think of it this way: comfort is so individualized we can never hope to make everyone in our building fully comfortable. But, interestingly, the engineering community is beginning to recognize that building occupant comfort is increased through climatic adaptation. As early as 1998, the American Society of Heating Refrigeration and Air-Conditioning Engineers (ASHRAE) unveiled a new building comfort guide called the "Adaptive Comfort Standard."[12] In short, this guide states that building occupants are willing to experience both higher and lower temperatures, expanding by a few degrees the high and low temperature ranges in a building, if they are given some element of control of building conditioning systems. For example, many building occupants, if given the ability to open a window, are willing to adapt to either cooler or warmer conditions (a few degrees up or down) than were previously considered acceptable.

It may be that our top productivity objective follows and expands on the "Adaptive Comfort" concept: Productivity will increase as building occupants are allowed to more actively participate and interact with the internal and external building environment. That is, give the people who work in buildings some level of control in choosing the attributes of their physical environment—from furniture to cubicle layout to control of temperature and ventilation. People want to be able to make their space cooler or warmer or perhaps more or less light and more quiet, personal, and private. They also want to make changes at any point in time to support their mood and their task. Ask any building manager, if they put up a thermostat and give a room occupant just 2 degrees of control, the occupant is satisfied and ceases to complain about temperature.

Society's recent history is one where buildings tried to thermally isolate people from the natural environment. Now, we are on the cusp of a breakthrough in building design. Making our spaces more interesting, delightful, healthy, and, ultimately, occupant interactive and controllable is our goal. With the momentum being established through the global green building movement, we have the opportunity to step back into strategies of the past century and pair them with technologies and processes of the twenty-first century.

THE GREEN BUILDING MOVEMENT

As a world culture we are certainly beginning to understand the significant role that buildings play in our lives. In the United Kingdom, for example, assessment tools such as the Building Research Establishment Environmental Assessment Method have been utilized for well over a decade to look at the environmental performance of certain types of buildings. Green Globes, a rating system for residential and nonresidential buildings, was recently established in Canada in direct competition to the U.S. Green Building Council's portfolio of programs. In the United States and several other countries, the USGBC, founded in 1993, and the LEED (Leadership in Energy and Environmental Design) program, first offered in 2000, for buildings has grown tremendously in only a few years.

The USGBC web site reports that as of 2005, 1751 new buildings representing 212 million square feet were registered with the intent to become LEED certified buildings. Whether this is a half-full or half-empty scenario is dependent on what lies ahead; will we continue to move toward this new architecture or will it remain a period or fad-oriented movement such as Bauhaus, post modernism, or expressionism? It is possible that this is different than these other architectures in that green building does not define a style of building. It is more of a philosophy. We have been moving toward this new green or high performance architecture because there are good reasons to do so. The primary motivating factors for building green include economics, environment, and people.

The economic supposition is that building green makes money. If the costs of building green can show a high return on investment, then it becomes easier to justify in the bottom line. This has proven to be true for many entrepreneurial developers. One of many worldwide, a British Columbia company, Windmill Development, has found good financial success by building green. So much so that they will no longer develop properties that do not follow green guidelines. What developers are discovering is that building green may, but does not necessarily, cost more to build, and green office space rents more quickly and for more per square foot. Many times there are federal and local incentives for building green, for example if a brownfield (polluted) area is cleaned up through development many jurisdictions will provide incentives in the form of tax relief for the building owner. In this way, green building directly adds value to both the developer and community as a whole, not just the building occupants, making them winning projects for entire community centers.

A second good reason for building green is to reduce a building's impact on the environment. The Leadership in Energy and Environmental Design program has six categories. Four of them (sustainable site, water efficiency, energy efficiency, and materials and resources) deal directly with the reduction of environmental impacts of buildings. Because of environmental concerns, many large national and international companies have made the decision to go green in both their new and existing buildings.

The third, and we believe most important, reason for building green is to support building occupants and their creativity and productivity. The potential for increased human productivity ties back to the first leg, or economic concerns. Studies from Carnegie Mellon Institute suggest that for a typical new office building, the greatest expenditure over a thirty-year life cycle is in people. In fact, about 92 percent of a company's costs are directly related to employee costs, including training new people to replace those dissatisfied employees who left for another company.[13]

Though you can view these three reasons for building green as separate rationale, in truth, they are fully connected to one another. From a business perspective, addressing the economic factors of green may at first seem to be the best course. But when we begin to understand the effect that a healthy and happy work force has on business health, the decision to do what is right for people and the environment comes easy. Consider these two examples.

In 2001 the University of Montana built a new daylighted addition onto their student fitness and recreation center. Set in Missoula, where the average rainfall is only 12 to 15 inches per year, the climate is arid. However, during the winter—which can be subzero—sunshine is limited to about 30 percent. But this is a "lemonade from lemons story" as overcast skies make for perfect daylighting strategies. The center is equipped with a workout room, climbing gym, multiple sports courts, and a cafeteria and sitting space on one end—all bathed in natural light. After the remodel, student visits to the center went from 790 to 3500 per day. According to the facility manager the students and faculty are attracted to the space because of the natural environment and natural light connections. The recreation center is now used as a recruiting tool for the University of Montana.

Another story comes from health care where the cost of professional staff turnover can be a big piece of the annual budget. Replacing and training one nurse can cost a whopping $64,000. Understanding the people/building connection, Bronson Methodist Hospital in Kalamazoo, Michigan, went for green features when they built a new unit in 2000. Since occupancy they have reported a 50 percent reduction in turnover among registered nurses. That is big savings for their business community. It is no surprise that effective hospital managers are beginning to pay attention to high performance features of their buildings.

The green building movement will hopefully continue to grow and mature. The benefits of green design are many, the disadvantages few. As owners, architects, and engineers become understanding of the rewards associated with designing for people, buildings should become more responsive to our need to be surrounded by the natural environment.

HUMAN RESPONSIVE DESIGN

Never doubt that our health and productivity is significantly affected by our building spaces.

Human responsive design refers to a new or existing building that is designed and constructed or altered to provide a high-quality habitat that supports the work and social, community and cultural needs of its occupants within the context of the natural environment: climate, vegetation, topography, and site parameters. Furthermore, buildings that are outcomes of human responsive design use natural and energy resources to the highest efficiency practical and are designed to employ human interactive passive and renewable strategies for heating, cooling, and ventilation.

From a totally human-centric standpoint, if people did not need shelter from the natural elements, if we did not need spaces in which to participate in community, share ideas and thoughts, practice our work or live, there would be no purpose for buildings. The other side of this statement is if we want or expect these experiences, our built environment should support them. Thus, buildings have to be designed with human beings in mind.

Human Responsive Factors

As suggested when we talked about green buildings, there is an emerging trend toward a new type of building that takes us beyond the inefficiencies and noninteractive designs of the past. In order for us to know how well a building measures up or compares to others, we need a ratings system that will let us establish a building's performance potential with reference to a baseline. Looking at current directions in research on productivity, Ken believes that there are three broad factors for ensuring a building's responsiveness to occupant needs:

1. Responsiveness to the physical site
2. Responsiveness to the climate
3. Responsiveness to the building's human culture

Responsiveness to the Physical Site

The first factor is how the building responds to the physical environment, including the location and footprint on the building site, site preparation for soil and erosion control, containment of rainfall, use of native materials, and vernacular construction methodologies. This is the point where the connection of the building to the environment is made. The more that the building encompasses or reflects the local flora and fauna through responsiveness to the site, and the less it interrupts natural water discharge, the easier it becomes to extend that connection to the building occupants. A great example of a building that meets this responsiveness to site criteria is the Bank of Astoria which is highlighted later in this chapter.

The physical site connection should consider both historical vegetation and the existing community of people and buildings that surround the site, thus giving the building a sense of belonging in its place. It should also consider and celebrate the community and culture that will occupy the building. You will see a good example of this expression in the Chapter 6 profile of the C.K. Choi building in Vancouver, British Columbia. The building is a research center for Asian studies and thus designers used generalized Asian cultural elements to define the structure's interior and exterior and not elements specific to just one culture.

Responsiveness to the Climate

The second factor deals with the building's response to the surrounding climate, sun, wind, rain, humidity, and so on. What is the impact of climate on the building envelope or "skin" and subsequent need for passive or active (mechanical) strategies to bring the interior of the building into the range of human comfort? The industry has coined an appropriate term for this: climate responsive design. In his book of the same name, Richard Hyde defines climate responsive design as strategies to moderate a building's interior climate for "human good and well-being."[14] This fits very well with the concept of human responsive design.

Unlike the physical site connection where historical culture, plants, and materials have influence, the climatic connection considers not just the macroclimate of the area or region but also the impact of the microclimate. The microclimate includes the climatic effect of adjacent buildings, parks, and human made waterways, building materials that either absorb or reflect energy from the sun, paving materials, sidewalks, and lawn areas. In fact, a new building under design should consider the impact that building will have on the local climate—will it change water discharge patterns, reflect or absorb heat, and so on.

Responsiveness to the Building's Human Culture

This is the essence or culmination of the three human responsive factors: the target if you will. This third factor considers how well a building responds to the people that use it, and how well it lets users interact with each other; with the microclimate that surrounds the building; and with a building's mechanisms for heating, cooling, and ventilation systems.

Questions to ask to determine if the building responds to the human culture include the following: Do building spaces, interior and exterior, feed the human senses—smell, touch, vision, hearing—through natural environment expressions of color, texture, sound, and light? Is the occupant able to open windows or otherwise control airflow and temperature within his or her personal workspace? Are furnishings comfortable and is there a variability of work areas that can be accessed by the occupants for working singly or in small or large groups? Can lighting and sound be adjusted by the occupants within their space? Are there exterior views either from the workspace or accessible from common areas to give the occupants visual contact with the great outdoors? Are there green spaces, internal and/or external, where the occupants can go to rest? Is there an exercise facility on-site? Is there a community space within and/or without the building, where occupants can socially interact with each other in a seemingly nonwork environment?

Human responsiveness is further enhanced if the building and site are responsive to the historical culture of the area where the building is located. This concept may be more difficult in both discovery and in expression—especially for an existing building—but the reader is encouraged to consider the importance of a cultural expression through some aspect of the building and/or building site. For a new building, the discovery of culture can be found during the programming phase of the design by asking questions during the design charrette[15] such as what is the history of our community and how could we best express that in our design; how has the evolution of our larger community had impact on who we are; and, through our building, how would we like to express this evolution to ourselves and to future generations? For an existing building, consider gathering a representative cross section of occupants to work through these same questions. It is best to have an experienced facilitator to assist in either process. In Chapter 7 we offer a process to guide your building or office team through selection of human responsive design strategies that would appeal to your work community.

Human Responsive Symbolism

Whether good or bad, every building expresses physical symbols of the culture that created it. These symbols are in the details of the structure and in the physical space and layout of the building and the site and act as a set of instructions for how to use and how to interact with the building.

In 2000, Barcelona, Spain, celebrated a renowned twentieth century architect Antonio Gaudi by opening up many of his designs to public tour. Gaudi was known for his human-centered architecture and human-scale details were integral to his buildings. Imagine walking through an apartment building and becoming aware that the bathrooms were designed to support more than what we normally consider the basic bathroom functions; for example a small shelf to hold a hairbrush strategically placed beside a sink so that to reach for it required intuition and not thought. Movement through Gaudi designed spaces is easy and flowing, again intuitive, and no space is so large that it overwhelms the user—very much the opposite of what we see today in North American homes.

These kinds of personal details (symbols) were not exclusive to Gaudi. Old-school architects used to design homes and other buildings with human-scale detailing—often including the design of furniture—but we seldom pay architects to do full-scale design anymore. Something else to consider is this: Our buildings of the past 20 years have become so large that we can only afford the lowest bid therefore leaving human-scale symbols by the wayside. We have so much space we cannot afford quality. Sarah Susanka has written at least two residential books about this topic, each proposing that new homes are too large.[16] Though from an outside view it seems we have forgotten what it is like to be surrounded by spaces that are simple, intuitive, soul feeding, and creatively inspiring; we all feel the calm, the restoration of body and mind that occurs when we have occasion to interact with such spaces.

Consider the simplicity side—that building spaces have become too complex, adding fodder to already full minds and thereby increasing our internal stress. In the past few years there has been a steadfast movement toward voluntary simplicity—taking intentional actions to rid our lives and our homes of unnecessary stuff. The premise is, the more you can give away, the freer you become to experience what is real and meaningful. We have to let go of the clutter to give our minds a break. When your mind is not working overtime processing all that stuff around you, there is literally more time available for you to participate in both work and play.

How does this noncomplexity apply to office spaces? The culture that develops within an office is influenced by the symbolism of place; the simplicity or quality of the décor; and the subtle invitations to interact that are expressed within the space. Further, it is quality more than quantity that provides a relaxed and creative environment. Chapter 5 will further pursue the contributions of sensory design elements that help to simplify human interaction with space.

Think about visiting a new office building in your community. Here is a probable scenario you would encounter when entering the building. As you walk through the entry large plastic trees stand to each side. They provide the only texture and color in the lobby. The space is large, open, and overlighted with hard white tile floors reflecting white walls. Does this feel like a comfortable space? Would it be a better space if the trees were real, the colors softer, and the space smaller and less bright. We could easily wonder how important it had been to the building owner to have such a large lobby; and what does this space convey to the workers that enter it five times a week, or to the first-time visitor? Probably not that this is a quality space; and perhaps that this is not a quality place in which to visit or work.

Interestingly, the vast majority of corporate and governmental agencies that are considering design of a new building would tell you that they want one that utilizes green or high performance strategies—as long as they do not have to sacrifice square footage. Quantity, square footage, almost always wins over quality of space. Consider that this push for large space over quality space could be a big mistake. What is the impact on people when building scale is out of proportion to the normal functions of a space? We lose the ability to bring human-scale symbols into the space; and with that loss we forfeit some of our ability to relax and focus; and we lose the sense of intimacy and ownership that a smaller more personal or task-oriented space could give us.

STRATEGIES FOR HUMAN RESPONSIVE DESIGN

The strategies we highlight in this section are mostly passive or hybrid and require combinations of natural and mechanical system interaction or human response in order to work most effectively. Passive strategy examples include appropriate use of available natural light and natural air movement that operate without power-driven mechanical equipment such as HVAC systems and electric lights. A hybrid system may use a mechanical system as a boost to operability—for example fans that assist the natural movement of air through an open window. A human response can be as simple as opening or closing a window or closing a window blind. The best strategies for conditioning and lighting our buildings would not require human interaction so much as invite it.

Daylighting Skylights and Windows

Daylighting forms the foundation of human responsive design strategies. We respond to the quality and variability of daylight in very productive ways. Perhaps the best daylighting studies performed in North America come from the Pacific Gas and Electric Company's Daylighting Initiative. In a groundbreaking study on the effect of daylighting in K–12 schools, researchers from the Heschong Mahone Group were able to document that students with the most daylighting in their classrooms progressed a full 20 percent faster on math tests and 26 percent faster on reading tests than students in classrooms with the least daylighting.[17]

Natural light enters our buildings through windows and skylights. It is not just the quantity of light that is important to us; it is the variability or change in light as the day proceeds and exterior conditions change. We want the connection to outdoor conditions that natural light brings. The visual cues allow us to maintain our natural circadian rhythm thus providing input and stimuli that our bodies need to function with appropriate alertness and more effectiveness. But windows and skylights can also let in direct sun that can bring heat and glare into a workspace and cause occupant discomfort. So the trick is to harvest the light in an indirect manner. The proper application of interior and exterior light shelves, shading devices, and vegetation become part of a good daylighting strategy.

Windows also serve other functions that are valued by occupants and affect worker productivity. In another study by the Heschong Mahone Group for the California Energy Commission, they found office workers that had the best views versus those with no view performed 10 to 25 percent better on tests.[18] Recall from the discussion in the introduction about creating alive meeting spaces that spoke to having window or landscape scenes on the walls.

Photo 2.1 Daylight harvesting strategies, Dalles Middle School, Dalles, Oregon, Boora Architects. An interior light shelf in the classroom shown here has two main functions: First, it eliminates glare by reflecting light from the upper window onto the ceiling, spreading the luminance over a larger area of the room and thus diminishing the contrast in light levels between the interior space and the window wall. Second, it brings natural light deeper into the building space, providing more occupants with natural light and reducing the need for electric lighting (Kevin Van Den Wymelenberg).

This is quite a significant finding and good reason to reconsider giving upper management all of the window space.

Though this section highlights the benefits of natural lighting we should not overlook the potential for lighting variability from our electric lighting systems. Strategies for putting electric lighting under occupant control are also effective. Studies of electric lighting in the 1950s did clearly show that electric light variability had a positive impact on worker productivity.[19] Remember, one key to productivity is to allow for occupant control of light, airflow, and temperature in their space. One way this is being accomplished in new and retrofitted buildings is to install an ambient or background lighting system in an office of around 20-foot candles (a measurement of light available to a horizontal surface such as a desk), instead of typical higher levels of 40- to 50-foot candles, and give workers good task lighting at their desks.

Photo 2.2 Exterior building shading strategies, Pierce County, Washington, Public Safety building, Miller Hull Architects. Depending on a building's orientation and size and location of windows in the exterior building wall, good exterior shading devices (or overhangs) like the one shown here can help to eliminate unwanted solar gain and glare. Notice also that exterior vegetation provides natural shading (Kevin Van Den Wymelenberg).

A good lighting strategy is to integrate electric systems with daylighting strategies. When photo-sensor controls are placed on the electric lighting to auto dim or brighten in response to natural light, electrical lighting can be reduced by an average of 40 percent.

Natural Ventilation

If given a choice, most of us would like a window in our workspace. We want natural light, we want a view, and many of us want the ability to open a window to control airflow and bring in scents and sounds. It is in our nature to want control. It is in our nature to want as much of a connection with the great outdoors as we can get while still being comfortable. Many, not all, would like to be able to sit back on a nice spring day, open a window, catch a fresh breeze, and hear the chirping of birds. Data supports an average of 1.8 percent productivity increase comes with an ability to control ventilation.[20]

Unfortunately, there can be problems with operable windows in an office environment. Security issues, noise (other than birds chirping), dust pollution, and energy loss top the list of reasons to not provide workers windows that open. It is especially important to be aware that some occupants may need their air filtered to remove pollutants and perceived and real odors. Ken used to work at a community college in the downtown Omaha area. At that time, Omaha was still known for its stockyards and the college sits adjacent to one of them. No one wanted operable windows because on most days the outside air was filled with the smells associated with rendering cowhides. A survey tool in Chapter 7 will help you determine if building occupants have issues with unfiltered outside air. But you will probably know if there are large-scale pollutants surrounding your building.

In lieu of operable windows, which we cannot all have anyway, what about bringing in good quantities of outside air for everyone? It seems to be a good strategy. According to ASHRAE, we only need about 1 cubic foot of air per minute to comfortably breath. We need an additional 14 CFM to flush the smells and odors from our environment. Buildings designed for natural ventilation may have high airflows, up to 300 CFM for buildings utilizing outside air for cooling a building's mass during the night or nonoccupied hours, according to G.Z. Brown, University of Oregon. But it may be difficult and costly to build natural ventilation into an existing building. So if good quantities of fresh air is a goal, and it is a good one, what choices are there other than natural ventilation?

A very cost effective and workable alternative may be to retrofit economizers, dampers on the cooling equipment that open to bring outside air directly into the air distribution system, on existing HVAC units. Depending on whether you have cooling towers, rooftop heating and cooling units, or other systems, economizers should be a first priority in many climates for bringing outdoor air into a building. You should check with a qualified and licensed HVAC contractor in your area to see if this option is viable.

Natural Cooling and Thermal Mass

This strategy is closely aligned with natural ventilation in that outside air is invited into the building through strategies of cross ventilation, perhaps operable windows on opposite sides of the building, or convective loops that are activated through a combination of high and low openings in the exterior building walls. The National Building Museum that was highlighted in Chapter 1 used both natural ventilation and cooling very effectively. It would be difficult to apply this strategy to an existing building that was not already "set up" to take advantage of outdoor air for cooling and airflow.

A good natural ventilation design will specify openings in the building that allow for either a cross flow of air—movement from a windward side of the building to a leeward side—or the establishment of a convective—high to low airflow. Depending on the difference in indoor and outdoor temperatures, and/or the prevailing winds, natural ventilated buildings can work very well. Like the rock walls of a cave, mass within the building structure can be cooled. This cooled mass has the capacity to absorb heat from bodies and equipment during daytime occupancy of the building. It is a very pleasant and comfortable cooling system. No direct productivity data exist that we know of, but a naturally cooled building is also naturally ventilated. If you have never been in a high-mass naturally cooled building just think about walking into a cave on a hot day. It is a similar experience.

Gardens and Quiet Space

One final and important strategy to consider as a way to make your building truly human responsive is the creation and use of garden and quiet or meditative spaces both within and without the building. If you browse gardening on the web, 76 million pages of information rest at your fingertips. It is the fourth most popular hobby in the United States after reading, watching TV, and spending time with your family. It is even more popular in the United Kingdom. Whether we actively garden or not, most of us enjoy garden spaces. Gardens ground us to the earth and help us to focus.

Garden spaces are right behind daylighting as a top human responsive design strategy and are more effective in establishing the human to natural environment connection than any other strategy. For one, garden areas, especially spaces with trees and shrubs, naturally provide shading and the lighting variability we discussed earlier. Obviously, planted areas can provide higher levels of oxygen, which is energizing. Even a small garden space that is set up with pathways can give one a sense of privacy and separation from the doldrums of the regular office environment, and if you are fortunate enough to have a large enough garden space, walking it may provide exercise or a place for walking contemplations. Many hospitals, senior residential, and assisted living facilities (which are also workspaces) include gardens, landscaped atria, and courtyards to ease pain and increase healing and quality of life.

Do not underestimate the benefits of adding a garden space to your office environment. It is nice to have both outside and inside gardens. Jana and Ken will provide more examples of the benefits of garden and quiet spaces in Chapter 5. But heed this cautionary note: Not all occupants enjoy plants, especially if those plants produce pollens. Before bringing plants into the building space, survey the building occupants to determine physical sensitivities and appropriateness of plant types.

BUILDINGS THAT ARE HUMAN RESPONSIVE

Now that we have brought some definition to human responsive design, let us look at some buildings representative of the features we have profiled. As you read through the following descriptions try to keep this thought tucked into your consciousness: the buildings profiled here were built purposely for some level of human activity and interaction with the natural environment.

While traveling, Ken visited two very nice, very beautiful and, in some but not all ways, very different libraries and one newly built branch bank that may well be one of the best examples of contextual human responsive design that can be found. One was a public library in Hood River, Oregon, with a new addition recently added to the turn-of-the-twentieth-century building. The other, a Benedictine seminary library was built during the 1960s at the Mount Angel Benedictine Abbey, Oregon. From the exterior, the architecture of the two buildings is significantly different in appearance. Once inside, both libraries retain that different feel though they both successfully utilize natural daylight as a primary architectural feature. The Bank of Astoria in Manzanita, Oregon, with its use of native materials, nature reflective color schemes, and natural lighting, provides an almost spiritual experience to those who view it from both outside and in.

Keep in mind that these buildings are located in a specific climatic area that may be much different than yours. Natural strategies for cooling, heating, daylighting, building orientation, and the like should vary by climate type. What is an effective strategy on a cloudy coastal region with 68 inches of rainfall per year is not appropriate for a high desert climate with hot summers and cold and sunny winters. Materials and resources and construction details and techniques will necessarily change with location too so that they compliment and reinforce the local conditions and native resources. Of course, the type of building, occupancy type, and use requires differing response in design.

The descriptions and photos of the three buildings are utilized to illustrate the potential connection between buildings, place, self, and work. Unless you have visited or worked in a building such as these, you may not be quite able to fully grasp the positive energy, high comfort, and invitations to creativity and productivity that they offer. These spaces can bring a very real sense of excitement to those who are aware of the human to nature connection and awareness to those who are not. The descriptions will hopefully bring you into the environment and spaces shown. You can help by allowing yourself to be open to the idea that a building really can affect a person's well-being, health, and productivity. In Chapter 5 you will learn how to identify these types of buildings in your community and gain a process for exploring them.

Hood River County Library

The small town of Hood River, population 6,020 in the 2001 census, is nestled into the Columbia River Gorge about 60 miles upstream from Portland, Oregon. This is the eastern side of the north-to-south-running Cascade mountain range. In its powerful drive to spill both small and mighty rivers of the northwest bioregion into the Pacific Ocean at Astoria, Oregon, the Columbia River has literally devoured its way through the mountains. Draining the north and east flanks of nearby 11,200-foot Mount Hood, the Hood River carved a narrow valley down into the Columbia. The climate is moderate, generally mild, with wet winters and warm and dry summers. Deep pockets of glacial till provide the opportunity to grow some of the best pears and apples on earth. Vineyards are spread across the upper valley—a part of Oregon's (a top U.S. wine producing state) landscape and economy. Set into a steep hillside, the town of Hood River peers across the wind-swept Columbia into the gray depth of the North Cascades. The Hood River library spreads east to west on a prominent bench a good 500 feet above sea level and 200 feet above the river. There are two distinct sections to the building where the new was linked to the old.

The old library, dating back to 1913, was one of the Carnegie libraries that are so prevalent around the United States thanks to the philanthropy of Andrew Carnegie. The look from the exterior is described as Jacobethan Tudor[21] style architecture—thick brick walls detailed with limestone columns and friezes at the entries and large windows framed heavily with limestone. On the north side the walls are broken with a central high vaulted window

Photo 2.3 The Hood River County Library. The old library is on the right-hand side of the exterior (view taken from the south). Notice the large percentage of window-to-wall area on both buildings. The new addition has high walls set with operable windows that draw air from lower openings, creating a convective flow of outside air through the building when ventilation and cooling are needed. The photo insets capture the interior to exterior view from the old and new spaces (Ken Baker).

flanked on either side with smaller (8 feet by 8 feet) windows set high enough that six-foot-tall bookshelves sit just below them on the building's interior. The high windows surround the perimeter of the building providing a dependable but ever-changing source of interior light during the daylight hours.

Operable windows, still on three of the four building exposures, offer the librarians easy access to the daily breezes moving up and down the river. The mass of the thick brick walls holds in the cooler nighttime temperatures during the summer providing a good level of comfort for librarians and patrons most days of the year. On a very hot summer day with full sunshine and no winds (unusual in the gorge), the building temperatures will climb into the high 80s. Partially because of its proximity to Portland, and certainly because of the beauty of the natural surroundings, but perhaps mainly because it became known as the wind surfing capital of North America, Hood River has grown rapidly over the past twenty years. The old library could no longer easily accommodate the changing population so a new wing was planned.

In 2001 programming and design of a new 11,145-square-foot addition and remodel of the 1913 building began. One main goal of the community and the librarians was for the addition to emulate the passive systems for lighting and cooling integrated into the 1913 building. Many architects would strive to aesthetically match a building addition with an older building, especially when the older building has strong architectural elements, as does the Carnegie library. But by intent this addition takes an even stronger natural environment approach than the older building. Natural light and views are enhanced in the reading spaces providing an inviting atmosphere to sit and read. Windows set in high walls are electronically controlled to open when interior conditions call for ventilation and cooling. The convective draw of the high windows also pulls air through the old building increasing its ability to ventilate and cool.

The library stands as a unique opportunity to view old and new responses to the natural environment and people, both appropriate and effective.

Mount Angel Abbey Library

A lot has been written about this beautiful daylight library finished in 1970. The architect Alvar Aalto was born in Finland in 1898 and so carried a turn-of-the-century perspective on building functionality refining his architecture to what has been referred to as an expressionist and human style. Simply put, this building was systematically designed and refined to capture and disperse daylight with a combination of grace and efficiency.

Sitting between Portland to the north and Oregon's capitol city Salem to the south, the drive to Mount Angel takes you to the center of Oregon's central valley. About 186 feet above sea level the town is protected by the Cascade Range to the east and the Coastal Range to the west and enjoys mild winters with lots of cloud cover and rain and warm, dry summers. Central to the township is a wooded bluff rising about 300 feet from the valley floor. On this hilltop, Benedictine monks founded a monastery in 1862. This is the highest ground for miles around and if you drive in from the south highway you can see the campus of buildings spread across the hilltop. The library sits close to the edge of the hilltop looking northeast over a small valley lake.

The curving road from the base of the mount up to the campus is canopied by large evergreens. At the top, the narrow roadway curves to the right, rounding the first set of buildings and opening to a small central campus of buildings circling the hilltop. If you have come to visit the library your inclination will be to look for features that stand out from the other buildings. You may be surprised to find there is no such distinction from this view. All

Photo 2.4 Composite photo of the Mount Angel Abbey Library. The background image is of the central library space. The large overhead skylight and light shelf is used to flood the central space with diffuse natural light. The lower left photo shows how daylight from the central library follows to the lower level. The exterior view (lower right) is taken from the north and shows the fanlike shape of the building that is oriented to gather natural light that is used to illuminate rows of books (Ken Baker and Kevin Van Den Wymelenberg).

of the exteriors are faced with a yellow clay brick so there is a cohesion or soft-ness to all directions the eye looks. Symmetry is low and rectangular. It is not until you walk the pathway to the lower campus road that you see the height and distinguishing fan-shaped façade of the library. Even then, it takes a curi-osity to understand the contrast in exterior elevations.

From the main campus, the library looks like a one-story building when in actuality there are two additional stories exposed on the southern hillside. A low, nondescript flat section of roof provides some shelter from the elements for patrons entering the library. The entrance opens into a low-ceilinged atrium, lobby, and gallery, separating the outdoors from the main library space. It is when you almost reach the inner glass wall and doorway of the atrium that you begin to see the magnificence of the space within. Architect Nathan Good aptly described the central library space in an article written for *Environmental Design and Construction* magazine: "After passing through another pair of doors along the north side of the lobby and entering a space with increased natural light levels, one can look out over the centralized receptionist's desk to the main reading and book stack areas, which visually unfold into a dramatic atriumlike environment. During the day, a crescent-shaped skylight over the multistory interior space bathes a series of radiating light shelves, reading desks, and multilevel floors in soft natural light."[22]

You would be hard-pressed to find a better example of using natural light in a library. During a power outage in the 1990s, the Mount Angel Library was the only building on campus able to remain open for work and study.

Bank of Astoria

Manzanita, Oregon, is a small and picturesque coastal town about 20 miles south of Astoria and the mouth of the Columbia River. It has a maritime climate with over 120 inches of rainfall annually. Tall fir trees line the streets and provide a dark green canopy over most of the areas outside of the small central downtown district. A short two blocks after the turn off of highway 101 onto the small peninsula that carries the town, the Bank sits to the north of the street. It would be difficult even for a nonarchitecturally aware person to miss because the small gabled building fits into its surroundings like a piece of art on a gallery wall. The small branch building was designed by architect and author Tom Bender and has been occupied since 2001.

The main entrance of the Bank sits close to the sidewalk separated by a twelve-foot wide island of native stones, grasses, and shrubs. The central portion of the island holds a pool of water landscaped to look like a small natural pond. Rising totemlike from large boulders on the building side of the pond is the bare trunk of a fir tree. The trunk is inverted so it grows from a slender twelve-inch trunk at its base to a spreading three-foot root ball reaching to the underside of a glass overhang that extends from the main roofline to protect the entry and customers from rain and weather.

The roof has east and west gables and gently curves pagoda style—a form also used by Native American coastal tribes—from end to end and eve to eve to the ridge. Drainage from the roof is channeled though gutters to a spout that sits directly above and just out from the tree trunk. When Ken visited, there was a light mist to the air, just enough so that a steady drip of water fell from the spout into the pond creating a small spray as it struck the water. It occurred to Ken then that this was a design feature to celebrate water. It also had a practical application as the pond served as a drainage area for the roof, allowing water to naturally percolate into the ground, thus reducing runoff into the storm system. The exterior walls are sheathed in already weathered cedar shingles, doors, and windows trimmed with native timber. Again, the look is reminiscent of the vernacular Native American

Photo 2.5 The Bank of Astoria, Manzanita, Oregon, Tom Bender, architect. The exterior views are taken from the west. In the background photo, note the slope of the roof's ridge. Natural roofing material is designed to grow moss. The bottom left inset highlights the columnar tree trunk that supports the roof's drainage pan. The interior photo captures the beauty of form and textures highlighted by natural daylighting. Windows provide a close view of trees and the street. The changing light conditions by day create connections for people to the outdoors (Tom Bender and Ken Baker).

architecture. An open-air glassed-in alcove protects the main entry from multiseasonal ocean winds. The building's interior trim was milled from wood harvested from the building site.

There is a simple entrance in the rear of the building to accommodate customers walking in from the parking lot. While viewing and photographing the building, Ken observed that people parked in the back lot but preferred to walk around the building to enter through the main entrance. Based on the building's front design and landscape, it seemed that people take the time to walk to the front door because they are drawn to the beauty of the nature placed there. Walking into the building from the front you are greeted by an open space bathed in natural light. A vaulted ceiling covered in natural colored wood planking set with recessed lights reaches gable to gable. Walls painted the color of fresh peaches hold an even glow, reflecting the natural light that enters from high-set windows on each gable and the five skylights that are cut into the southwest roof façade. In the center of the building an inverted cedar trunk provides a central support column for the building's structure. Built circularly around this massive column is a customer desk where, standing, you can pen banking slips (see Photo 2.5). Behind the column to the eastern perimeter a ten-inch diameter bent trunk reaches floor to ceiling framing a circular alcove where customers can sit in private to view the contents of their safe-deposit boxes.

On the north end, there are more traditional teller stations; to the south are the open offices where customers sit with the banking staff. From employees' desks the gable windows frame a wonderful view of sky and trees. Ask them how they like the building and these veterans eagerly relate that this is the best place they have ever worked. You can see why. The space is magical and Ken found himself not wanting to leave.[23]

CONCLUSION

Providing office workers some control over the workspace environment and providing them an opportunity to connect with the great outdoors is a good business strategy. We spend much of our lives in buildings and wish to work in spaces that honor our need to be in relationship with nature. Buildings that utilize daylighting and provide worker views to the outside have been shown to significantly increase productivity and learning. The human connection to the building and building spaces, and the buildings connection to the climate, site, local community, and historical culture should be of primary consideration when architects program a new building design or existing building remodel.

This chapter provided a good grounding in "green building" and a better understanding of human responsive design and building technologies. Hopefully you were prodded by the top productivity-creating goal of giving building occupants control and interaction with the building and environment. The elements occupants want control over include light, air, space layout, and temperature. Cost concerns winning out over quality design really do negatively affect the happiness and productivity of a building's workforce. Jana and Ken sincerely believe that buildings can incorporate and observe the sacred and the creative and that sound building approaches that celebrate the spiritual connection between people, buildings, and the natural environment are critical to our personal well-being and to our ability to be productive.

Part II: The Art of Creating Culture in Towers

THIS SECTION EXPLORES the development of community and organizational culture in relation to place and space. The focus is on people and the creation of community in an ever-changing world of built environments.

3 / Workplace Lessons from Working and Living in Towers

ONCE A BUILDING passes the two-story mark, people start getting onto elevators and stop walking past others, which means that the human connection is lost and the potential for community and creativity is diminished. Unless structures for human interaction are built into each day, people and buildings become barriers to each other. This chapter explores examples of building communities from companies such as Fortune 500 companies and other best places to work, as well as stories and lessons from residential communities such as nursing homes, apartments, and planned neighborhoods and from social enterprises such as churches, libraries, and neighborhood gyms.

WORKPLACES AS LIFE CENTERS

In Minneapolis, Minnesota, the Target Corporation headquarters building has implemented a life center approach for employees. The Target headquarters has an office of the Department of Motor Vehicles (open weekly) in it so that employees can get or renew a license. It has dry-cleaning services, photofinishing, a cafeteria (where prepaid food cards can be purchased), printing, and credit union services. Also found on-site are ATMS, a coffee shop, places to buy bus passes and stamps and to mail packages. Further, as a variety of corporations have, the Target Corporation has a company store with company-branded merchandise and a day-care center for employees' children. The headquarters office holds blood drives too. All of these offerings help make employees' lives easier and create an inspiring community.

The creation of life centers at work includes university campus settings where studying is the student's work and where teaching is the professor's work. For example, Idaho's land grant institution, the University of Idaho, spent years creating their Living Learning Community on campus. The University of Idaho's Director of University Residences, Michael Griffel, speaks passionately about what has been created, how it has changed student housing and learning on campus, and how new communities of living and learning now exist.

The process by which the Living Learning Community came into being was comprehensive, inclusive, and timed. Because of years of student housing use declines, student housing occupancy had dropped to about 75 percent of capacity. As a result of occupancy being low, the money to improve buildings was not there and a spiral of challenges ensued. In addition, because student feedback included unhappiness with the housing building aesthetics and functionality, and because of years of feedback from students, faculty, and staff as well as the more recent formal student surveys and the resulting poor satisfaction with housing ratings, the goal became clear. The goal was to build new housing that was student and learning centered so that students, faculty, and staff want to live, learn, and work in the resulting built environment. The stakeholder input gathering process began with 120 students, faculty, and prospective students meeting in about 20 focus groups to discuss what a living learning center would include and how it would look and work. "Picture how you want it to be" was the guiding opening statement. Additionally, about 600 surveys were completed to gather input from students, student government, faculty, and staff. A consulting firm was hired to help provide guidance and form to the project and the resulting building proposal. Over a nearly two-year period, there was a core group of 20–25, that Director Griffel refers to as the "dream team," that did research and literature reviews about what achieves academic success in an environment, visited with friends and other campuses, brainstormed, reviewed the focus group information, and met every week to determine what should be included in the living learning center. The time spent researching and gathering information meant that the team used good research, good best-practice information on learning and building design, and sufficient market research with students. The volume of research was reviewed and synthesized with all the stakeholders at the decision-making table.

At some institutions, student housing is handled by two separate divisions within a university: resident life departments, which address student needs, life, and success issues; and financial departments, which focus on operations and costs. In this project at the University of Idaho, the discussions and domains of responsibility were merged. The university became focused on living communities and on learning based on the premise that learning happens when people live and work together in shared communities. Traditionally, campus living communities take on a theme: international house; the name and life of a famous person; the College of Natural Resources house; College of Engineering house; religious studies house; or even multidisciplinary study communities.

University environments around the world have discovered that when people are grouped together, the characteristics of that group of people are enhanced whether they are positive characteristics are not. So the goal is to create group environments that enhance, enlarge, and improve academics, problem-solving skills, language skills, human interactions, and overall life success skills.

Before new and wholly remodeled space was constructed, the University of Idaho started out by getting rid of 40-year-old mattresses and painting the residence hall rooms. Both the improvements and the now lack in available on-campus living space eventually led to a campus housing situation in which there was not enough space on campus for students to live and the university ended up with students temporarily living in local hotels.

As improvements on all fronts were being made, a high sense of community was developing. In order to build on the new-found changes, the university created affinity programs that were about mutual self-interest for students and their colleges. The university needed to have each of its colleges be able to keep good students, and the housing communities helped with both the learning and retention of students. To continually improve and enhance the housing community experience, the University of Idaho pursued a grant from the U.S. Department of Education that focused on improving student retention and graduation rates. Part of the grant was used to assess students' self-reported behavior and their perceptions of their peers on a variety of scales including study habits. One of the resulting goals was to change the environment in the residence halls. Another goal was to have residence hall communities clearly visualize and demonstrate care, listening, and a sense of shared purpose in learning. The idea was that there was a need to feel the qualitative differences in the residence hall or living center. Yes, the feeling of being cared for and about, along with strong academic experiences, makes a difference. People tend to stay in environments where they feel cared about, safe, and academically focused.

In the quest of always looking for ways to create new environments to create academic success, the need for balance between private and group space became clear: the living learning centers include group or community space as well as private rooms. Director Griffel says of the private rooms: "They are a retreat from the outside world. In order to be good community members we need to be sane and need time and space to be personally well too. We need to have private space." The group spaces allow for ideas to be exchanged, stories to be told, group study sessions, social time, and play. The living learning communities are about striking a balance between community and individual/private space.

Throughout the design, build-out, and occupancy periods, stakeholders were involved. Staff felt engaged and listened to in the building and preparation process. During the input phase for instance, it was discovered that what is practical for custodial—totally easy cleaning—is not really inviting to live in. So, there was some healthy tension about building for cost, versus easy cleaning, versus aesthetics. Director Griffel indicates that "The residences have more of a residential grade appearance and build-out than a commercial feel—and that as a result the space has been harder to keep clean. Yet the groups are working together and have gained an understanding that buildings need to be softer in order to be warmer."

On the University of Idaho campus, as on other campuses, some of the campus buildings have been referred to as prison cells versus these new living learning communities. The difference in the new living learning center construction does cause a difference in the wear of and use of the buildings. For instance 10 p.m. to 7 a.m. is when most of the buildings on campus are cleaned. But the residence halls are cleaned at their least busy times, 7 a.m. to 4 p.m., and this difference in cleaning time has staff and students interacting with each other. There is now a sense of having a "residence life team" in which every member feels equally important to a student's success because now everyone has a chance to interact with each other as people contributing to the overall success of students. With this high level of engagement, the staff members both contribute to and receive energy from the interactions with students. Students, faculty, and staff on campus, as well as visiting students and parents, see and feel the difference between dormitories and these new living learning centers. The centers have become a part of the recruiting tools the university has to offer.

One of the challenges in the living learning community has had to do with creating both a sense of openness, sharing, and learning at the same time as creating a sense of privacy and security. There is a need to have safety and security for everyone and yet to still create an open, community-oriented space. Griffel states that the steps they have taken focus on being "vigilant but invisible." For instance, the entry- and exit-ways of buildings having cameras, and there are cameras on elevators. The student room suite doors have lock-security on a key-pad and each of the individual bedroom doors has an electronic-lock too. On the other hand, the community spaces are completely open.

The University of Idaho's Living Learning Community project is located on prime real estate in the center of the campus. The original design for the project included an on-grade parking lot with the buildings on a podium beginning one story above grade. The original project design was aimed at meeting the LEED's requirement for Bronze or Silver certification. But it would have required more steel, and the soil water table was found to be at about three and a half or four feet. Then, the bids for the total project including the parking lot with the building on a podium above came in 20 to 60 percent over the budget goal. So the project team had to regroup with a renewed focus on the budget and still get close to the design dream that had been worked on for years. While the completed project missed the Bronze LEED certification by a few points due to some of the lumber versus steel uses and to some of the costs, in other ways, the finished project would have met LEED Bronze standards: heating and air systems that run very efficiently with lots of controls, inclusion of high energy-efficient washers and dryers, reclaiming water for things like watering the grass while avoiding the living areas, and other unique features. While Director Griffel thinks that the Living Learning Community may be one of the most environmentally sound campus buildings in the state, he knows that even more can be done as they look to future campus buildings.

Looking to the future, while drawing from the past, far from the University of Idaho, the University of Pittsburgh's Cathedral of Learning, dedicated in 1937, embodies another approach to learning centers and community creation. Built during the depression era in the United States, the Cathedral of Learning is recognized as the world's second tallest education building at 42 stories and 535 feet in height. The building includes a ground-level commons room that is three-stories high, classrooms, administrative offices, libraries, computer centers, and a restaurant. In other words, the building includes spaces for study, for group interactions, and for socializing.

STORIES FROM *FORTUNE*-RANKED COMPANIES AND BEST PLACES TO WORK

Hewlett Packard, Boise, Idaho, Site Stories

Globally recognized technology company Hewlett Packard has over 140,000 employees in 178 countries. Being familiar with the community-centered and team-oriented work accomplished at Hewlett Packard's (HP) Boise site, we interviewed HP Vice President of Human Resources Denise Kohtz about the site's strategy and approaches for creating community in their buildings and on their campus. Following are key excerpts from the interview.

Baker and Kemp: How do you build a sense of community for your work teams at HP?

Kohtz: We are interested in building community at various levels in our organization. At the organizational unit level, we aspire to ensure that each of our employees has a position plan with roles, responsibilities, and metrics that clearly align to our higher purpose and objectives—this begins to build a sense of community through focusing on a common goal. Then, as plans are formed and implemented, "how" we work together is filled with community-building events that occur frequently to foster two-way communications (meetings, coffee talks, communication sessions, MBWA—management by walking around, and so on) and to measure and celebrate progress and results (checkpoints, reviews, celebrations). At the smaller, work team level, we also foster community by encouraging a strong manager/ employee relationship and colleague collaboration and teamwork. At a "site" or location level, we encourage community among employees at the same geographic location—whether they work with one another in the same organizational unit or not. This community building emphasizes relationships with people in our buildings, and with the external community. Company initiatives and leadership advocate for site councils, employee action teams, networking, community volunteerism, and other actions that help employees feel engaged in the multiple communities within which they operate.

Baker and Kemp: How do you build a sense of shared community within the whole of the HP corporation?

Kohtz: Within all of HP, frequent communications from senior leadership (in person, web casts, memos, etc.); gatherings of work teams; visits with customers and partners; celebratory events; morale surveys; continuous work on our culture, on the behaviors that keep our values alive; encouraging all to give back to our communities; all help our sense of shared community.

Baker and Kemp: What do employees say means the most to them in their pursuit of community?

Kohtz: As a result of employee feedback, surveying, and listening sessions, we have discovered that employees feel the greatest sense of community from the following things: the ability to come to a work environment where all are respected and valued for the talents and contributions they bring; the opportunity to network with, learn from, interact with colleagues; the chance to know what is being done in their location, in their organization; having fun at work; having a sense of pride of who HP is and what HP does in the community.

Baker and Kemp: What does your company do to define and reinforce its internal culture?

Kohtz: HP has defined and communicated our values in addition to our company objectives and goals to all employees. In addition, to reinforce HP's culture, employee performance behaviors on "how" work is done at HP (in addition to what is done) are articulated and included in performance reviews. HP actively trains managers and employees on the "HP Way," on HP values, on ways to live out and perform to these values. HP also conducts an annual morale survey, which we call "Voice of the Workforce," which includes action plans and follow up/mid-year "pulse" surveys to check progress. Part of the "HP Way" is a strong focus on two-way communications, gatherings, learning opportunities, and valuing diversity. The company also holds summits and special meetings focused directly on improving our culture and work environment. Another part of the HP values includes the encouragement of open and honest communications and a focus on integrity (within values, leadership messages, ethics training, open door policy, etc.).

Baker and Kemp: HP has a very modular approach to organizing workspace and cubicles. In fact, HP teams are often reorganized physically once a project is completed and a new one is begun. How do employees feel about working in your building(s)?

Kohtz: Employees like the open cubicle space, it seems to match the working style of most employees. They also like the "break" areas and the open meeting areas for collaborative work. Employees have also made clear that they like and want the facilities and grounds to be clean, neat, and updated. However, some of the drawbacks include higher background noise levels, lack of privacy, lack of local climate control and lighting levels. Common areas and closed-door meeting rooms that can be scheduled are available that provide some relief for those conditions and requirements. The overall objective is to provide a work environment that allows the employee to be productive. Standard programs are administered to maintain consistent levels of cleanliness and kept-up facility conditions.

Baker and Kemp: Do employees in different buildings have a different sense of productivity and community? How are the outlooks different?

Kohtz: At the HP Boise site, our campus has buildings that are somewhat spread out, so it is common to not visit all of the buildings in the normal course of work —which may cause some to feel like they do not know what is happening in other parts of HP. Throughout the years we have had workgroups located in nearby "satellite" locations and from our main headquarters campus come to work at the Boise site. These groups have expressed mixed feelings—some very much miss the main campus as it provides more services than the satellite locations. Some love the independence and chance to have a smaller, possibly different feel than they have experienced at our site.

Baker and Kemp: Do customers, clients, vendors, and contractors comment on how different your space feels compared to other places they conduct business? What do they say or mention?

Kohtz: We most often hear that HP is HP, that anywhere in the world you visit, there are many similarities—you know when you are in a HP facility. Contractors and consultants feel comfortable operating within our environment. Many of them have office environments that are much different than ours. Tools and data are accessible and available. In our open environment, the consultants often times adapt their work style to a less formal "roll up your sleeves" approach.

Baker and Kemp: Did your original and/or remodel architecture plan include environmental concerns? Resource use concerns? People productivity concerns? If so, how?

Kohtz: Most of the buildings on our campus were designed to be configured with modular type furniture systems (partitions and cubicles). The building core and shell are open, with very few interior walls. There are no enclosed offices and few private spaces such as closed-door conference rooms that can be reserved. The majority of the population is assigned a cubicle of similar size (8 feet by 10 feet), and outfitted with work surfaces, etc., that make efficient use of the space. The cubicle concept is a way of life for most employees and is embraced as a symbol of equality among management and teams, as well as promotes open communication and collaboration. We try to locate most work groups contiguously.   Common areas such as break rooms, open conference areas, breakout areas, and free address cubicles (LAN and phone available) are designed into the group layouts and are used frequently. The atmosphere is informal, and employees like the flexibility to utilize this type of space "on demand," rather than have to reserve it in advance. The cafeteria seating area is utilized similarly, as are seating areas established in a number of our building links. Most large department (or site-wide) communication sessions are conducted in one of these open type environments rather than in more traditional conference rooms.   The utility systems such as lighting, HVAC, and power distribution have been designed with the flexibility to accommodate a number of furniture layouts, reconfigurations, and minor outfitting without major upgrades. We have reduced the number of moves in recent years but historically have moved employees frequently, as teams are formed and/or product cycles change.   The office environment described is a real match with the personality of our employees, and our company. It is open, informal, productive, and promotes communication and teamwork.

Baker and Kemp: Does your building include interior or exterior quiet spaces, gardens, landscaped sitting areas, or walking paths for employee use? How much space is dedicated to them, and what do they look like?

Kohtz: Our interior building space includes break areas, classroom-like and informal meeting areas, recreational area (video games, ping-pong, etc.), cafeteria, coffee stations, coffee bar, vending areas, microwaves, fitness center, and a lactation room. Our external campus includes a walking path/par course with exercise stations; soccer and baseball fields; volleyball and baseball courts; horseshoe pits; a giant chess board; an attractive park space with pond, trees, picnic-table area, playground, cooking facilities, rest rooms; and landscaping that includes trees, shrubs, flowers, and commemorative statues for HP and our partners.

At the conclusion of the interview, Kohtz shared the following story about the Boise HP site, which has several thousand employees:

On the Boise site, many employees were feeling a need to be more connected— with each other and with our external community. A few years ago, to meet this need, we held a "search conference,"—a meeting methodology that takes a diagonal slice of our organization, a mix of people from various backgrounds, experiences, roles, and brings them into an open conversation. What they do have in common is that they are thought leaders—willing to think differently, see the possibilities, are creative, and are action oriented. After honoring our past, outlining the realities of today, and imagining the future we hope for, a number of action teams were formed. The process began in 2004 or so. Then, in early 2006, we held a formal "renewal" meeting to celebrate the successes these teams have had and to evaluate our teams for relevancy looking into our new future. Key past successes include the following: formation of a site leadership council which oversees work environment, business, and community happenings for our HP Boise-based teams. They meet every six weeks to review local giving and business impacts on our site. They bring all managers together twice a year to discuss what is happening, and to ask for their engagement and leadership in helping to enable any change. They bring all employees together one to two times a year for the same reason. Another communication improvement came in the form of bringing back a local-site paper-based newsletter. In our days of e-mail, this publication had gone by the wayside a number of years ago. The return of our "InSite" newsletter has reminded us of great days in our company history and has helped keep us connected through human interest stories about our fellow employees.

Kohtz continues:

At HP we also discovered that "fun" was an important factor for employees. So, we brought a myriad of fun things to our site. For example: a giant chess board is in our courtyard, we have added video-game stations and game tables to break areas, there are water bottles in our fitness area. We have theme days, increased advertising to employees about the employee discounts they are eligible for. And, we've focused on increasing our involvement of large volunteer groups in community events, fund raisers, and community service projects. Then we celebrate the high level of volunteerism our employees give to the community. HP has held an innovation fair to encourage new business ideas from employees. And, we keep exploring more ways to build and maintain community in our workplace. For instance, the action teams are continuing with a focus on these areas: external community, internal community, growth and innovation, and communication.

Longaberger Headquarters Building Models Its Product

An extraordinary example of a building reflecting a company's purpose, mission, and culture is the Longaberger Home Office in Newark, Ohio (see Photo 3.1). That is right, the building is shaped like a giant picnic basket and baskets are the company's business. Rose Anzalone, a Longaberger employee and Jana's original introduction to Longaberger, says that "Working in the 'big basket' is actually kind of neat. It is always a great conversation piece when people ask you where you work. Our lobby is beautiful and we have some of our products displayed. We always have tours and visitors in our lobby which can sometimes bring another layer of excitement to the workday. It is nice to see people admiring our craft and our company."

Photo 3.1 The Longaberger Home Office is a seven-story building that replicates the company's trademarked Longaberger Basket (The Longaberger Company).

Here are some facts about the Longaberger Home Office: In October 1995, construction began on The Longaberger Company's seven-story home office, a replica of the company's Medium Market Basket and a building dream of company founder Dave Longaberger. Construction was completed in December 1997. The 180,000-square-foot office building is situated on a 25-acre, parklike setting off State Route 16 in Newark, Ohio (35 miles east of Columbus). The cherry woodwork used throughout the building was harvested from the Longaberger Golf Club property and was milled, sawed, and shaped by Longaberger employees. In addition, Longaberger employees designed the exterior and interior of the building, managed the entire project, and constructed more than 50 percent of the building. The sense of pride and ownership in the building and the work done in it is high. The building is visited by hundreds of thousands each year, including Longaberger home consultants, customers, and many others desiring a closer look at this one-of-a-kind structure. What people come to see is the "basket" that encases offices which are situated around a seven-story, 30,000-square-foot atrium filled with natural daylight from the skylight overhead and includes two basket handles that are attached to the top of the building with copper and wooden rivets replicating those on a Longaberger Basket. The handles, which weigh about 150 tons, are heated to prevent ice from forming.

Farm Bureau Companies of Idaho's Headquarters Building Mirrors Its Mission

Meeting space, wall art, office cubes, company lobbies, and even entire building design can mirror the mission of the organization. For instance, the Farm Bureau Companies of Idaho in Pocatello, Idaho, has built a headquarters building that is reminiscent of agriculture. The curved, stainless steel-faced towers are symbolic of plowshares and the building's lobby is symbolic of a grain silo and is entered by walking over a paving pattern designed to look like gears from farm implements. The reception desk design mirrors the overall shape of the building and the interior atrium brings natural light into the building. The interior railings along open walkways are made of cable and replicate the image of wire fencing. Throughout the building, twenty-first-century wiring, heating, cooling, phone systems, and individual workstation climate controls have been installed. This building models human responsive design because of the attention paid to both the building's style being reflective of the mission and to providing tools and comfort controls for individuals to do their best possible work.

Pfizer Research and Development Listens to Their Research Scientists Before Building

Having built a reputation for building work environments that are conducive to scientific work and to scientists, we also interviewed facility managers at Pfizer. Pfizer has manufacturing sites in 83 countries. In 1996 when Viagra was just about to hit the market, Pfizer Inc. was focused on designing an innovative lab building to address four goals according to Michael J. Mirabito who has been with Pfizer for 14 years and is responsible for delivering global facility projects for the multinational pharmaceutical company. Mirabito is on a team which supports research and development facilities in St. Louis, Missouri, and La Jolla, California. So, the first goal was to be number one in the world in the pharmaceutical market: as a result, the best employees would have to be recruited and retained in order to reach the goal. This included providing work environments that could give Pfizer a competitive advantage for finding and keeping great employees, researchers, and scientists. An equally important and top goal was, and still is, safety. The next goal was to create a quality of life for people at work that would cause them to say "this is where I want to be working." And the final goal was to build office and laboratory space that would be able to accommodate change in a short period of time plus be able to handle the science anticipated over the next 15 years.

Pfizer's desire was to recruit more scientists and the additional scientists would have to come from the same talent pool upon which other companies were drawing. So, Pfizer recognized that the building design could become an employee recruitment tool. In order to innovate with the building design, scientists were brought into the conversation so that their needs for safety, conducive office and write-up space, and space for collaboration could be incorporated. The real difference in the new lab and office design came from listening to Pfizer scientists who stressed the importance of close office proximity to the labs without compromising safety and while improving the overall quality of life in their workspace.

Mirabito says "Most building designs are typical. They are about bricks and mortar and efficient use of space. In our business, research is where we focus. So we focus on our employees, their management style, and on what makes people productive." He goes on to say that Pfizer realized "co-locating chemists and biologists, rather than keeping them separated by floors or buildings, to ensure interactions were frequent" was important to enhancing knowledge sharing. As a result, Pfizer put scientists from different disciplines on the same floor and across from each other where they could see one another working and could come together to collaborate in a "town square" that has copy machines, tack-surface walls, meeting space, and a communal area that allows getting together informally and exchanging ideas and talking. The reorganization of people and space was based on the belief that science will be advanced as a result of sharing information, talking to each other, and exploring what is happening with their experiments. In essence says Mirabito, "By design, we foster collaboration by enabling people to come to the center of the building and encourage human interaction."

In the building redesign, the office is now exterior to the lab, so scientists access their labs through their offices rather than through the lab itself. This makes the office space more aesthetic, quiet, and comfortable due to the use of acoustic tiles and carpeting in the offices. Now, scientists can have coffee and food at their desks while writing up reports or planning their experiments. The improved quality of work life, plus the increased daylight into both the office and lab spaces, has made a marked improvement. Daylight was viewed as very important and desired in connection to the labs, common science, and office spaces. Thus the building has glass windows to the outdoors, into the company atrium, and into the labs themselves.

The Pfizer Groton, Connecticut, building is known as Building 220. It has 550,000 square feet and is home to 600 people. Building 220 has a central atrium that is bordered by labs, all of which are glass walled. It is a high-functioning building and it feels and looks good. From the exterior of the building, visitors have commented that Building 220, which is the centerpiece building of the Groton campus, opens its arms up to the site's front gate entry to the several dozen buildings and 100 acres of campus that include walking trails. The building gives a warm feeling to the large site in that it looks a bit like a butterfly, with the lab spaces being the wings and the central lobby atrium being the body. The Building 220 atrium serves as the space for site and company-wide meetings.

Creating a sense of community in such a large building was a challenge. Pfizer did it by creating neighborhoods and town squares on each floor—spaces where people could be comfortable, and where they would bump into each other thereby fostering collaboration. Each town square area feels like its own neighborhood of thought and people. This contributes to a sense of community and to a quality of life that is enjoyable. Eliminating as many distractions of daily life as possible—on the chore front—has also helped work to be more enjoyable. Other things done in the building to make life easier include having a business travel agency, a bank, a company store, and a computer center. Several days a month vendors are on-site providing a variety of products for purchase: one day it is CDs, another day kids' books, and around the holidays there are specific items for sale. Employee electronic newsletters and special clubs such as ski clubs or theater clubs are also a part of the mix of employee amenities. Additionally, the site includes a fitness center, a medical center and health services, a central cafeteria—with satellite locations in other campus buildings—and a child care center that is off-site but nearby. Lessening distractions and providing options at work is an important part of Pfizer's creation of quality of life for its employees.

When talking to Mirabito about what employees say means the most to them in their pursuit of community, he responds that employees are "driven by the science and finding breakthrough medicine. It is their life mission to help people live longer and healthier lives." To that end, the lab space itself is big enough to accommodate a lot of high technology scientific equipment that is needed for people to do this important work. Because of the increased use of scientific equipment, the element of human safety is increased as well. Additionally, Pfizer utilizes the clean-corridor, dirty-corridor approach. This preserves the people space. The clean corridor is where the office space and town squares are accessed and allows the clean space to be more user friendly, which speaks to the human element. The dirty corridor is designed and treated for handling chemicals in and out—door guards, wall guards, and all of the architectural treatment is very different. There is linoleum rather than carpeting on the floor and the air movement is increased over that in the office areas. The dirty corridor is for the movement of materials. Mirabito says "Pfizer has made a commitment to build this way. It speaks to the importance of the individual employees and allows preservation of the core of the building."

Pfizer is very focused on sustainability and continues to improve and enhance its infrastructure systems in order to reduce waste and energy consumption. Generally, laboratory buildings are high consumers of energy. For instance, laboratory building air is 100 percent fresh air which cannot be recirculated. In a lab environment the air change rate is 12–15 times per hour versus 6 changes per hour in an office. Pfizer can build great buildings, but if they are not functional and science is not productive, then the company has not made a good investment.

Another Pfizer employee adds his commentary about building community in buildings. David Greunke, Director, Global Strategic Facilities Planning, supports the planning and design for all major research and development building projects. His team benchmarks what makes a good office and lab environment and assists in the master planning process for all research and development sites. Greunke has been with the company for 10 years and has seen lots of corporate changes in employee culture during that time. Even with the ongoing change, it has remained important to keep listening to the scientists and their needs. Scientists are involved in the needs assessment phase and the discussions for the design of buildings. Input gathered by Pfizer planners who speak with individual scientists, their functional workgroups, and focus groups about a new building plan is a part of the process. When it comes to using the neighborhood and town square spaces in the Pfizer buildings, management encourages people to use the spaces for interaction. Most interaction zones or neighborhoods have electronic setups for use of technology so that problem solving can continue. Integrated design and full participation from the design team and the building occupants and users are now Pfizer hallmarks.

Interaction with the human resources team also is a vital part of the process, which focuses on the corporation's human resource requirements and on identifying needed building amenities at a site level. For instance, some sites have child care and some have more conference centers than others. The focus has been on how to get researchers more productive and create a space where they are comfortable working. Science research takes a lot of time and concentration; it must be conducted in a safe manner within a safe work environment. Greunke also would encourage people looking to design buildings to keep both the people and work-function elements in mind:

> There is no magic or single solution. You have to understand what your business is about. A Pfizer building does not necessarily work for State Farm. Know the business. Know what needs to be done and achieved and design the building for that. Again, you have to know what the business is doing and what each site's culture is in order to design the best building.

Pfizer has plants and research sites all over the world. Greunke goes on to say that you

> don't just impose strict standards globally. Work with the culture of each site and the culture of the country they are located in. In La Jolla, California, outdoor space can be used year round which is different than the sites in Ann Arbor, Michigan, or Groton, Connecticut, where indoor passages between buildings have to exist for people to move between buildings in the winter. Each of these sites is different than the sites in Europe or Asia. At the 200-acre Pfizer site in Sandwich, England, in Kent, amenities are critical to creating community and retaining talent at the site. For instance, there is a social club near the campus so employees can interact after hours.

HUMAN RESOURCES AND BUILDINGS GO TOGETHER

During the interviews for this book, a repeated theme was that human resource managers were most involved in the amenities and special service areas included in the building's design. In other words, to cost-oriented, architectural, and construction types, human resources people were involved in the fluff and stuff to make people feel good and the things which create added costs in a building. Yet, as is the premise of this book, the increased productivity, creativity, morale, and employee retention found makes it worth investing in buildings that are energy efficient, cost effective, highly functional, and people focused. Human resources managers can contribute to the overall success of a building's employee population by participating in the design process as well as in the ongoing building and maintenance of employee culture and community.

Human resources professionals continue to be responsible for human resource policy documentation, implementation, and enforcement; recruiting and retaining great employees; training and development; benefits; safety; and recognition of employees. In addition to all of the legally and organizationally required aspects of human resource professional jobs, the typical and critical human resource domains for building communities in buildings are corporate consciousness, citizenship, and philanthropic giving; on-site amenities; people and training; conversation spaces and workout places; unique employee benefits; celebrations and recognition; team meetings; and even corporate alumni groups. Each of these areas are discussed in the following pages and could of course have books devoted to them in their own rights.

Corporate and Community Consciousness

From the Aveda Corporation in New York, New York, to McDonald's Corporation in Oakbrook, Illinois, and Starbucks in Seattle, Washington, companies like these communicate their consciousness and values with employees, vendors, shareholders, and customers by communicating on packages, in advertisements, and in their retail locations about what they are doing to make the world a better place for all of us. Take for instance the community giving campaigns that fund schools, literacy, recycling, and housing programs—these beyond-the-workplace-giving undertakings are communicated. Also consider the volunteer days set aside by corporations—employees are encouraged to take one to three days off a year to volunteer in the community and away from work. Some corporations sponsor events by providing staff teams who can serve as ushers at theatrical events, sporting events, parades, and fun-runs. Community sponsorships include encouraging staff teams to get involved in raking up a yard or paint-a-thons for needy and disabled or elderly people.

Aveda Corporation expressed part of its corporate employee consciousness by working with architect Maya Lin to create a workplace that Lin describes as "a nurturing work environment that connects people to the out-of-doors. A work environment that is about shared space and a sense of community." In much the same way, Pfizer, Inc. the world-wide pharmaceutical company described earlier in this chapter, focused its innovative research building on meeting both the research work and human interaction and connection needs of scientists focused on finding cures for many of the world's health problems.

Starbucks has a flier in its stores that discusses "Starbucks commitment to social responsibility" and presents the annual highlights of Starbucks corporate socially responsible behavior. The story unfolded is one of coffee, coffee communities, responsiveness to communities and customers, environmental responsibility, and the creation of a great work environment. As a result of sticking to its story and following through in its behavior, Starbucks's customers and employees alike appreciate knowing the story and feel more connected to the Starbucks brand, the Starbucks way of doing business, and to the Starbucks stores.

Starbucks and McDonald's Corporation share a common approach to in-store communications with customers, employees, and prospective employees. McDonald's stores include brochure racks with job applications that communicate the company brand and philosophy; customer comment cards that reinforce the corporate values toward community; commitment to the customer flyers that share founder Ray Kroc's vision and commitment to giving back to the communities that have made their business possible; and a flyer that is a social give-back report of sorts that details where and how McDonald's has given back to communities, how it has partnered and with whom; and how employee training and opportunities play into the well-being of the community at large.

Corporate consciousness also includes the giving of dollars to support arts groups, schools, ongoing education, and community social needs. For instance, Union Pacific has made a commitment to American education and America's future workforce by sponsoring The Principal's Partnership for ongoing education of public high school principals in 23 states west of the Mississippi River. Knowing that the corporation hires about 5,000 people a year and sees about 1,700 people a year retire, Union Pacific executives decided that part of their corporate citizenship would be the sponsorship of this program. Philanthropic giving to a community ranges from new programs being created, as Union Pacific has done, to giving to established cultural, nonprofit, social-service needs-driven organizations already at work in a city, county, or region.

Community involvement and corporate citizenship include sponsoring events held by nonprofits and allowing time for employees to serve in the community. For instance, the Allstate Corporation, a Fortune 50 company, publishes an annual report titled *Corporate Social Responsibility Report.* It details the company's involvement in its office communities, its commitment to giving through The Allstate Foundation which has a mission to support and improve neighborhoods, schools, communities and other nonprofit organizations, and employee giving through community outreach programs.

Corporate citizenship applies to businesses of all sizes, from the one-person company working from home to the Fortune 10 company with global locations. Corporate citizenship includes having a social vision, developing a focused strategy for being a corporate citizen, and partnering with the community in the ways that best meet its needs. It also includes listening to employees and supporting their efforts in the community and annually reviewing and assessing the contributions being made to the community to ensure that the giving is in keeping with your company values and mission. Companies of all sizes can demonstrate community consciousness and citizenship by teaming with other businesses, creating partnerships around the community where company sites are located and that the organization touches or can touch anywhere in the world, and by encouraging employees to volunteer.

On-Site Amenities

Companies, advertising agencies, governmental entities have in various ways brought human energy alive in workplaces by incorporating business campus walking trails, running trails, basketball, racquetball, and volleyball courts, along with showering facilities. Sometimes these activity spaces are outdoors on the ground, other times on rooftops, and still other times right inside the office area: spaces for play, for meetings, for individual work, for team work and collaboration, for creative conversation. Concierge services, on-site or nearby child care, elder care, and sick-child assistance make a difference in employee well-being too. Each of the companies interviewed for this book have incorporated a variety of spaces into their overall office and work environments. In the United States and in China, some corporations have included movie theaters in their workspace designs so as to create employee camaraderie and company-sponsored movie space for employees and their families to gather on their own time.

People and Training

Both for-profit and governmental organizations over the last two decades have established minimum numbers of days to be spent each year by employees learning new skills and participating in training sessions. Depending on the organization, the minimums have ranged from 8 hours to 40 hours a year for employee training. Collectively, since 2000, companies are annually spending billions of dollars on employee training. Employee training subsets include mentoring, coaching, teamwork development, leadership development, executive development, skill-specific training, product training, and safety training.

Conversation Spaces and Workout Places—Unique Employee Benefits

From art-filled break rooms to fully equipped workout facilities, employers of all sizes look for ways to provide unique employee benefits that will help in the recruitment and retention of employees. The traditional and now expected medical and vacation related benefits are not enough in competitive job markets. Now, employees ask about such benefits as child care, elder care, flextime, counseling programs, extra vacation days and comp days, tuition reimbursement, on-site gym space, off-site gym memberships, discount programs, company sports teams, and employee-oriented trips. Attention to office ergonomics might even be considered a part of the benefits package when viewed from the standpoints of preventing medical problems and injury and of improving workplace productivity. Concierge services that ease errand-running stress on employees are an option too, as are holistic wellness programs and services. Flextime includes flexible use of working hours to allow personal appointments, school appointments, time with family, the ability to juggle child care and elder care issues, and the ability to work at highest-energy times of day for each employee. The National Sleep Foundation's research suggests that sleep-deprived workers costs U.S. companies about $18 billion a year in lost productivity, injuries, and other workplace challenges—so, perhaps the benefit program can include sleep-pattern improvements. Educational programs for smoking cessation and weight loss for the employee or for family members also fit into a potential benefits package.

Celebrations and Recognitions

In order to celebrate diversity, a company could consider a monthly or quarterly theme such as Art History Month, Women's History Month, Company History Month, Cultures of the World Month, Earth Day, Energy Awareness Week, Carpooling Month, or any other theme that helps to convey new ideas and express the company's values about both human and biological diversity. Be aware, however, that themes of the year can sometimes work against an organization when the theme becomes a distracter rather than a reinforcement for doing business. Focus on themes that relate to your business, carry clear messages, and lead to specific actions that serve and benefit employees, customers, and the company.

Recognition of individual and team contributions help keep employees working for you. Recognitions can include thank you notes, employee of the month awards, parking privileges, and bonuses. They also can include sales incentive award trips, educational meetings, and conference attendance. Consider the fact that people most often leave jobs for emotional reasons rather than for pay or monetary reasons. Others have said "people do not work for money, they work for a cause, a sense of life purpose, for a greater good and a high goal." Employee performance reviews can be utilized much more effectively when used as a reinforcement for performance rather than as a punishment for lack of performance. Or, how about more time in the garden space, on a walking path, planting a tree in honor of employee achievement, or providing better access to daylight, outdoor views, or pieces of art as ideas for recognition? Then, there are low-cost and great ways to say "Thank you": notes, cards, e-mails, phone calls, lunch, dinner, gift certificates, trendy items, electronics, trips, spa certificates, humorous rewards such as a singing fish or a brass bell with a funny quote, and company logo clothing and items all can be welcome forms of recognition. Logo clothing helps to create a sense of community because some companies are so big, that employees do not all know each other and yet when they see the logo on a shirt or jacket an immediate sense of connection and a community can spring forth. In other words, let people know how what they are doing is contributing to the success of the organization and that their work is appreciated.

Workplace rituals are another form of celebration and recognition that help to create community. Celebrations of birthdays, company anniversaries, life milestones such as having a child or a grandchild, a marriage; starting the day with exercise as is done in Asian-led companies around the world; daily work-planning meetings; quarterly all-employee meetings to share company results; and annual incentive and reward meetings are examples. Even rituals taken from neighborhoods, such as the weekly Flamingo Fridays in one Minnesota neighborhood keep people and their kids acquainted and connected during the warm summer months; while monthly cocktail hour events in New York, New York, and in other metropolitan city apartment and condominium complexes keep tower dwellers talking. At work, incorporate spontaneity: the first spring day the temperatures reach 70 degrees give everyone an extra half-hour for lunch, or celebrate because of needed rain fall.

Workplace traditions are yet another way to recognize and call attention to your unique way of doing business. Longaberger has done this in many ways with its headquarters office building. Many companies have discovered that their new approach to doing something becomes their workplace tradition for providing service, getting work done, and even for working together. For instance, establishing a once-a-quarter or once-a-year "clean-out-the-files day" is a tradition that forces a cleaning out and a regrouping for new work. Or, celebrating birthdays once a month at a staff meeting rather than every day there is a birthday can bring productivity up without loosing sight of valuing people. Another example is giving away candy and even dog biscuits at the bank and bank drive-through window. Neighborhoods and business places alike create community through picnics, Neighborhood Watch and team-focused security efforts, associations, clubs, activity groups, parades, contests, and theme events. Work-related traditions can include these activities and regular exhibits at or participation in trade associations, conferences, and business associations such as chambers of commerce.

FROM THE HUMAN RESOURCES FIELD

One of Jana's high-tech clients is AMI Semiconductor, a half-a-billion-dollar-a-year company, which has offices in North America, Europe, and Asia. Terri Timberman, Senior Vice President of Human Resources at AMI Semiconductor's world headquarters shares some of her experiences in building community for work teams.

Timberman says:

> I have done a number of things over the years that have been successful. Communities end up with their own language, history, hero/heroines, etc. Rituals are key to building and maintaining community. In one company, we had "food rituals" where on Wednesdays before payday we'd gather for breakfast at a local inexpensive place. It was an open invite and whoever could, showed up. Then, Friday lunch was at a Mexican restaurant, or we'd meet for Friday drinks after work. Potlucks celebrating various ethnic backgrounds of the employees were also a hit. Casual-dress day, t-shirts day, or Friday Hawaiian shirt day also brought some fun into the workplace. These rituals helped create a sense of belonging and of community

while providing an informal platform for communication, problem solving, and relationship building.

When asked what employees say means the most to them in their pursuit of community, Timberman says:

Feeling like they are a part of something bigger than themselves. Show employees how their work connects to the whole and how the whole impacts the larger community and even the world and how your products impact the world community. Samples of your products or the customer's end products, posters, pictures, testimonials from customers, are just some of the ways to help employees connect their community to the larger community.

When commenting on how different buildings in the company facility inventory feel to employees and visitors, Timberman reports that "One of our facilities is an older building that gets comments on how it looks and feels like something from the 1970s." She goes on to observe that,

I think it is harder for change to take place if the physical environment does not change with the times as well. You can change the environment without a new building. Simple upgrades such as paint or carpet, removal of internal walls or barriers, or the addition of artwork, posters or an "awards" wall are just a few low-cost examples of changing the physical environment to support a broader change in or support of a company's culture.

Communicate, Communication, and Communicated

The communication tools and vehicles used to reach employees can contribute to the creation of workplace community. E-mailed newsletters are great for people who read and process their electronic mail and who feel connected via electronic items rather than hard copy items. E-mailed communication can save printing costs. Company web sites for techno-driven customer and employee communications can work well. Web sites with internal security access codes can communicate the same messages. Not every learning style and age group will gravitate to your web site, so be sure the mix of your communication strategies is right for your employees and customers. Some companies, as you read about HP's experience earlier, have returned to hard copy newsletters in order to bring a more local flavor to communications. Hard copy newsletters, delivered at work or at home, can help family members feel like a part of the workplace community. For employees, include the following kinds of information in your communications: company news, employee recognition, employee opportunities, activities and discounts, stories profiling employees, stories about volunteerism by employees of the organization. External communications to customers and prospective customers are printed by insurance companies, hospitals, companies selling products and services; communications to citizens and taxpayers, such as school newsletters, create community knowledge and shared vision.

Corporate Alumni Groups

Just as graduating classes from high schools, private schools and colleges form alumni groups, so do some former corporate employees. With more than 500 known ex-employee groups in existence, these groups can become sources for businesses to tap to bring people back into a workplace. Companies may or may not endorse the groups' formations but people eager to form kindred communities form the groups anyway. Company alumni groups exist for the purpose of keeping people connected, doing new business networking, and for story telling and social purposes. Examples of groups include the Microsoft Alumni Network, Nabisco Alumni, Arthur Anderson Alumni, Ernst & Young, Hewlett-Packard, and Texas Instruments.

WORKPLACE LESSONS FROM NURSING HOMES AND CARE FACILITIES

Nursing homes also offer lessons in creating community. Just before the turn of the century, care facilities began recognizing the power of home-like settings: living rooms, dining areas that include private dining space options for families. Family room centers that incorporate dining room functions, television sitting areas, card playing areas, and conversation areas create a sense of place and of community in a larger building. Separate activity-specific rooms for crafts, for prayer, meditation, and reflection, and library/den-type spaces for reading also create community gathering places. Some care facilities have even discovered that bringing child care facilities into close proximity with and even co-location in the nursing home brought more life and good health to the residents of the living centers. Parents of the children in the day care began reporting that they liked the sense of grandparents that their children were gaining.

Activities designed for good physical and mental health are regularly scheduled in most care facilities. Some facilities actually take their residents camping in the summer, which is a huge undertaking, but with family, staff, and volunteer support it is doable. Any type of field trip you can imagine for any other group is possible for residents. Consider, for instance, scenic drives, shopping trips, tours of a capitol building, movies at a local theater, post office tours, fire or police station tours, fishing day trips, tours that showcase a specific profession or the community's latest technology, athletic event attendance at any level—high school, college, or professional teams—the circus, visiting an elementary school or high school to tell stories, and the list for off-site activities goes on. These shared trips keep people active, alert, engaged in life, and participating in community. Special events are also schedule at "home" in the care facilities themselves in order to create a sense of community in the places where people are living, and of course staff team members are working. Events include, for example, craft fairs by the community in the facility as well as craft fairs showcasing residents' work for the community; indoor trick-or-treating down the halls with children stopping at each resident's room for candy; on-site concerts and educational seminars; contests, bake offs, staff wheelchair races and relays; decorating an activity room like an old theatre, serving popcorn, and showing old silent movies with organ accompaniment; dances with high school or college students; motorcycle rides from a Harley Davidson club; BBQ's; community fairs for Grandparent's Day, Mother's Day, or Father's Day and so on.

Ongoing activities are a part of resident community life. Indoor and outdoor, garden spaces, craft areas, woodworking shops, library space, group television-watching space, areas for putting puzzles together, yoga classes, exercises classes, and other group activity spaces that are kept scheduled are all examples. Unscheduled group space is also a part of the available space. Things like fountains, gazebos, and sitting areas, both inside buildings and outside on the grounds are inviting for alone time and for time with family and friends. The décor of the environment people are living in makes a difference too. The goal is to reflect a home rather than a facility or institutional environment. The carpeting, paint, wallpaper, furniture, pictures and paintings, knickknacks, and anything used to decorate can reflect a home rather than a facility and are a part of creating a home-like feeling. Some nursing home residents are allowed to have pets, or they have a "community pet" that they take turns caring for. Some nursing homes encourage residents to care for plants as well. The staff takes care to switch struggling plants with healthy plants and rehabilitate those that need it. Although plants and pets demand significant staff and volunteer support, they also create more personal interactions between patients and staff. Having plants and pets around and as a part of conversation helps to strengthen the home-like feeling and can help eliminate the facility feeling where the majority of patient-staff communication is related to a clinical condition.

WORKPLACE COMMUNITY IDEAS FROM CITY PLANNING

For several centuries, the principles of maintaining community order, safety and image, as well as a sense of friendliness in neighborhoods have been applied to living and working environments. With an early focus on walking to and from work, church, school, and social activities, that then shifted to an organizational focus on horse-drawn carriages and public modes of transportation, and then on city and road organization that was car centered, now neighborhood and city planning has returned to a more walking, bicycling, and public transportation-centered focus. City planners suggest that elements such as the following contribute to the success of community and neighborhoods: a variety of age groups; cultural diversity; friendly, open design; a relatively small population cluster; community leisure and learning activity spaces; community meeting areas; affordable housing that is also of good quality; community garden areas: narrow streets with traffic calming devices such as islands of plants; child care resources; and high-technology resources demanded by today's workers and entrepreneurs.

Some developers of mixed use community centers have taken history lessons and incorporated them into their developments in order to create a sense of human community that feels good to live, work, shop and play in. For example, some developers look to the owners of the land they have purchased for potential stories, names, and actual events that can be incorporated into the newly constructed space as road names, as historical markers, building names, and told as stories along pathways and walkways. Businesses often do the same thing in an effort to create a sense of history by naming meeting rooms after company founders, after key product lines, or after geographic features from the locale in which the building is situated to create a real and lasting sense of community, using relevant and accurate naming devices so that historical and geographic integrity is maintained. For instance, developments in the desert that have names better belonging to oceanside communities create an unreal and unsatisfied set of expectations.

The lessons from city planning include the mixed use of individual buildings, with both city and urban building, including retail space on the ground floors, parking space below ground or midway up the height of the building, office space starting on the second or third floor of the building and taking up a selected number of floors, followed by apartment and condominium floors up to the penthouse suite or suites at the top of the building. What does this mean for our workplaces? It means that greater attention to the creation of physical work, play, individual, and interaction space is needed so that people feel as comfortable and creative in their workspaces as they do in their living and playing spaces. And yes, this can be accomplished without losing a sense of professionalism and productivity.

Just as neighborhood development and planning around community/living centers has gained attention during the transition into the twenty-first century in the United States, city planning is in vogue again in Asia for the first time since the 1970s when it was last in vogue around the world in high population centers. Taking a lesson from hotels and hotel/apartments, for decades, apartment complexes in major cities have offered concierge services to make life easier for residents. Similar to the Target Corporation service offerings mentioned earlier, residential services include dry cleaning, running errands, dog walking, grocery delivery, package acceptance, travel arranging, and even party planning. Fitness centers, libraries, and churches also have gotten into neighborhood creation on their sites by including private space for working out, studying, or praying, group space for the site-designed activities, and group social spaces. The group social spaces include coffee shops, restaurants, meeting rooms, and meeting or special function halls. The idea behind all of this social space creation is that the more comfortable and safe people feel visiting places on their own and visiting places for the purpose of interacting with others, the more likely people are to come in the first place and the more likely they are to stay in the space longer, and then keep returning for visits well into the future. Of course it is the combination of both the comfort of the space and the friendliness and care of people with whom interactions occur that keeps people coming back.

RETURN THE STAIRCASE

In an effort to encourage physical activity, university and business buildings have returned to the use of stairways as a part of daily walkways rather than relying so heavily on elevators for floor navigation. Some locations have even installed mirrors that make people look more thin as they climb up stairs to a stairway landing. When stairway and stairwell space provides an incentive for use, people are more likely to take the stairs. Artwork, painted murals, the slimming mirror, or employee notice bulletin boards can be incorporated into stairways so that there are multiple reasons to use a staircase each day, rather than waiting for emergency evacuation use only.

Researchers are even discovering that people who live in sprawling developments are less likely to walk, are more likely to weigh more, and may even have higher blood pressure than those who do not live in sprawl.[1] When work was more body and brawn dependent, physical exercise was simply a part of each workday. As work became more sedentary and desk-bound in the middle of the twentieth century, people got less and less physical activity into their workday. Then, beginning in the 1980s, following the urging that running was touted as the way to get and stay in shape, corporations began looking at how to provide incentives for employees to exercise. National associations for employee wellness and fitness became popular. Rand Corporation has conducted studies on suburban sprawl too and discovered that when people live where the distance between residential and commercial areas inhibits walking, they are at greater risk for health problems such as asthma, headaches, and hypertension than city dwellers who actively walk each day.

Sprawl and Space

Cities around the world are so densely populated that the only direction to build is up, up into towers for living, shopping, playing, eating, recreating, and working. In some places too, business parks and educational campuses are also constricted by limited land space and are restricted then to building up. The more upward we build the more critical it is to design, implement, and evolve space that is human responsive and not just space-efficient focused. Some of the ways to promote physical activity in workplaces include the use of stairs, walking paths on-site, locating near parks, rooftop areas to walk or run, and court areas. Additionally, businesses can provide health education and programs offered through human resources departments.

CONCLUSION

Community is about a variety of ideas, outlooks, perspectives, cultures, age groups, and interest groups coming together to find common abilities for and interests in interacting together because of living and working together. Whether human beings live together, work together, or in some places both live and work together, everyone has a need to feel a part of a larger group and community at least occasionally. In fact, world recognized management consultant and author Peter Drucker (who died in 2005 after 60 years of research, authorship, and consulting) posited with Fortune companies around the world that in their quest to improve workplace productivity, it is imperative to create the conditions that allow employees to do their best work.

Creating a sense of community at work can take the form of activities; company newsletters and magazines; web sites; payroll notice inclusions; sports teams; posters in lobby reception or other common areas that communicate what the business does, where it is located, and what its goals are; and it can come from having time to talk to each other to solve the problems of the day's work assignment. Time to talk in a community or group oriented space is important as Pfizer discovered. Community is also encouraged through the attributes of the physical space as you will discover in Chapter 5. Community space created through parklike campuses and rooftop gardens and walking trails adds to employee well-being. For instance, an Apple Computer store in Chicago, Illinois, has grass on the roof, as does the Schiphol International Airport in Amsterdam, Netherlands. While green roofs have been popular in Europe for decades, they have only just now begun catching on in the United States. As you will read more about in Chapter 5, mindfulness in the built environment works to improve worker health, creativity, and productivity. The stories presented in this chapter are a reminder that community is important to the corporate bottom line. Companies that pay attention to their people and create space for community to develop have found the investment to be worthwhile.

4 / Turn of the Twenty-first-Century Workplace Communities

FROM WORKING AT all times of the day and night in common workspaces to working in virtual teams spread out all over the globe, our world of work has brought new challenges. Beyond the physical dimensions of our workspaces, organizations are now created around "communities of interest"—like-minded people who seek out each other regardless of physical boundaries. Electricity allows us to work 24 hours a day but we cannot stay awake that long. Dozens of institutes and associations have spent decades studying the affects of long workdays and shortened hours of sleep. The resounding results: human beings still need to get six to nine hours of sleep a night. Tied to our length of workday is the time of workday that falls in an individual's highest energy level and therefore, hopefully, highest productivity time. Morning people are typically at their peak productivity between 6 a.m. and noon and then again later in the afternoon. Afternoon people are at their peak between noon and 6 p.m. with a second-wind peak time in the evening. And night owls are at their peak time from 6 p.m. to nearly midnight with a mid-morning peak around 10 a.m. to noon. What does all of this mean? It means that grouping people with common high-energy work times into workspaces with common lighting and noise controls and available tools and equipment raises productivity for individuals and teams.

CUBES CHANGED WORK LIFE AND WORK

Office furniture maker Herman Miller introduced the world to open-plan furniture systems, or what is now known as cube life, back in the 1960s. In an effort to create new workplace productivity and creativity along with a flexible and effective use of building real estate over the last 40 years, cubes were introduced in companies across all industries and countries and of all sizes. In search of personal productivity, people use headsets, radio sets, and earpieces for phones to drown out cubicle surround-sound interruptions, life noises, and human interactions. The challenge is to create a workspace environment in which we can work together rather than feeling compelled to drown each other out. Feelings of depression also can be a challenge for some cube dwellers. Feeling cut off from natural light in the middle of a cube complex, some employees bring light into their spaces by adding special daylight electric light boxes so that lack of light does not bring them into dark or depressed moods. Remodeling and light tube companies bring natural light via the ceiling by installing skylights or roof tubes. Bringing in family photos and personalizing cube space décor can keep employees feeling lighthearted and creative. Another way to lighten the mood is to bring music into the space, on an individual level or by way of a company-wide music system.

In an effort to create equality, some bosses have now left their closed-door offices and moved out among employees into cubes. For some organizations this works. For others it creates a sense of spying and oversight that actually dampens productivity. Cubes can work. Closed door office space also has a place in our workplaces. Some conversations among employees are private, should be private, and as a result should be held in private. For instance, employee reviews, discipline or coaching discussions, or personal issues needing to be discussed with a manager all merit a closed door, wall-surrounded environment in which to talk. Unfortunately, cubes can create a sense of being one of many, a number in the profit-making game the company pursues, and of being lost in a maze of halls and cubbyholes looking for treasure just as a mouse looking for cheese in a maze is seen in cartoons.

Newspaper and magazine cartoons as well as running comic strips have lampooned the life of office workers' lives in cubes. When a building is unfriendly, employees' sense of safety, belonging, and creativity diminish. However, cube life can be improved. When employees are invited to make the space their own, within the limits set by company policy, personal photos, paint, moveable furniture, couch/sitting areas, posters, and sound-dampening devices and panels can work together to increase productivity. Good company policy includes items of cube etiquette such as not listening in on others' conversations, not clipping fingernails (hard to believe but true), and not smacking your lips when chewing gum or eating at your desk.

As long as we live and work, there are times when people need to come together in one place to accomplish work and times that people want to come together to explore ideas, create, and problem solve. Said another way, as long as people work together in buildings, there is a need to come together in meeting space, as well as to work in individual spaces. Individual office space is as much a reflection of a company's culture as is the lobby and meeting space of a company. In group workspaces, incorporate the look, feel, brand, logo, and service marks of the organization so that people who visit and work in the space remember who the company is, what it does, and what the company values. Reflect back to the alive meeting rooms in the Introduction. Remember to equip meeting space with the right tools and space for working, thinking, and problem solving. Graffiti walls in group space can be white-boards, flip charts, tack boards, chalkboards and networked display, conferencing, and shared software-driven tools. Stimulate imagination and creativity in group space with paintings, posters, employee art, art collections, and the furniture and décor. Invite employees to contribute to furniture arrangement, music selections, and décor implementation.

MUSIC AS A SOURCE OF STRESS RELIEF AT WORK

Cube workers, solitary workers, and workers in stress-filled jobs have turned to music as a way to reduce distractions and stress. Some environments allow music to be played audibly, others require headsets or earpieces to be worn. Still other environments, such as long-term care facilities encourage time to be spent in recreational music making, or the act of making music for fun, having discovered that playing music also reduces stress, reinvigorates, and energizes people for creativity. Concerts in city centers, in company auditoriums and in school gymnasiums also create a sense of community. Take the story of automobile consultant and owner of WomenBuyCars.com Trish Terranova, a frequent business traveler who, while in Poland, came across an outdoor concert where a pianist was playing Chopin near a statue of Chopin. "Watching people's faces change while they listened to the music even as rain sprinkles started falling from the sky was a transformative experience. The stress from my traveling and meetings melted away as I became a part of a community experience that transcended my inability to speak the language and that energized me for the rest of the meetings and events ahead." Music became a means for bringing people together, onto a same level of experience, thereby creating moments of shared community.

Additionally, expanding the affects of cube music into customer environments, Terranova shares that in automobile dealerships the playing of music that staff likes may actually alienate customers. The use of overhead public announcements while helpful to staff becomes annoying to customers. The availability of cell phones means overhead announcements can be eliminated, creating a more customer-oriented sales environment. Terranova says, "We know that the longer a person stays in a dealership, the chances that they will buy from this dealership will go up exponentially. So dealers are encouraged to play music that customers enjoy and to eliminate the use of the overhead pages. The environment improves for customers and for employees and more sales are made." In other words the whole environment becomes more productive when attention is paid to the often-overlooked details of a work and buying environment.

Cube life has become so stressful and distracting to people wishing to tune others out and to be more productive that an industry has grown around creating quiet and privacy in work cubes: products range from sound-dampening and absorbing cubicle panels to sound systems. In 2005, to introduce a sense of cube privacy, a voice privacy technology called "Babble" from, of all companies, Herman Miller was introduced to help people working in cubes have a confidential telephone conversation in their cubes. What happened to walls for privacy? What happened to our sense of space and of meeting human needs alongside with meeting real estate needs? Somewhere things went wrong, that is right—wrong. Buildings became masters of space just as media, computer, and communication technologies have become masters over so many peoples' attitudes and time. It is time to take back our buildings and make them responsive to people.

FROM FIXED WALLS TO NO WALLS TO NO BRICKS

From enclosed door offices, to cubes in brick-and-mortar buildings, to working off-site, working virtually or distally, working from home, and from client sites, the places in which work happens have changed. The need for community and human interaction continues. The more technology has entered the workplace and created individual cubes of project work, the more people search for things they have in common. As a result, television, movies, and broadcast media contribute to the creation of community cultures too. In the early 1990s, evening workshop attendees would ask Jana "Will we be done in time to get home and watch *ER*?" Then, in the late 1990s, *Sex in the City* became a must-watch show. As did the television shows *Seinfeld*, *Friends*, and *Who Wants to Be a Millionaire*. In the 2000s, the latest talent-show-contest program, *American Idol*, created conversation circles, as did the *Survivor* program and spin-off shows. Why is this important to our workplaces? Because (1) media shapes our conversations and our interactions during free time and social conversation as well as during workplace conversations; (2) media delivery mechanisms are a part of doing business. In the 1950s through the 1990s, consumer advertisements in broadcast media outlets were the focus. Broadcast media are a new form (1950s and forward) of physical and sociological architecture. Because they create a sense of community by providing common stories to talk about in the workplace, common interests, learning, and travels are discovered among peers and colleagues. Beginning in the 1980s and still in active use today, media became pervasively used for employee training, company messaging, video conferencing, and teleconferencing in meeting rooms. Now broadcasts touch employees and customers in grocery aisles, at cashier checkout stands, in post office waiting lines, in airport passenger gates, in restaurants, pubs, and bars, in hospital rooms, in overhead music systems in retail stores, on manufacturing floors, and as a part of workplace security systems. In the twenty-first century, networked systems, internet-based systems, desktop web cams and individual video phones make conference calls and distal collaborative work instantly available.

Whether or not a workplace is inundated with broadcasted media, nearly every workplace is dependent on computers and computer-driven networks and architecture. In both office and manufacturing environments, workplace improvement lessons can be drawn from the field work of lean manufacturing. The characteristics of the "5S Visual Workplace," developed to improve manufacturing work flow, can be applied in any workplace to better meet the needs of visual and kinesthetic workers and to increase productivity for all workers. The five-step "5S" system for reorganizing and improving work flow follows:

1. Sort through, sort out, and separate—This is the work flow analysis and inventory-taking step done to determine what is at hand, what is needed at hand, and what needs to be separated for easy finding, and what needs to be gotten rid of.
2. Set in order or select and specify locations—Once the sorting has happened now it is time to put things in their right places so that order is maintained and productivity improved.
3. Shine, sweep, and scrub—A clean workspace is more inspiring to work in, more safe, and more productive.
4. Standardize—Create standard systems and processes so that work can be replicated.
5. Sustain—Reach agreement on what needs to be done to sustain the improvements already made and the ongoing improvements that will be needed to keep all systems working.

Improved work flows contribute to both improved productivity and often an increased sense of community because work processes are flowing better, allowing for ever greater accomplishments and quality of work. Whether working together in face-to-face environments, working in different countries via technology-driven connections, or working distally in the same city, the need for clear communications, clear plans of work, and agreed-upon project accomplishments remains. In the twenty-first century, myriad technologies allow work to be accomplished in buildings, around buildings, outside of buildings, and without buildings.

FROM NO BRICKS TO DISTAL WORK

Some workplace technology analysts have suggested that in the next few decades 35 percent of work will be done virtually, or distally, meaning "situated away from the point of attachment or origin," in other words, away from the home office or altogether away from an office building. A virtual community can be described as "a genuine social group that assembles around the use of e-mail, web pages, online games, and other networked resources." From people doing innovative design work, to customer service work and order taking, virtual and distal work is already occurring. For instance, drive-through restaurants are using order takers who are not even in the store location to take orders and key those orders back to the store via a computer network. This will continue to change the way we build workspaces, wire them for work, and create community in the places we live.

Shauna Wilson, president of Amazon Consulting, Inc., and author of *InterneTeaming.com: Tools to Create High Performance Remote Teams* (Inkwater Press, 2005), works globally with organizations that have moved to incorporate distal (or virtual) work into their strategic accomplishment of work. Wilson shares this story of creating a newfound sense of community with an intact work team:

> My favorite story is about a team that worked in the same location for years with little turnover or job changes. They called me to help them with a project to reduce turnaround time. Though this team served many distal clients, they still had each other in the same local construct (building) for project assistance. This group had a couple of people that monopolized face-to-face meetings. Understanding this, I asked them if they would mind trying to solve their turnaround-time problem using online tools. In the initial meeting, we used a daisy diagram as a tool to brainstorm elements that related to the extended turnaround time. The daisy diagram challenges the user to come up with eight ideas per subcategory, which would total 72 ideas. I ran this exercise in a NetMeeting (a Microsoft product) Whiteboard and gave them five minutes to complete the daisy diagram. Removing the team from their normal environment to a virtual meeting environment opened up the possibility for everyone to get their ideas across without interruption. My next step was to have a round-robin discussion where everyone had a chance to summarize their ideas on the daisy diagram. Outside of this specific meeting, this team is somewhat dysfunctional because of the manipulation and bitterness felt toward two time-monopolizing team members. The construct of internet teams can change the dynamics among the team members in that it levels out the playing field where all can be heard and provide input.

In typical work teams, who are the people not heard or at least feeling that way? Wilson says that she has found that it is both the silent analytical nonconfronting types, and also people feeling physically challenged and/or judged by others who have found comfort working on internet teams due to the removal of biases and judgment that often looms in face-to-face interaction. When an individual feels part of their own workplace community, then that community begins to build trust and an improved ability to work together. Wilson goes on to say that,

> When an environment changes from face-to-face conventions to distal formats, how the internet teams learn, how communication flows, and core competency definitions all need to be understood. For example, most people learn by visual observation. In distal formats, however, people are thrown into a world where audio (telephone) is the primary means of communication. Distal team members are inundated with multiple e-mails and sit through countless "show and tell" Power-Point (a Microsoft product) presentations on NetMeeting. Distal teams need to learn how to create a visual learning environment while working over the internet.

The first step in setting up a distal team is to assess the team member's strengths and weaknesses in the areas of using quality problem-solving tools (like flowcharts, affinity diagrams, or mind mapping), facilitation skills for conducting meetings online, and using collaborative software. What talents do team members already possess that can be applied easily to create a visual learning exercise while working with distance? What core competencies are needed to develop into a high-performance distal team? How wide is the performance gap? How important is the performance gap? What portion of the performance gap is a result of deficiencies in distal team members' knowledge, skills, attitudes, and technological support? All of these questions are for human resource managers, employee managers, and team leaders to work through as a part of twenty-first-century workforce accomplishment and productivity.

When it comes to designing interior facilities that meet the ever-changing work being done, Wilson's experience indicates that "it is very difficult to manage work and productivity when the proper communication processes are not established. This is tough when contained in a face-to-face convention and even more challenging when virtual. Many times the remote team has no visibility to their other team members, what their responsibilities are, and how change impacts each of them." Wilson continues,

> I find when teams create a communication escalation process that defines the event trigger, responsible contact information and any paperwork that should be completed to process the event, a team relationship is established that can build trust when the team is working through the issue. Remote teams that direct issue escalations to problem-solving teams for current or future products or services form new communities of learning and research where issues can be studied further. When change occurs as a result of an escalation or improvement, the appropriate level of approval and notification about the change needs to be defined to ensure remote team members are informed. My experience is when these three processes, issue

escalation, problem solving, and change management are linked into one tracking database, it allows for records to be easily updated and kept current. The tracking database then becomes a relied on tool for communication about change and how it is affecting each remote team member.

In order to design and maintain distal facilities and technologies that create a sense of community, Wilson provides this image of what happens:

Often when teams disperse, they rely mostly on e-mail, fax, and phone to pick up on all the communication that used to take place in their face-to-face office settings. But, when you look around your face-to-face office, passive communication is occurring on wall-posted calendars with weeks crossed out with someone's name on it staking out their vacation time, newspaper clippings, comics, and the posters that hang on the wall, all of which passively share information. SharePoint (a Microsoft product) offices can provide this and I believe provide more opportunity for passive communication. SharePoint offices allow for centralized file sharing, discussion boards, calendars, databases, and team surveys. Since most teams are thrown into their remote teams without preparation, my experience is most teams only use the centralized file sharing. This is a waste of a very expensive tool because remote teams could improve their performance by reducing their e-mails using the discussion boards to converse about topics at hand. They could also use the calendar and announcement function to keep everyone informed about up-coming meetings or events and the survey function for decision making. Contact lists could be used to provide personal and business information as well as using company-secured chat rooms to replace hallway conversations. When the SharePoint office is designed to replace the prior face-to-face office, the users just log into their SharePoint office each morning to review the changes that have occurred. Rather than checking e-mail for conversations, users would check the discussion board leaving e-mail for personal or escalation type of communication. This system can save time rather than causing employees to sort through 100's of e-mails daily. But, everyone has to adapt for this type of internet office to be successful. A distal community needs to adapt new communication rules, especially around e-mail, to make the distal office work.

When asked if there were any other areas to comment on in relation to the *Building Community in Buildings'* premise that buildings without people do not matter, here is how Wilson closed:

Since I am a small business owner and consultant, I have three computers, five different types of printers, a well stocked office supply cabinet, DSL, and a smart cell phone. Most of the clients I work with, I have never met or seen in person, yet we work very well together. Working from home as a distal worker takes discipline. I used to have my office in my living room and have found that it is important to create an office away from the living space. When I worked in my living room, I actually worked while I watched TV at night. Since moving the office into a spare bedroom, I have better-defined office hours and when I leave, I do not check my e-mails again at night. To break up my workspace, I usually go to a coffee shop (walk) when I need to think or brainstorm about a subject. I make lists to complete daily. I dress causally, but I do get dressed for work, I don't work in my pajamas. I exercise at a gym and find that when I participate in a class I do better not only in exercising but in meeting and talking with people face-to-face. I also volunteer my services with nonprofit groups, again to converse face-to-face. I have been working from home nine years and can't imagine working in a brick location!

No matter how virtually a workforce exists, managers who care about their employees show up at regular intervals on every floor, at every work site, in every team meeting, to check in, to listen, to respond to questions, to remind people of how their contributions fit into the organization's accomplishments, and to cheer people on. Managers seeking productivity and results-oriented creativity ensure that each employee has clear accountability statement for their work, whether they are working virtually, in a distal setting, or on a company site.

ONLINE GAMING TELLS OF COMMUNITY FORMATION TOO

From technology-driven twenty-first-century work accomplishment to online multiuser gaming systems, communities are forming in ways that challenge conventional thinking about face-to-face community formation and about communities of practice. Myspace.com and group chat rooms like it, instant messaging, text messaging, cell phones, wireless technologies for laptops and hand-held telecommunication tools are all allowing for human interactions that support and maintain a sense of community. In this age of digital convergence, the cell phone that became your web access is now also your radio and television as well as movie-on-demand player. Walking, shopping, driving, waiting for buses, planes, and trains has all changed because now we can do these things with barely an interaction with the people right next to us and yet with ongoing interaction with people not physically with us. As a result, some argue that our technologies are not helping us to connect human-to-human, mind-to-mind, and heart-to-heart in ways that allow us to be more creative, more human responsive, and more productive.

Others, however, argue that online communities are viable communities too. For instance, computer technology expert Kevin Graham, who is a CISSP (certified information system security professional) enterprise security architect, suggests that community can form independently of buildings and yet interdependently with the architecture of computer systems while still supporting and maintaining human communities. Graham says:

> Communities within so-called "virtual" worlds differ little from those in the physical world. In fact, virtual communities may be community in the purest sense. More traditional views seem to conflict with this. They seem to argue that key to community is the idea of face-to-face interaction and common experience, community thus dependent on physical proximity and organization. It is a reasonable assumption, but with the advance of technology it is also increasingly self-limiting. Certainly physical proximity can be one basis of a community. But distance doesn't necessarily prevent community either. In fact, communities can arise

out of the mere fact of distance as they do out of the mere fact of proximity (support groups for military families and message boards where this common bond brings people together to share fears, hopes, and experience). In either case, whether people are near or far, the key element is again focused on finding commonality.

Presuming that no other method other than physical proximity in this case allows for the communication and awareness of commonality, then the segmentation of internal space in a way that prevents access between individuals who form a community might undermine the strength of that community by undermining the mechanisms underlying its formation, not the original commonalities, but the ease or difficulty in which the interaction of the individuals in a community may express those commonalities in the context of the group. So, key to the origination of community is commonality, but key to the creation, growth and strength of community is communication. A structure seemingly then can facilitate the creation of community by expressing a form that fosters and reinforces the interactions necessary for the sense and recognition of commonalities and "belonging."

Graham, whose experience ranges over 20 years of working with computers, networks, and network architecture and security, continues by saying:

Virtual communities are, in essence, a sort of building. They are structures that build on commonalities by providing a medium to facilitate communication to recognize and build on the commonalities that give rise to community. Virtual communities don't have physical walls and rooms. They don't even necessarily exist in a single place. But some of the strongest communities form here. For example, when a company builds a business office they may have several competing drivers. The first is the corporate image they wish to convey (location of the offices, the exterior and interior decor, etc.). Offices are often organized by departments: accounting, second floor; executives, top floor of course; mail room and delivery, as out of the way as possible. The primary purpose of a business office is to conduct business. The community precedes that purpose and the building is an extension of that purpose. The business seeks to create an environment that enhances shareholder value, makes a profit, and perhaps serves some greater noble purpose in the eyes of the founders. To be effective at exercising this purpose, alignment and communication play a critical role—hierarchy and chains of command aside (symbols of this emphasis in buildings include separation by floors, differences in office sizes, parking privileges, the existence of exclusivity in access to common services [executive wash rooms, lunch rooms, company cars]). In building an effective community, the original purpose that gave rise to the building along with the segmentation that serves to satisfy ego and self-actualization cannot be allowed to interfere with the more fundamental elements of community that have to do with belonging, inclusion, safety, and stability.

From the divisions, organization, and structure of built-space, virtual communities follow for the most part the same properties and even use the same terminology as buildings, giving a hint as to the relationship between buildings, communication, and community. Graham provides these examples of online communication and community: chat rooms, bulletin boards, news groups (groups around a specific subject of interest) and says,

But they add key elements of selective anonymity, the availability of multiple roles that would not normally be accessible and ways of communicating "out-of-band," even when in a group. They also allow for a much greater variety of people to explore commonality and a richer ground for ideas to foster, in part because of the previous aspects. Most importantly, they allow a purity and mutability of form, along with an accessibility that enhances communication and community in a way that a physical building cannot. Don't have the right chat channel or news group? Then create a new one. Don't feel at home with anybody in this virtual world? Then switch. This is a lot easier in a virtual space than in a physical one.

Based on the distal work that Wilson is doing and drawing from the following comments from Graham, the twenty-first century begins to look like a place we have read about in books and seen in futuristic movies: to look like a place in which people can work from anywhere, with one or a million connections to each other all happening on, with, and through some form of technology. Graham provides insight into the complex world of virtual communities known as "the massively multiuser online role-playing games (MMORPG)." Graham says:

The psychology and drivers around these communities are incredibly complex, and even in some cases the subject of psychology research for the complex social interaction and communities that develop. Much more than the analogy of a building, these are virtual environments that seek to create entire worlds. Usually the commonalities that lead people to seek these environments are relatively simple: the urge to escape daily "real life" pressures, the desire to share adventures or common goals in a complex world that allows them to create their interactions and destinies. It turns out that MMORPGs are in fact highly social environments where new relationships are forged and existing relationships are reinforced.

Graham continues the MMORPG story:

The first community is that of the game, or world, to which one wants to become affiliated—part of this is escapism, but I think part is also affiliation with a common idea or purpose, in a world where one controls who they are and starts (for the most part) on level footing with everyone else. Typical things which can get in the way of community (age, race, sex, appearance) don't show up here. Everyone starts out equal and (mostly) the world is built in such a way that equal opportunity is built in. For instance, you don't get greater access or capabilities by virtue of being male, at least in terms of the rules governing the "reality" of the virtual environment. Once in the virtual world other communities quickly form. I mentioned the needs of the individual; there are necessities of progression in the virtual environment, just as in real life: virtual money, training costs, often rent and repair to equipment damaged in battle or with use are factors in the environment that encourage interaction that leads to communities—a social structure of specialization creating a whole community that is greater than the sum of its parts. This interdependence is artificial of course. It would be just as easy for the creators of the virtual world to make each player completely self-sufficient, with no need to buy, sell, or interact. Curiously, this need for others to reach one's own full potential (although frequently complained about) is critical to the reinforcement of community; even those "loners" who for the most part experience the game on their own, do so only in the context of a greater community which forms a basis of stability, affiliation, interdependence and the ultimate promise of support when things get tough.

In a MMORPG environment, not everyone has to walk in lockstep; regimentation, while good in real-life armies, does not necessarily accomplish the same thing in virtual reality (or for a business). Graham suggests "everything has to support this idea of multiple avenues of contribution to the community, provided it does not undermine the original purpose of the larger community (world, guild) to which the individual belongs. Once this variety has been established, the same rewards and recognition apply. In other words, you allow people and teams to interact in the way most pleasing and effective for them but hold them to the same measures of performance and reward so that these differences in style do not create division that undermines the larger community." Sounds just like the world of work in a brick-and-mortar building does it not?

Graham's observations of the parallels between built and virtual environments follow:

> At some point the building and virtual world alike become nothing more than frameworks with their own purpose, reflecting a structure belonging to a community different from the one that comes to populate them. Virtual worlds have the advantage in that (within reason) they can easily change to reflect the evolving values and goals of the communities within them and the larger environment of which they are a part. So in communicating values and goals, and creating environments that support the alignment of smaller communities with the mission of the larger community of which they are a part, it is important that the larger community evolve as well. Throughout, everything is measured by the original mission and, as long as the primary mission is met, people are pretty much free to approach meeting it as they like. Rank in MMORPG worlds as well as in workplaces is necessary as groups and organizations get larger but is clearly associated with greater responsibility and not given out of preference or awarded inconsistently. This sense of equitable structure and fairness allows exclusivity associated with being a member of a smaller group in the larger community to function in support of the larger goals of the group or organization. Something else to consider, the structure created in the virtual world allows a wide range of human interaction that reinforces the feeling of belonging and community.

Continuing the virtual lesson, Graham shares this:

> People who say they feel engaged or disengaged from a virtual world generally cite three things: immersion (how effective is the environment in making them believe in its premise, how interesting and challenging does it remain over time?); flexibility (how flexible is the environment in providing alternatives to progression and reward?); and stability (does the environment remain consistent and equitable enough to depend on the efforts today leading to known rewards tomorrow?). Both virtual buildings and real ones reflect an idea and purpose that may or may not have

direct relationship to the people that inhabit them. Beyond the original commonality that led individuals to become a part of the structure, there are many other factors that have to be allowed for in order to build and keep communities within it. These factors include fostering communication through common areas and structures within the building, providing for a variety of interaction suited to different communication and work/play styles, a sense of equality supported by the structure itself that suggests everyone is really part of the same community, and an equitable structure of reward and advancement that reflects both the larger purpose of the community and collectively the values of those that serve it.

Graham concludes:

The continuity of meaning, purpose and form are more important than the built structure itself. Buildings may help build the community within them, but the buildings themselves are extensions of some greater structure that arose from the perceptions and intent of the community itself. For that reason, the ability to spontaneously create and organize virtual space in similar ways to how one might approach physical space is a powerful medium in which to provide structure for community. Such a community is not inhibited by distance, may be driven entirely by ideas, and depending on the will of its creators, may provide an honesty, speed, and flexibility of interaction that simply is inaccessible in the context of a physical building.

Consider too that just as gated communities sprung up in residential areas during the last three decades of the twentieth century, in the twenty-first century that gated-for-protection model has been applied to online communities where special memberships, user identifications, and passwords are required in order to access order information, chat rooms, blogs, information-sharing centers, photographs, catalogs, and anything to which anyone wants to limit access. A twenty-first-century communication phenomena, a blog is short for the words web log, which is a journal or newsletter that is sometimes a stream of consciousness or a news report approach to story telling. A blog is frequently, sometimes even hourly, updated so that people feel "in on something" that others do not yet know. The information posted on a blog is meant for public viewing, consumption, and discussion. Messages to employees and customers, whether in the form of a blog, a newsletter, e-mail, or special mailing also demand a gate keeping of sorts—a determination of how much is too much and a monitoring of accurate message communication. Monitoring, for instance, when and how community is built by messages and when community is being undermined. Consider all of the pop-up ads interrupting web site visits that most now have blocked. Consider too company bulletin boards, message walls, e-mail announcements, posters in work areas and break-rooms, and even posters in bathrooms. After awhile the onslaught of messaging numbs us rather than helps to build a sense of shared information and a sense of company community. Adding to a sense of personal control over events is the news channel offering of online weather services with "zip code accuracy." This "accuracy" leads to a technology-driven gathering of geographically local community information that can provide a sense of self-control and choice within a local environment. Another approach to technology-driven choices and opt-in self-control comes from one of the newest forms of team building and learning: "geo-caching." In 2005, geocaching gained popularity as people turned their global positioning system devices into treasure-hunting game tools. This is a way to create community and teamwork with virtual teams. Conduct your own web search to learn more. Other web-based forms of community creation include web-based dating and networking. Again, in online interactions, beware of what is missing: body language, tone of voice, facial expression, in-person identification of the person's approximate age, gender, and background. Is this person real or fictitious, safe or dangerous, genuine or deceiving? And is community creation based on these potentially divergent realities of safety and human reality and the potentially dangerous realities that can be hidden when online?

What this means for workplace buildings in the twenty-first century is that the buildings themselves must provide the wiring, cabling, networks, tele-communication systems, interoperability, software. and hardware systems of computer-driven work and the virtual worlds that can be created as a result of technology. A century ago, electricity was for lights. In the twenty-first cen-tury, offices, manufacturing floors, and even retail and restaurant environ-ments need electricity everywhere for computers, printers, security systems, machinery, chargers, copiers, fax machines, cash registers and, of course, for lighting. The way that employees work and learn is largely dependent on computer systems too. Online communications and classes taken from desk-tops, in classroom environments, or from laptops while traveling are a part of nearly every workday. To prepare future workers, some states are even requir-ing high school students to take online classes before graduating. Whether workplace communities are built online or in buildings, dependence on elec-tricity and on human beings capable of continuous learning will continue.

ALL MODES OF WORK LEAD BACK TO HUMAN INTERACTIONS AND LEARNING STYLES

The online cultures and gaming communities commented on by Kevin Graham lead us back to human, face-to-face cultures and distal communities. However work gets done, human interactions are a part of every workday. For 20 years, Jana has been involved with working and learning style approaches and studies. From recognizing the difference between a Western sense of privacy and need for large personal space and an Eastern emphasis on communal identity and shared space to understanding multicultural and learning style differences, more than ever, due to travel, in multinational corporate ownership and distal work environments, all employees are called upon to understand and work with differences.

Cultural tools abound for determining the cultural needs of a group. Some of the measures found in cultural tools include high-context, high-relationship and multiactive, reactive, linear-active. These measures of culture are helpful in defining office space sizes and arrangements as well as for organizing people for work. Again, people's relationships to things and to other people differs based on their country of origin as well as the regions within a country where people were raised, spent most of their lives, or found the greatest affinity for themselves. For instance, U.S. born individuals tend to have a greater sense of personal space (up to six feet) than those who are European or Asian born (two to four feet). This space difference affects interpersonal relationships and workplace interactions as well as the perceived need for the sizes of offices, cubicle workspace, and meeting room sizes.

Another workplace difference that comes from both cultural and personality studies of individuals focuses on decision making. Whether or not employees are making decisions based on community needs first, each employee has a need to be understood for his or her point of view and how that point of view can help a team workplace decision to be reached. Behavior during decision making and in action looks and works differently depending on this decision-making frame of mind. For instance, community-first decision makers tend to talk, act, and decide in terms of keeping team harmony and productivity, ensuring group interactions continue, and organizing both work and people in ways that the community's needs are served. Individual-first decision makers can appear to leave others out and move ahead with work on an individual level without appearing to share any concern for the larger team, group, or community. On the other hand, community-first decision makers can appear to be indecisive while working to get everyone into agreement about what needs to be done. These decision styles can affect the built environment because the time spent in individual work versus in group meetings or conversations differs greatly, resulting in different space needs in a building or in a virtual workplace system.

From decision-making styles, to learning styles, the way that people think, act, and process information has an effect on the organization and on equipping and uses of workspaces. For instance, people who view the world primarily with their "left brain" tend to think and organize in a linear, analytical, and logical way. Because "right brain" people tend to focus on being creative, recognizing feelings, and trusting intuition, overly ordered and rule-bound workspace can constrict a right-brain creative person. On the other hand, a creative person's workspace can feel chaotic and unproductive to a left-brain person. Even car advertisements have appealed to left-brain and right-brain decision-making styles, so why should we not also consider these differences in workplace needs and in decision-making styles?

There are also "relating styles." Some people prefer tasks and things, others prefer people. The relating focus an individual begins from affects the use of space, decisions about the use of time and the need for a workspace that allows for individual task work accomplishment as well as team time and space for work. Separately, the Gregoric Learning Styles, created by Anthony Gregoric, have been in use for decades to help people understand how they perceive and order information. Gregoric posits that there are four learning styles: concrete-sequential (linear and sequential learning—fact based and research oriented), concrete-random (concrete and intuitive learning—problem solving), abstract-sequential (abstract and analytical learning that requires an ordered environment); abstract-random (emotional and imaginative learning—active and informal learning environments). These four approaches to ordering information influence how people organize their offices, files, desktops, projects, and work flow. Without an understanding of these styles as well as of multiple intelligences and learning styles, employees are less productive than they can be individually and in teams. An understanding of all these styles and approaches is critical to productivity—building organization and flexibility, determining who can comfortably and effectively work off-site, in distal mode, and who will work better on-site (around people)—and to creative workplace communities.

The above mentioned "multiple intelligences" refer to the eight learning modalities proposed in 1983 by Dr. Howard Gardner. He defined and labeled these eight "multiple intelligences" in order to better describe the broad range of human potential. As you read through these eight modalities, consider where you, your boss, your architect, your contractor, your employees and co-workers tend to feel most comfortable in interacting with the world. The "intelligence" approach that feels most comfortable becomes the basis by which experience, interaction, and organization is pursued. The multiple intelligences are

- verbal/linguistic intelligence—words, reading, and writing;
- logical/mathematical intelligence—numbers, logic, and reasoning;
- visual/spatial intelligence—pictures, drawing, and painting;
- bodily kinesthetic intelligence—bodily aware, hands-on interactive, and building things;
- musical intelligence—music, creating it and listening to it;
- interpersonal intelligence—people smart, discussion oriented, and collaborative;

- intrapersonal intelligence—self-aware, reflective, and able to work alone;
- naturalist intelligence—nature smart and environment aware.

Again, these provide insight into how people organize their individual spaces and how groups are likely to organize and need order in their spaces. We do not all need to behave the same way, however, people benefit individually and collectively when the strengths of all styles, approaches, and attitudes are recognized so that work can be completed more effectively, productively, and creatively together. While the temptation is strong to overlap these tools for understanding how people approach thinking, learning, problem solving, and living life, do not do it. Here is why: Each tool is designed to measure and describe different aspects of being human. These tools for understanding ourselves and others line up next to each other to provide a well-rounded view of how human beings approach getting things done.

Consider these pairings for describing people: optimist, pessimist; realist, idealist; analyst, synthesizer; pragmatist, spirit-guided. Which phrases would best describe you and how you interact with the world? How you view yourself affects the way that you organize the things in your life and how you relate to the people in your life. The way you invest time, the way you keep things or discard of them, the way you ask for help or do not and the way you work alone or work with a team is affected by the way that you are, the way that you see yourself, and the way that others perceive you. So whether or not you are on the design team for the buildout or rebuild of the workplace you currently work in, if you are reading this book it is because you have a desire to influence the way that workplaces are built and to influence their ability to provide productive and creative space in which people can work.

RECOGNIZING INDIVIDUALS, CREATING COMMUNITY

The 2006 Idaho Teacher of the Year, John Sharkey, says, "Valued employees produce more with more commitment and loyalty." For about a century, the employee incentive and reward industry has been around encouraging companies to show how well employees are valued and appreciated. Focused on helping companies reward and retain strong performing employees and even frequent purchasing customers, the industry suggests a variety of ways for motivating and rewarding employees. Including that if you want to keep road warriors (business travelers) motivated, it is important to recognize individuals and their passions: electronics, home-appliances, trips, and gift certificates for shopping seem to be motivating.

For other employees, creating workplaces that feel like home is motivating. Some people actually do work at home, full time, year round, with kids, pets, and neighbors abounding. According to the Families and Work Institute, about 43 percent of employees who do not currently have the flexibility to work from home on some days would like to have the option to do so. Some people work in buildings and towers within a five minute walk or a two hour drive from home and also desire to create a sense of home at work. Investment firms, resort-town retail shops, bookstores, and churches have established policies that allow employees to bring their pets and even infants to work. For still other employees who put in long hours and plenty of overtime, or simply need flexibility, being given time off as a reward for productivity and hours worked is motivating. Working evenings and weekends puts some people into a low-productivity spin; days run into each other and the simple structure of working Monday through Friday and completing household chores and attending church on the weekends disappears. Replaced by every-day-seems-the-same and therefore the days and weeks run together, the sense of being rested and the ability to be creative and productive are soon lost.

As discussed throughout this section, individual space and group spaces are both necessary elements to fostering productive and creative work environments whether the focus is on brick-and-mortar physical office environments or on distal workplaces. Human interactions do drive workspace planning and design, office furniture construction and purchasing, and ultimately the use of built spaces and virtual spaces. Individual workspace includes cubes, closed door offices, and personal computer systems. Group space includes sitting areas, idea-session areas, neighborhood space, meeting rooms, and auditoriums. Mixed-use spaces include workstation clusters for teams where individual desks have a nearby or central team meeting space (as described in Chapter 3 when presenting the Pfizer workspace).

During the 1990s, communities of practice began forming in companies, across companies, and across industries in order to bring people of like disciplines together to share ideas, gain updated skills, and explore trends for the future. Communities of practice form around specific fields such as human resources, architecture, chemistry, engineering, information technology, law enforcement, and medicine. The size of a community may range from under a dozen to tens of thousands. The community meeting places range from on-line exchanges and phone calls to international conference events. In keeping with the concept of creating communities of practice, community libraries include individual, classroom, and meeting spaces for personal reading and reflection as well as group interactions. The library in Seattle, Washington, incorporates a daylight atrium space known as the living room. Built to reflect its neighboring landscape, the Phoenix, Arizona, library was built to resemble a copper mesa split by a stainless steel canyon and has a reading room that is over an acre in size. And the Hood River County, Oregon, library described in Chapter 2 includes both individual and group space for people to gather, talk, explore ideas and brainstorm solutions for the world.

VILLAGE MENTALITY

While community-first thinking and decision making has its advantages, sometimes asking whether the village mentality is helping or hurting your organization is important. In other words, is the group-thinking going on helping people to be productive and creative, or is water cooler talk dampening morale and creating in-fighting, frustration, and destruction? Consider the cultures created in workplaces, communities, and families when families live apart due to job demands. In this case, a village mentality that looks out for the good of everyone is helpful; it includes organizational considerations such as spouse support, child care, special training about the culture(s) being lived in for both the relocated employee and the family left in another location, company-paid trips home for frequent visits, and clear and firm end dates of the job that has split a family up can all help ease the fractured sense of community.

Individual employees sometimes get caught up in the work-community-first mentality, with cell phones, pagers, faxes, e-mails, voice mails, hands free, hands on, electronic calendaring, project managing, conference calls, and all the technology-driven promises of productivity improvement constantly at hand. Twenty-first-century workers are more overwhelmed with the task of managing all these tools than sometimes they are with the actual work to be done. Empty rooms filled with human bodies are created when each person plugs in to headsets, earpieces, and laptop driven work and videos. Community is dependent on human interaction, whether it is in person or via technological communication. Taking work on a vacation does not help productivity or community. Create company policies or agreements about down time, off time, and vacation time so that employees really do experience both physical and mental time away from the workplace. Without these breaks, burnout runs high, productivity wanes, and interpersonal tensions can rise. Strategies for leaving work at work before heading out on vacation include leaving the laptop and cell phone at home, or, having a clear "who can call" to get problems resolved with your input. If you do break down and take the laptop with you, check e-mail only once a day. Limit your work activities to an hour or less. Leave voice mail and auto-reply e-mail messages that let people know that you are away, when they can expect to hear from you, and whom they can contact in the meantime.

Getting back to workplace teams, in-office teams as well as virtual or distal teams all form around information, common project goals, and communication circles. Companies that work to keep communication lines open rather than channeled into cliques are the ones most likely to succeed in accomplishing their business goals. Furthermore, companies that organize built workspace to meet the needs of both individuals and groups are more likely to experience creativity and productivity while accomplishing business goals.

FROM THE FIELD OF BUILDINGS

In an interview with John Watts, Director of Facility Construction for Portneuf Medical Center in Pocatello, Idaho, the team approach for accomplishing human responsively designed buildings that lead to improved patient care becomes clear.

Baker and Kemp: How do your construction teams work together as a community?

Watts: In my typical design-build situations, there are at least six different work teams at work under one overarching project team. First, at the daily, basic, detailed end of teamwork you have the "OAC" team. The OAC team is the owner-architect-contractor team which is similar to a three-legged stool partnership. If one leg falls out, then the remaining two legs fail. We built a team that clearly understands the need to work as a team, not as individual contractors. Attaining that goal, in part, is completed with the personality and dedication of the primary team members. Additionally, the binding contractual relationship of the owner to the architect or construction folks is a key ingredient. The lump sum, low bid method of construction contracting demands an adversarial relationship, even in the best of situations. We used a construction manager type of contract, thus eliminating much of the adversarial roles. There are pros and cons for each type of contract method, so selecting the correct contractual instrument is very important. Next is the project team and users. For each level of the scope of work (SOW) we try to identify the team members. Typically this is at the department level. Most of the time that process is clear cut, but politics sometimes make it more of a challenge. The key issue to the user team is education: on the process, on where they fit, and on their duties, and then to be responsive to their needs. That does not mean you are going to incorporate all of their needs, but you still need to be responsive and provide them a good understanding of the issues. Most of our interaction is dependent upon the phase of the development: for example, program for design and concepts, budget development, plan reviews during the design development and construction document stage, equipment planning, transition planning, and occupancy. Should the user be engaged during the project, then it is a very rewarding process as they "direct" the designers and get "their" clinic built. The buy-in is very important as the users gain ownership and feel the rewards of the completed space. The project team is happy as they have an engaged owner, but the project team actually controls the budget, time line, and outcome of the overall program in order to make a satisfied customer. The third team is the project team and "AHJ." The AHJ are the authorities having jurisdiction and they are everywhere. The AHJ issues come in all forms: hospital, city, county, state, national, and special subject groups. Without detailing these, the general principle still is valid: identify, educate, understand, and adhere to compliance issues, meet their deadlines, and communicate. The fourth team is the project team and management. The buck must stop somewhere and most often it is this level of the "working teams." The role of management is end-state project control, goal setting, setting responsibility levels, and delegation of authority to execute. Should any one of these elements become unbalanced, then the "system" fails or significantly hampers the project team. Should the project team have no or little oversight by the management, then management loses control of the project and places too much control at a level too low. The project team needs to insure formalized reporting; budget and SOW control are the basic ingredients to clear communications to management. From a management aspect, an imbalance of project team "authority versus responsibility" spells micromanagement and sti-fling of the dynamics needed by the project team in a fast pace design and construc-tion situation.   The fifth team is the management and board. The program control and accomplishment is often the clear mandate of the board. They expect manage-ment to accomplish those programs that are authorized. Of course, management uses the project team to execute and control the individual projects that comprise an authorized program. Clear communication of the holistic issues, time lines, and funding needs to be accomplished in a formalized setting. Excluding the board in major dollar situations will initialize issues of distrust or lack of control. Over-communicating details of the projects/programs will invite micromanagement. Pro-viding working minutia of a project overwhelms the board with details not appropriate for that level.   The sixth team is made up of the hospital and public. The public can be your best or worst friend in any project. The best course of action is clear communication and education, where warranted. A viable public affairs effort can greatly help to keep the public informed (for those that listen) and have them proud that they have a progressive hospital that will provide them great medi-cal care. Lack of communication invites rumors and distrust.

Baker and Kemp: How do you build a sense of shared community within the whole company as projects are being worked on?

Watts: Listening, interaction, communication, availability, clear direction, goal setting, and sharing in the rewards (or losses).

Baker and Kemp: Did your original and/or remodel architectural plans include environmental concerns and human productivity concerns? If so, how?

Watts: Yes. We included both environmental and productivity concerns in our considerations. Environmental concerns: All environmental laws will be enforced and accomplished in the hospital construction programs, even if such are not com-plied with by neighboring developers. We will take the high road and our respect for, and implementation of, environmental issues will be proactive in response to the community and legal authorities. Separately, supplemental environmentally friendly programs that are available to participate in, and be recognized as being certified, are not generally implemented, for example "Green Programs" or "Energy Star," as they add significant costs and use our limited funding resources. If a pro-gram is not mandated or does not have a clear cost-saving payback ratio, we will not incorporate the voluntary programs.

Full time equivalent employee concerns are a significant issue in building design and utilization. The need to be much more effective in our productivity is a major element in making money or not. Also, the aging of the professional staff (especially nursing) is a design criterion with which to be concerned. The productivity concerns that run the gamut of design include but are not limited to interior finish selection, automation, and proximity of nurse station to patient rooms. Supplementing the facility infrastructure with optional building elements such as digital controls, pneumatic tube systems, wireless communications (data/nurse-call/voice) is most often decided in terms of productivity enhancing service-to-cost ratios.

Creating healing environments for patients, medical teams, and care givers has been an objective of hospital designers from the time the first hospital was being built. Beyond continuing medical advancements, what has changed most are the hospital buildings themselves. More money than ever is being spent on hallways, wayfinding (more in Chapter 5), and patient rooms. The improvements in the physical spaces people are working and recovering in are reducing the length of hospital stays, which saves money for everyone. And why do parking lots and parking structures have to look so dour? Hospitals and some cities are leading the way with beautification of parking structures, including artwork, planters, and ground-level retail space implemented in the design. When companies and governmental entities are willing to spend some money and make the parking areas blend more with the surrounding buildings, a reinforcement of the community center can be formed. For instance, the Darden School of Business on the University of Virginia campus has paid careful attention to the built environments of classrooms, eating areas, meeting auditoriums, sleeping quarters, and yes, the parking structure. Each of the business school's buildings is red brick with painted white wood trim, including the two-story parking garage which at first, second, and even third glance looks like another two-story dormitory building. Keeping the focus on people and learning, the parking garage building's design along with a limited driveway system of roads guides thought away from getting in the car and leaving and keeps minds tuned to the ideas, concepts, and studies at hand.

Today's flexible workspaces run the gamut of warehouse style office spaces with "cube cities" that get rearranged every time a project is completed and team members are reassigned to fixed-desk workstations that are wired for both cable-tethered and wireless technology to be used by full-time employees assigned to the desk or by the rotating door of employees, contractors, vendors, and even customers who may want to sit down and work for a few minutes or for the day. In the latter environments, one locked drawer at a desk station may be all the private space available. In all office environments, flat work surfaces for spreading out work and safely settling computers are requisite. Along with the needed work surfaces of course are ergonomically designed furniture and accessible workspaces, meeting rooms, and rest rooms. Speaking of meeting and conference rooms, twenty-first-century meeting space demands more electricity and more technology: electronic whiteboard systems; projection systems; and even specially cooled AV rooms are to be found in meeting spaces around the world. In hospitals, in office buildings, off manufacturing floors, in police station briefing rooms, and even in companies with 50 to 100 employees, high-tech conference rooms are offered.

CONCLUSION

The twenty-first-century economies have evolved from the history of agrarian, industrial, information-age economies incorporating the best of each and now including a molecular focus in the life, bio-, and nano-technology fields that heretofore was not technologically possible. This changes the places in which work occurs because clean rooms, labs, and idea-driven work become the norm. We have moved from predictable, place-fixed, physically demanding work, to unpredictable, nonplace bound, and mentally demanding work that takes an emotional toll on body and spirit when the right supporting workplace environments do not exist. Helping to ensure the well-being of employees is the human resource professional. The National Association of Workforce Development Professionals, which serves human resources, benefits, and training professionals, suggests that the work-force development professional is responsible for helping individuals identify, prepare for, obtain, and maintain employment in career fields that lead to self-sufficiency and to help business develop, hire, and retain a workforce while helping the business maintain and improve its economic competitive-ness. Additionally, human resource professionals are now called upon to actively participate in the area of building design and virtual workplace design so that human beings are recruited, retained, developed, encouraged, sup-ported, and valued so that creativity and productivity follow. Of course, everything in Chapters 3 and 4 can be book and web researched to your heart's content. The discussions here are meant to merge the built environ-ment and human environment discussions into an integrated implementa-tion approach that fosters greatest productivity and creativity for human beings—which are the more detailed subjects of Chapters 6 and 7.

Part III: The Science and Art of Increased Productivity in Buildings

THIS SECTION BLENDS the elements of the first two sections, making recommendations for the creation of more productive workspaces.

5 / Building Mindfulness and the Humanization of Buildings

WHAT IS IT about a building space that speaks most directly to you—the pathways through cubicles, easy access to fellow workers, the style and comfort of furnishings, textures and colors of walls, floors, and ceilings, good lighting, daylighting, thermal comfort, private spaces for working or resting, public spaces? "Wow," you may be thinking, "there is a lot to building spaces that I don't really think about." You are in good company. Consider whether this is true for you; most of us think about those attributes of a building that either annoy us or make us unhappy. We do not necessarily actively think about the good aspects of our buildings, we just experience them and go about our work. But the experience of the nicer attributes of a building, a view for example, can be negated by negative thoughts about other space attributes—such as glare from the very window that provides that view or the phone chatter of your office mate on the other side of the shared cubicle wall.

What does it really mean when we say we experience something? Does it mean that we participated in an event; is it something we have actively pursued? Experience is an interesting word (as a noun) and even more interesting concept and worth a short exploration here. The Microsoft Encarta dictionary[1] that most of us find on our computer has several definitions for experience. One definition suggests that you would have an active interaction over time with events or people and by doing so could expect to increase your knowledge or skill in a certain area. Another definition frames experience as something that "happens" to someone—it could be spilling your coffee or just talking to a co-worker; and still another suggests that experience is a "direct personal awareness of or contact with a particular thing." This definition moves from the accidental or incidental occurrences of just being somewhere, hanging out with no focus, to actually participating consciously with your actions; and it aligns closely with another definition that seems to celebrate a more mindful element of experience—acquiring knowledge "through the senses rather than through abstract reasoning." This suggests you may be involved in a more direct or participatory set of actions in contrast to a generalized thinking process. Think about this: we can set up thousands of what-ifs in our mind, but unless we take action we will not learn. You may recall this famous quote from Confucius, "I hear and I forget. I see and I remember. I do and I understand." Add this thought to that: "I think and the thought passes; I participate and I learn." Jana provides this additional insight to help us deepen our understanding of the experiential process: "We understand what we pay attention to."

In this chapter you will have the opportunity to learn some mindful approaches to the built environment and to the creation of productive workspaces. Mindfulness is the practice of being fully awake and aware—for our purpose here, awareness of your surroundings and awareness of your work and the people with whom you work. The practice of being mindful can actually require great courage because it means you are willing to at least try to live within each moment that is daily given to you; that is, to not live in the realm of thoughts of past experiences or continued dwelling on a mistake you made yesterday; and it means not letting yourself escape the present moment by pondering or dreaming about future events. Contemplate this statement and see if it feels truthful: "Being mindful at work will not only ensure that my efforts are more focused, efficient, and productive, but it also will have the added benefit of making each day more personally satisfying." Does it make sense that if you choose to be more present with your work, the quality of your work and your personal satisfaction will increase accordingly? Most of us find it very difficult to live with full attention to each moment, but by giving it our best attempt, each and every day, we can build a practice that will, day by day, affect change. For some of us, workplace buildings can help us to be mindful. Spaces that are designed with intent to be human responsive use colors, light, airflow, movement patterns, plants, and other design elements to invite human interaction, build awareness, and awaken our senses to creativity, innovation, and productivity.

YOU BECOME WHAT YOU PRACTICE

Not every building or space is designed or set up to assist us in being mindful. In fact, most are not. A mindfulness practice cannot change the building but it can change your perceptions and thus your ability to see and experience the good aspects of your space.

Another way to consider this is that, ultimately, you are responsible for developing your skill sets; and all it takes to do so is a resolve to practice. Consider that everything in life that brings you new knowledge or skill requires a willingness to participate, and to experience—again and again. Whether with mindfulness or not, you engage in practices each and every day; and without doubt, you become what you practice. It is true. We can only be what we are willing to practice; so choosing what we practice becomes important to our development as a person.

If you want to get better at some activity, if you want to "gain experience" and the implied skills and knowledge that come with it, how do you go about it? Let us say you wanted to learn to play the guitar. Can you acquire the knowledge you need to play by going to concerts or recitals featuring guitars? Probably not, though you may be able to begin to understand the range of sounds and music a guitar can make, you probably would not gain much of an understanding of the fret board unless you put your hands on a guitar and practice. In the beginning you would practice reading and playing notes and then build up to basic chord structures; you would need to learn tempo and rhythm and be able to move both hands in proper sequence with each other. It would quickly become obvious that, in order to play, you must first practice. The more you practiced the more you would know the guitar—even if you never became an accomplished player, the more you practiced the more you would begin to truly understand the subtleties and nature of the instrument.

Following is a story about practice. It is a fictional story about a person— to be fair let us call him/her Person—but you probably will recognize Person well. Person, a lower-level manager in the company has been at the job for 30 years and has become gruff and short with new people who "don't know the ropes" and who ask questions about "things they should know" (see, you already know Person). Person is sometimes short tempered and will get on someone else's nerves if something irritating is happening (and that seems to be a moving target). In fact, many in the office are intimidated by Person and would like to avoid interactions at all costs. But another co-worker who has been around for a long time and has known Person for years tells you, "Person's okay. Grumpy sometimes but has a heart of gold underneath it all." Do you believe that? Maybe Person was born with a good heart but forgot to practice using it. You become what you practice, and, if your practice takes you down a certain path for long enough, you can only respond from that pathway you have walked whether it is a pathway of grumpiness or kindness, pessimism or optimism, or complaining or problem solving. You will respond from whom you have become.

If, in a building space, your practice is to complain about what is wrong, you will learn to become a complainer, perhaps a very good one. There are choices to make. If you practice mindfulness, paying attention to your moment-by-moment work and communication activities, your levels of experience and subsequent knowledge and skills can deepen. There is a bonus. As you learn to deepen your focus on the present—not the past, nor the future—stress is reduced.[2]

At the end of this chapter we will look at some practices you can adopt to assist your growth toward mindfulness. But for now, let us look at the role the building space can play; it is pretty significant.

ELEMENTS OF MINDFULNESS IN BUILT SPACE

Although, as stated earlier, individuals ultimately take responsibility for their practices, the building space can and should support organizational values, intent, and goals. Intent is reflected in the space through those elements of human responsive design and human resource development. Ideally, what we want is a space that nurtures our physical and mental health; provides a safe and secure environment in which to work; builds on our sense of community; rewards us; gives us some control over our personal comfort; and, provides a physical environment that stimulates creativity and boosts our morale (you will find more detail on these and other productivity variables in Chapter 6). For now, let us consider how these variables blend with the physical elements of space, thus setting the stage for mindful action.

In order for a space to help us be more mindful, it must first engage our senses in a manner that more easily allows us to focus and act in the present. Ideally, a building is broken into activity zones with each zone decorated to support a specific set of activities. For example, a workspace zone, where cubicles are the rule, may utilize maximum daylighting, color schemes that are energizing and view areas—either windows or artwork—that allow for mini breaks at your desk. A conversation gathering place, a break room or cafeteria, may use daylight that is filtered through plants and trees to provide a more relaxed or social atmosphere. Wall colors may be more muted than office area colors; textures would change and furnishings would be of a design and layout to support human interaction.

This is really a practice of sensory design. Sensory design—designing spaces that tap our senses or cognitive mind as opposed to our rational mind—is not complicated, though it does require rational mind thought and process to achieve intended goals; and as you will see later in the chapter with the hospital example, sensory design is becoming standard practice for some building types. Gardens are wonderful sensory spaces. Sensory design is among the most critical of concepts needed to carry through in creating a mindful space.

Another aspect of mindful design is worth exploring here. The documented history of the built environment and human mindfulness connection goes back several thousand years, to one connection being the ancient Chinese art of feng shui. Over the past few decades this concept has found firmer ground in Western culture but it continues to be a misunderstood term. Once again we can look to the Microsoft Encarta dictionary on our computer and see feng shui described as a "Chinese system that studies people's relationships to the environment in which they live, especially their dwelling or workspace, in order to achieve maximum harmony with the spiritual forces believed to influence all places." Unfortunately, this addressing of "spiritual forces" holds many of us at a distance because it seemingly requires adoption of not only a new belief system but also of a new spiritual belief system—and you may not be ready to adopt a new set of beliefs.

However, a search on the World Wide Web finds a site[3] that provides a definition and understanding about feng shui that is much more pragmatic and perhaps easier to implement. The term feng shui simply means wind and water. Several thousand years ago, the Chinese people first used the principles of feng shui—the effect of wind and water—to determine the best site for a new village. It later became a process for guiding building actions with a respect for the flow of nature. The spiritual is still there for those who want that expression, but action on the basic principle can be much more practical —build with an understanding of the relationship of the building and space to the surrounding flora, fauna, geography, and weather patterns. It fits well with human responsive design.

Here is a story that supports the content related in the last two paragraphs from Ken about how he came to develop a better understanding of feng shui:

I first heard about the Bank of Astoria building (see Chapter 2) from a friend and colleague Terry Egnor. I was telling him about this book and he became excited and insisted that I borrow and look through a couple of his books by architect and author Tom Bender. Terry told me that the Bank of Astoria in Manzanita, Oregon, was built using many materials native to the Oregon Coast, and that a main support column in the central space and another dividing wall were trunks and branches of trees that were specifically grown for this kind of use. It sounded interesting to me. We met up again the next week and true to his word, he had brought two Bender books for me to review. Reading through one of the books I was soon convinced that architect Bender was also very much a visionary. The book I read spoke to the potential for and observation of sacredness in the built environment, the spiritual connection between people, buildings, and the natural environment —very closely following the Microsoft Encarta definition of feng shui given earlier. In my reading I came to consider that the following passage from Bender's *Silence Song and Shadows: Our Need for the Sacred in Our Surroundings* clearly presents the ideal reason for a community, developer, or owner to build with mindfulness. "Our surroundings act as mirrors, truly reflecting the values, dreams, fears, and fascinations of the individuals and societies that have shaped them. We can, if we wish, read them like a book, pointing out item by item what was in the minds and hearts of those who created and shaped a place."[4]

When I first read this passage I was struck with the simple logic it contains. It seemed apparent to me that our buildings are truly reflections of who we are. If, as Immanuel Kant wrote, "Eyes are the windows to the soul," then surely our built environment, those structures that society has erected to shelter and house the living community, must truly show us a pathway to the mind if not the very heart of the community. And it made me ponder, where else do we have such opportunity to express ourselves as we do with our built environment?

Interesting to me, when I went to the bookstore to order the *Silence Song and Shadows* book for myself I found it listed under feng shui. I would have been surprised to see the book's association to this concept if it hadn't been for a recent experience. Previous to that experience, even though I knew feng shui was rooted in some form of oriental belief system, my small understanding of the concept told me it was new-age mysticism referencing the psychic energy of furniture placement, colors, orientations, etc. I understood that there may be a deeper expression but from the information that I had allowed myself to encounter I dismissed it as just more fluff.

But as good fortune would have it, something happened to profoundly change my understanding of feng shui. In 2004, while attending the U.S. Green Building Council Green Build Conference[5] in Portland, Oregon, I was making my way through the poster session presentations. This was a time during the conference when the authors were standing by to explain the information encapsulated in the posters. As I rounded a corner I came into eye contact with a poster having "Feng Shui" as the title. I found myself cautiously (I can be seriously cynical about what I perceive as fluff) stopping to look. A woman quickly introduced herself as the author and told me that she was from China. Continuing, she asked me to look at the poster and use the information presented to decide where I would site a small village.

The poster was a large map with ocean on one end and a mountain range on the other. A river flowed from the mountains, broadened into a delta and emptied into the ocean. As I recall there were five letters—A through E—placed in various locations on the map. One letter was in the mountains, another at the very base, another was at the point where the river delta ran into the sea, yet another on a high ridge, and the final located in a broad valley above the river. I considered only for a minute deciding that the broad valley below the ridge was protected from both coastal and mountain weather, was above the river's flood plain, was not so exposed to cold and winds as the ridge location, and would have access to good river bottom farmland, mountain wood, and food from the ocean. "This location I said." "Yes," she replied, "and that is Feng Shui." It was a good and simple lesson on the placement of community, marrying human logic to the spirit of place.

So, as you read the upcoming information on color, texture, light, and sound, consider that there is historical and evolutionary support as well as logic and science that can be applied when selecting these interior and exterior space attributes; and that their contributions to space should not be left to chance because they can and do effect everyone's ability to find security and health and to practice creativity and productivity within a space.

INTEGRATED DESIGN

A space that supports mindful practices has to be designed in a mindful manner. Perhaps the best approach to this is through the practice of integrated design. Integrated design refers to a design process that sets a broad and strong foundation for communication among an extended design team made up of architects, engineers, interior designers, building owners, workplace users, the building contractor, maintenance and operation staff, human resource professionals, and sometimes vendors and members of the community. The intent of integrated design is to allow this extended team opportunity to review and discuss the owner's goals and objectives for the overall building design, including those goals and objectives that address human responsive design, and to thereby select systems that meet the goals and objectives in the most simple and elegant[6] manner possible. It is important to note that everyone on the team has a voice in the design.

For example, if an owner's goal for a new building or addition is to provide every building occupant with at a minimum of 25 percent of their ambient lighting from a daylighting source, an integrated design process would ensure that the full team including the architect, lighting contractor, and mechanical contractor would have good opportunity to discuss the most simple and elegant strategies for initiating the light-related design elements. To meet this 25 percent goal, the architect would need to consider elements such as the building cross section (depth), building orientation (north, south, east, west), the number and size of windows, and whether light shelves or exterior/interior shading devices would be appropriate. The lighting designer would provide input to the architect regarding lighting types, fixtures, and control systems that would be most compatible with the design and provide the best transitional—between electric and daylight—lighting for occupants. The mechanical contractor would discuss the opportunities for heating, cooling, and ventilation strategies that are compatible with the lighting and envelope (insulation, wall materials, windows, etc.) design elements; heat gain from the windows could increase the need for cooling the building's perimeter, but the reduction of electrical lighting could reduce the overall need for cooling the building. An end result should be a mechanical and electrical system that is as simple as it can be, one that fits the needs of the building and the people that will occupy it.

If when reading these last paragraphs you have thought to yourself that, "Of course this is only logical; isn't this how buildings are generally designed?" the answers are "Yes, this is logical," and "No, it is not a typical design process." Even today, as green building comes to the forefront of building design, the most difficult task encountered in the design process is allowing the design team the time and flexibility to engage in integrated design. But if we are hoping to evolve to buildings that appropriately respond to the site, the climate, and the human community, integrated design has to be given top priority so that buildings that support mindfulness and productivity are constructed and appointed.[7]

Sensory Design—Color, Texture, Light, and Sound

With better understanding of the importance of paying attention to design elements (color, texture, light, sound, and smell) within a building's interior and exterior, better human-centered buildings are built. These sensory factors help to fashion spaces that are more supportive of the humans occupying them and the subsequent activities that are performed within workplaces. As much as a building's physical structure, heating and cooling systems, and so on, are important to consider in a building's design, sensory design is equally important and requires a willingness to explore new ideas and concepts and to share and develop them within the integrated design team. And, as always, the occupant plays a key role in sensory design. A building space can only support mindful action to the extent that the occupant is willing to wake up to participate and work in the space.

Every object is made up of energy or matter that vibrates at a certain electromagnetic frequency based on input of sound, light, and color. Colors are measurable wavelengths of light and influence the vibration of an object. Since our bodies are made up of matter, we have frequencies at which we vibrate. This is not a constant frequency, as balance and equilibrium are constantly in motion based on the input of other energy sources (color, light, and sound) that surround us. Just as being in a warm room affects the rate of heat energy moving from our bodies, sound, light, and color influence our levels of vibration. Consider then that colors affect our moods, our well-being, and ultimately our health. For example, the color red is said to represent energy and vitality and represents a strong healing energy for certain maladies. Red can also bring anxiety. Peach, like interior wall colors used in the Bank of Astoria (Chapter 2) is said to represent truth and balance. Almost the opposite of red, peach elicits feelings of peacefulness and calm. Green is a healing color and also brings about a sense of calm. Think about how you feel when surrounded by the green of nature in a park, garden, or forest. Blue is a cool color, like water and sky, and is thus good for reducing the heat in both our minds and bodies.

Color Healing—Clothing

The colors you wear affect your mood and that of the people around you. You may be drawn to wear a certain color on a particular day. It usually means that color is needed by your inner-self to change your mood. Think about the colors you choose to wear each day. Look at the colors you are wearing today. They were probably selected on a subconscious level. However, see how it applies to your activities of today! Just what is it that you were seeking today? Have your energy levels been low? Are you wearing that red tie or dress that gives you energy and confidence? Or are you seeking to calm your mind by wearing green or peach? Think about it.

Color Healing and Your Surroundings

The color of your surroundings, at home, at work, or in your car, can determine your mood. Selecting the correct color for your bedroom can help you sleep better. Jana knows someone who orders flowers for her own office once a week as a way to inspire herself and others. Picture the hotel lobbies you have been in that have real flower arrangements greeting you as you enter. Did your mood not lighten as you entered? Recall the business lobbies that had fresh flowers on the reception desk. You and the employees that pass by are all buoyed by the color, life, and joy that radiates from an arrangement of fresh flowers.

In the fall of 2005, Rutgers University released the flower research done by Jeannette Haviland-Jones, professor of psychology and the director of the Human Emotions Lab at Rutgers University. The first question researched was "Do flowers affect mood in a positive way?" The answer, a resounding, "yes—flowers make people smile" was the result. A conclusion drawn was that "while we don't think we need or want flowers, we do." Flowers do have an emotional impact on people, and it is a positive effect. If you work in a space that feels impersonal and unsupportive of your needs for color and delight, try making a small change—bring flowers or some object of color that you enjoy into your space. It is important to tie personal choices to the act of shaping our environments, even when the environment feels out of our control.

What You Eat Colors You Too

Eating food of certain colors can actually balance your energies. Yellow and orange skinned vegetables such as squash and carrots add carotenes to your diet and help you see better; dark green leafy vegetables are full of calcium and vitamin D which strengthen your bones. Eating seasonal foods, fresh fruits, and vegetables, and local foods when they are available, add to your health, and when you are healthy you are more likely to be tuned in to your surroundings and your work.

Perhaps the most important aspect of food is how you eat. If you eat your food unconsciously, powering down the apple while your mind is at work on a project, you will miss the opportunity to fully appreciate the experience of eating. One of the reasons many of us tend to overeat is because we are not mindful of eating while eating and thus are not aware when we are full or satisfied.

Light

Light is a basic need. We need it in order to see, to work, to play. When natural light is on the wane during the winter months, many of us suffer a form of depression known as seasonal affective disorder (SAD). SAD is noted as a "mood" disorder that we can suffer when seasons change and our natural circadian rhythm shifts throwing us out of emotional balance. The Seasonal Affective Disorder Association claims that a half million of North Americans are affected by SAD. How many people do you know that would not admit feeling a bit of the blues in midwinter?

This is one reason—a very good one—why daylighting strategies and view-windows are important considerations for workspaces. If you go to work in the dark, have no or little access to windows during the day, and then leave work in the dark, day after day after day...well, you get the picture; it can become a depressing situation for most of us. The virtues of daylighting and views were already discussed in Chapter 2. Know too that the sensory input from daylighting and view-windows can help people to be perceptive, creative, mindful, and productive.

Sound and Noise

Breezes, white noise, no noise, or music noise are all considerations that play into the creation of a space that is mindful of its occupants. Is your space alive and creative? Or is it dying and deadening? You immediately know the answers to these questions because this is something you have at least internalized if not thought and spoken of. Try this quick experiment: Focus your attention on two things: your internal feelings about sound and the effect of sound on your feelings. Now go on a walk around your office and see what feelings and perceptions come up. Where do the sounds feel energizing? What sounds do you like most—people talking, music from a radio? What spaces are too quiet and need sound? Can you find somewhere that is noisy and distracting? Hopefully you will find the sounds in your personal space compatible with your work style and productivity needs.

What is important about sound and the office space? First, privacy is a key consideration for most of us. We want to sit at our workstation, whether it is in a cubicle or closed office, and know that we can have either a phone or person-to-person conversation without having to whisper and without being overheard by our neighbors.

Second, we do not like sound that is unpleasant, such as the sound of a squeaking door, but we learn to ignore it on the conscious level. We have a great capacity to live with the noises that come our way but noise can be irritating on a subconscious level causing us to be irritable or to feel stressed. We may not even recognize the source of our discomfort when it is coming from subtle background type noises.

Third, noise is especially distracting when it keeps us from being able to hear each other. Air blowing from an overhead diffuser, the vibration of a rooftop mechanical system, the chatter of co-workers as they catch up in the hallway adjacent to our space; all of these can be distracting or worse, can drown out a work conversation or meeting. Most of us lose some hearing as we age, especially in the higher frequencies, and background noise can literally block our auditory senses. It is like trying to see with your eyes half closed.

Some of you may want to be able to listen to music while you work but that generally does not work well for cubicle spaces because the music cannot be contained to the space. If everyone played their favorite radio station or music the office would be a strange mix of noise. Of course, with our personal music devices and headphones we are pretty free to rock-out in privacy as long as company policy does not limit their use.

Over the years, Jana and Ken have been to museums, meeting sites, offices, and retail spaces looking for good and poor examples of building design that clearly illustrate how buildings do have an affect on people's ability to work productively in them. Sound and noise has always been a factor they have considered when experiencing a space.

Here is a story from Jana's experience.

> While delivering a time management workshop at a client site on the 15th floor of an office tower in Chicago, a periodic rumbling finally caused me to stop the instruction to ask, "What is that sound—it sounds like the train running beneath the building." The employees in the room smiled and said, "That's the elevator shaft, just on the other side of this wall." And some said "Oh, we don't even notice it anymore." Honestly, the reverberating elevator sounds and wall vibrations sounded and felt like a train was passing. I'll never forget this experience because for the four short hours I was in the meeting space I was physically and mentally distracted. Imagine what people—even though they said they don't notice it anymore—are actually experiencing as a result of the noise and vibration stress in their daily work environments.

SPACES THAT SUPPORT MINDFUL PRACTICES AND COMMUNITY

If you have ever traveled through the southwestern United States—southern Colorado, southwest Utah, northern New Mexico, and northern Arizona—you may have had the opportunity to visit some of the Native American ruins, such as those of the Ancestral Puebloans or Anasazi[8] people. You would probably remember it as a very sensory experience. The earthen dwellings of these native peoples were built into naturally formed rock alcoves. They were not only exposed to nature, they were of nature in texture and hue and physical makeup and appearance. They were built of the natural world and are wonderful examples of both climate responsive and human responsive design. The cliff dwellings above the Colorado River within Mesa Verde, for example, are the ultimate in simplicity and elegance in that their function and structure were in harmony with both the climate of the region and the native culture. In fact, much of what we know of that culture comes from the visible ruins.

Photo 5.1 Anasazi ruins at Mesa Verde, Colorado. These ruins portray typical Anasazi dwellings. The natural geography of the land blends almost seamlessly with the built structure. Earth, wind, and light were integrated to create a very comfortable and livable community space. Security also played a big part in choosing and developing the site. Once in the dwelling area, people were safely separated from others outside of the Pueblo (Ken Baker).

What do these 3,000-year-old buildings tell us about creating mindful spaces today? The message is simple: We are extensions of the natural environment just as the Anastasi were. It is biological truth that—whatever else we may believe in—we are a part of nature. For the past 100 years western society has developed an architecture that tries to separate humanity from nature when in fact there is no need for separation—there is a need to unify. We are not the Anastasi, but our buildings should be, as theirs were, equally reflective of the larger environment, the geography and biology, climate and history of place. The colors and hues and textures that are most likely to support our being mindful are those that are reflective of our local biosystems.

Why? Whether we are conscious of it being so or not, connecting with nature is familiar. We feel most safe and secure, relaxed and confident when in familiar territory. What could be more familiar than a building that reflects the natural environment? Think of this: If you could choose between a two-hour drive through a quiet and picturesque countryside or a two-hour drive through a traffic-jammed big city, what would you choose? Our buildings are traffic jams. Full of distracting sounds, sights, and color.

So buildings that support mindful practices are buildings that provide spaces that help us to feel safe and secure on the cognitive or intuitive/perceptual level. Consider that while the cognitive mind is fed by the elements of the building space, helping you to maintain your sense of well-being and helping to feed your creativity, your rational mind remains free to think and process on work tasks instead of focusing on solving issues with the building space. Let us look at some examples of mindful spaces.

Hospitals

Portneuf Medical Center, in Pocatello, Idaho, demonstrated a mindful approach in its building remodel. The hospital management team and board decided to create a healing environment that was pleasant to work in, to visit, and to recover in. Design sessions and focus groups were held that included nursing staff and doctors who would be using the area to determine needs and make sure the new areas would be efficient as well as pleasant and relaxing to work in. Focus groups were also held with community members to learn what consumers were looking for in a hospital. A repeated comment was that people would prefer hospitals to be more homelike.

Ceiling panels of pictures from the surrounding landscape—mountains, flowers, fountains—are over patient beds and are in hallways at intersections called decision points. Decision points are places where people choose what direction to head. They are marked differently and provide direction with little or no need to read. Patients can easily become disoriented in the hallways of hospitals so signage that does not require rational but rather cognitive or intuitive response works well.

The term for this more perceptual or sensory method of finding one's way is appropriately called wayfinding. In wayfinding, visual (cognitive) cues are given to the patient and visitors to assist their navigation of spaces inside and outside the building. Colors and textures are key indicators of particular pathways. Ceiling tiles, wall colors, floor coverings, and lighting are designed to direct movement throughout the hospital. Where corridors intersect corners, they may be built at 45-degree angles, creating a larger foyer type of space. Nurse stations are many times placed at these intersections to offer friendly and personal direction to wayfarers.

Natural light and outside views play an important role in wayfinding. Instead of sterile, closed-in corridors that are reminiscent of a maze, imagine traversing a space that provides exterior visual cues to your location and destination. The natural light also provides sensory cues to the staff working in the hospital. At Portneuf Medical Center, skylights have been placed above each nurse station to provide staff with a visual connection to the outdoors. Otherwise, during the winter, staff working long shifts may never see light.

Photo 5.2 Hospital wayfinding. St. Luke's Children's Hospital in Boise, Idaho, shows wonderful aspects of wayfinding. The central desk, flooring, and ceiling are full of warm pastels that provide an atmosphere that is both cheerful and calming. Footprints that depict natural environment elements such as salmon and trees lead visitors to various hospital locations (Ken Baker).

Hospital rooms have changed significantly over the past 30 years to family-centered spaces. In the 1970s a typical room was 90 square feet in size with two beds. A room today may have between 200 and 300 square feet and one bed. The room is broken into three distinct zones. The entry is a work zone for the medical staff. It gives them a place and reason to spend time in the patient's room. The patient has a zone that surrounds the bed and includes the bathroom and even the ceiling above the bed as they may spend a lot of time looking up. The third zone belongs to family. The family zone generally resides along the window wall next to the patient's bed. Furnishings such as recliners, desks, and computers are common.

The spring/summer edition of *Northwest Public Health*[9] is devoted to articles on sensory design and healing landscapes. One article in the magazine, *The Healing Nature of Landscapes*, points out that hospital garden spaces were seen as far back as the late nineteenth century, and that hospital gardens of today are healing spaces not only because of the nature connection as provider of a healing sensory input, but also because they have become exercise spaces where the physical body is strengthened.[10]

Consider that hospitals are humanizing and naturalizing their facilities with artwork, healing gardens, sun rooms, and earth tone color schemes. Why have all of this wayfinding, daylighting, healing gardens, and family zones in rooms? For two reasons: First, the average stay time for patients has been reduced. This is more cost effective for the patient and for the hospital. Second, the big reason is implied in the first: patients are healing more quickly in these sensory designed environments.

Churches and Coffee Shops

Recently Ken worked with an architect who was designing a new church. He was surprised when he saw that a sizeable coffee shop was part of the plan. The architect, also a lay minister for the church, explained that it had become common for religious institutions to offer an extended community experience after participating in the sermon. Coffee shops figure predominately in that experience. The purpose, according to the architect, is to expand the opportunity for the parishioners to interact as friends, as family, and as community.

Tom Bender, whose Bank of Astoria was profiled in Chapter 2, speaks of the community potential of coffee houses and other spaces. According to Bender, there is a coffee house in Manzanita, Oregon, that offers patrons a "community table" to sit down at and join in community. The large table is recognized as community space so when a person sits at it they are intentionally opening themselves to dialogue with others. It is not where you would sit if studying for a test, reading a book, or plugging into music or the internet.

This simple space, a table, is a symbol of our desire to break from our individual thoughts and to engage with each other. It begs the question of why this easy access to each other is not more clearly embedded throughout our workspaces as described in Chapter 3 in the Pfizer building discussion about neighborhoods in which scientists can gather.

Offices

One recognized way for office buildings to support employee relaxation and mindfulness is through green spaces and gardens. More and more, large corporations are recognizing that green spaces help office workers to feel better about their work environment. They are places that allow you to leave the confines of the cubicle without having to leave the office. They can be configured as quiet spaces—perhaps a single bench at the end of a plant-lined corridor—or as community spaces in lobbies and interior atria with plants and sitting space arranged for larger group interaction. Ideally, both individual and group space would be supported within the green environment.

THE INTENT TO EXPERIENCE—WALKING IN CONSCIOUSNESS

Let us do a thought experiment and imagine that we are going to tour a building that was built to respond to the needs of occupants within its environment. Here is something you can do: Find a library, school, or community center in your area that was built at the turn of the last century. If you are in the United States, try to find a Carnegie library—they were built across the United States around the turn of the twentieth century so there may be one in your community or nearby.

With most of these older institutional buildings you can experience a clear example of architect Louis Sullivan's[11] idea of "form ever follows function." In essence, the physical architecture of the building was in direct response to the building's use. Most likely it was built with a vernacular architecture, from material resources found within the region. Further, the materials and building methods were probably selected based on predominate climatic conditions of the area such as hot and dry, hot and humid, cold and dry, cold and wet, and so on. Because it was an institutional or "community" building, the materials and construction methods used were selected for qualities of endurance. In other words, these buildings were built to last for more than a couple of generations.

So let us say that you have located one of these buildings close to where you live and now you plan to experience it in a mindful way. As you approach the building, look at the way it sits on the site and notice its orientation to the sun and wind. Does it seem to be sited to respond to the most predominate

Photo 5.3 Building green space. This simple green space in the atrium of Portland Community College–Sylvania, Portland, Oregon, was well designed. As a lobby space, it is central and available to all building occupants and visitors. There is a small walkway where you can actually enter the green space and walk to a central fountain. A break area is adjacent to the space and can be used for work or social conversations or as a quiet space for individual focus. Notice the beautiful play of natural light across the greenery (Kevin Van Den Wymelenberg).

climatic conditions of the area—cold and heat, wind, rain, and sun and sky conditions? Big windows generally faced north and south with smaller windows facing the east and west where the low angle of the sun is more penetrating and thus more apt to cause discomfort due to glare or solar heat gain. To reduce unwanted heat gain in hot northern latitude climates, the southern exposure may have less glass than you see on the north façade. What do you see from the outside that suggests the architecture responds to the climate and site?

Begin to slowly walk around the building allowing yourself to be fully aware of the feeling of temperature change and any air movement. Walk around the entire building if possible. Is the sun shining, or is it cloudy outside? Think about the time of day, the season of the year. Where is it warm and where is it cool, dark, and light? What exposure feels the most comfortable and which the least, and think about how that would change with the hour of day and the month of the year.

As you circle the building, look at the landscape. Consider what may remain of the original plantings, those now century-old trees and shrubs.

They were most likely planted to assist the building with its heat and cooling load. High spreading trees filter the sun, allowing mostly indirect light to strike the windows and provide shading for the exterior walls helping them to remain cool for much of the day during the summer. The trees and shrubs also may have been placed to block or divert colder winter winds from the building or to funnel breezes into windows during warmer seasons. Vegetation and soil slope could have been designed to divert water from the building and the site. Try to gage how well the building and the surrounding environment seem to work together.

Circle the building until you are back at the main entrance. It is time to enter the building. Do so with the intent to experience the space, light or dark, warm or cool. Be aware of your feelings as you step from outside to inside. Note the difference in temperature and light as you walk into the central corridor or lobby. What about the space feels inviting? Are you motivated to keep moving through the space?

Walk from room to room with awareness of air, light, color, sound, and texture. What do you notice? Does the space feel comfortable? Does the space support the activities for which it was designed?

If you have chosen a Carnegie library you will notice the high wide-set windows allowing light to penetrate into building interiors for reading and other functional activities. Operable windows should be on either end of the building facilitating some occupant control of building ventilation and cooling. Is it working today? The thick brick walls provide a thermal mass that tempers the changes in outdoor temperature, and the building is most likely oriented to optimize the climatic conditions in which it was sited. Does this seem true for the building you have selected?

Another experiment would be to select a building of the 1970s or 1980s, perhaps a library of that era, and to perform the same walkabout. What are the differences between the two buildings? Which one would you prefer to work in?

As a last experiment, find a new "green" building in your area and exercise your mindfulness walk-through. Try to find a building that was built to a green building standard such as the LEED[12] guidelines that were mentioned in Chapter 2. How does this building feel to you—good or bad or somewhere in between?

Any and all of these buildings may have aspects you like or dislike. The purpose of these explorations is to bring your awareness of the built environment into focus; to gain knowledge of what features would best support your senses of security, creativity, comfort, and delight, and what best supports your company's or organization's work needs. Where would you choose to work?

PERSONAL MINDFULNESS

Building space aside, personal mindfulness is a choice. One of the most common laws of physics is called the second law of thermodynamics. It says in part that energy always moves from a complex to a more simple state. Good examples of this would be the burning of fossil fuels in your automobiles. The expired gas turns to hydrocarbons, which are simpler molecules than was the petroleum. Think of this as a metaphor for life. The simpler your life—the less stuff, whether material items or internal agendas, that you have to think about and care for—the more easy it is for you to focus on those tasks or issues that are present at any given moment.

One of the five yoga yamas or moral teachings speaks directly to this same theory of life simplicity. Aparigraha (a para gra ha) means nonhoarding or noncollecting. From the yogic perspective, holding onto or coveting "things" keeps us from experiencing the wholeness of consciousness. This same theme is carried by all major religions (consider that Christianity's Ten Commandments, the Vedas of Buddhism, and the Islamic Talmud all warn against attachment to the physical and to coveting what belongs to another); yet this message can be difficult to heed in societies where materialism is considered a personal right.

Here is the connection of "not coveting" to our work. The actions of coveting require our thought energy, and when at work our thoughts turn to buying that new car, scheduling our evening, or planting our garden, we are probably not focused on our work. We are daydreaming. Is that so bad? No, not really bad, everyone daydreams. It is almost impossible to focus 100 percent of your time on your work. We need breaks, both mental and physical. But the more we can stay in the moment, work while working, rest while resting, scheduling tonight's activities during a break and then move on, the greater will be our productivity and personal satisfaction. We will be less wasteful of our time and really less wasteful of our lives if we learn to become aware of where our focus is and where it can be at any moment.

Though it would be great if every building provided you with the perfect environment for creativity, health, happiness, and productivity, that situation may never fully materialize. Although we can know there are aspects to spaces that feed our well-being, these aspects will always have some degree of subjectivity. What works for you in your work space may not work for another, or not as well. What feeds you fully today may leave you half empty or distracted tomorrow. Things happen in our lives that affect our moods and attitudes day to day and we cannot fully rely on nor give blame to our space for our feelings and perceptions.

So, while it is important for space to support us, it is even more important for us to support ourselves. This is the key: the more you practice being open to accepting things for what they are, the easier it becomes to accept things for what they are. Is this a "duh, I knew that" moment for you or a "flash of enlightenment?" You are the one person responsible for your ability to be and stay present in any situation. Probably the biggest thing you can hope to do is change your own attitude about what you are capable of accomplishing. It is your choice and will require effort and practice.

Following are some ideas to assist your intent to become more mindful.

Dress Differently

It is not necessary that you go out and buy new clothes, but consider what certain pieces of clothing do for us mentally. Do you have a favorite shirt or outfit? Is it something you wear frequently? Ask yourself why; is it because it is comfortable, or because you have gained weight and these particular clothes fit better; are the colors more to your liking; or are you just too tired while dressing in the morning to care? Also ask yourself how these clothes make you feel. Do they make you feel more certain of yourself, more assertive or professional, handsome or pretty, or do they make you feel unprofessional, vulnerable, and powerless? Just as a building's space, colors, textures, and light can affect our moods and support mindfulness, so can our choice of clothing. Think about your choice in clothing and if it does not feel right, or does not support the person you are, make some changes. If you are not sure how to make a change, then ask someone you trust to help. It may be someone you admire or a person that is known around the office for dressing professionally. If you are not too sure about asking, then observe those whose dress seems to fit them well and copy an idea or two for yourself. This is about finding a style that supports you both personally and professionally.

Get Out of the Building

One of the most direct and effective actions you can make to become more aware is find a park and walk through it with the intent to be aware and open to what surrounds you. Walking contemplations are a wonderfully relaxing and rewarding way to build mindfulness. You can do walking contemplations anywhere, on the sidewalk or the office will work, but first try a space that you find pleasant. Also, please find a place that is safe, possibly a space that other people frequent, that is well lit and open. Consider taking a friend or two with you to share the experience and create a "safety in numbers" environment.

A park works well for walking contemplations because they are generally attractive spaces that we enjoy visiting. They also can provide a break or change from the ordinary or usual routine. Here is what to do: Go to the same park each day, perhaps at lunch, or just previous to or after work. You can alternate the time of day you go to fit schedule needs but try to go each day because you will be building a practice.

First, set your intent. Each day as you arrive at the park tell yourself that your intent for being there is to observe the nature of the place. Leave behind your thoughts of the office, home, or anything outside of the park. You are there to be only there, to observe the flow of life around you.

Walk slowly and observe. You are not out for exercise or even for a leisurely stroll, this is about building a practice of mindfulness, so pay attention to moving slowly and to using all of your senses. Listen to the sound of leaves rustling in the breeze; be aware how sounds and smells change while you are walking. Let your eyes find detail that you would usually ignore. Look closely at a shrub and observe the texture of the plant, the colors of the stems as well as the leaves, allowing yourself to fully experience this moment over all else. Most of all remain open to a deeper set of experiences. You may be surprised at what unfolds before your senses. Commit to doing this contemplation for six months—going back to the same park day after day during the workweek. You will be surprised how each and every day is different from the last with new discoveries and insights. Though each day is a separate journey, the practice builds, opening the contemplative person within you. This is a very subtle but very powerful practice and if taken seriously will change your perception about life and work.

Drink Less Caffeine, Eat Less Sugar

Whoops! Now it gets personal, but if we are looking to change our perceptions and become more mindful, why not consider altering those habits that have the power to act on our physical and mental self? Caffeine has an effect on us or else why would we drink it? Everything we put into our bodies has the potential to affect our moods and attitudes. Consider that if you are already stressed, drinking one more cup of coffee or eating one more cookie may only magnify that feeling of being stressed. If your mind is already wandering, will caffeine help it to be more still, more focused? Perhaps it could but perhaps it will not. If you are a coffee drinker, when you go for that second cup of coffee in the morning ask yourself what you hope it will do for you; wake you, make you more alert? Now have that second cup but do so with a mindfulness of how it makes you feel. Try to only drink when you have or are willing to take time to be aware of your drinking, sip by sip. At the very least you may find yourself enjoying the coffee more than usual; you may find that by drinking with awareness you need to drink less.

If you drink coffee from habit, if you need a cup sitting within your grasp during most of the day, consider altering what you drink. Try switching your drink to something noncaffeinated such as a herbal tea. If you drink to be alert try a cup of green tea. See how it feels. Ginseng tea is a noncaffeinated alternative to coffee that can provide a pleasant and uplifting mood shift. Or, if you are feeling stressed, try a ginger tea. It can be very calming without taking away your mental edge. Ginger also has been shown to reduce inflammation in muscle and tissue, the opposite effect of acidic coffee.

Limit Information

We sit amid information. It surrounds us and engulfs our minds giving rise to thought after thought after thought. Surrounded by media, from newspapers, television, computers, magazines, cell phones, radios, and even co-workers, you can become so overwhelmed that you are powerless to act. How can you counter this constant barrage? First, decide to separate and limit the input. Separate your interests into categories: entertainment, family, work, national, international, local, and so on. Now sit down, at your computer or with a pen and paper and make a list of what is important and necessary for you to know under each of these categories. For example, list what you know is the best media source for providing you with national/international news. Where do you go to find the most reliable local news? What journals, data sources, people, or internet sites are most helpful for your work? What media best supplies you with entertainment news? Post this list somewhere where you can see it every day and see what happens when you try to follow it for a week. After one week decide what you need to add and what can come off. Change the list as often as you want or need to do so, but keep in mind that you can limit the type and kind of information that gets through to you. Find those few good media sources for providing you with the information you need in order to live and work well.

Most importantly, try to be aware of how news affects you. Is it something that you need to know or is it just more "noise" adding content to your life without providing value? Once in a while, take a media break. Dr. Andrew Weil, author of *Spontaneous Healing* and several other outstanding wellness books, suggests that, for our health, we spend a week without the television or a week without reading the newspaper. Try it and see if it helps you to relax and gain insight into other aspects of your life.

Single Task

Most of us have multiple tasks in which we need to engage each day. In the last couple of decades we have somehow decided that the ability to multitask, that is, take on several tasks simultaneously, is the ultimate expression of efficiency. Do you think this is true? To help you answer that question, think about your work tasks and what is most true about them. Are your tasks to be performed with speed or with efficiency? Speed does not necessarily guarantee accuracy but accuracy is implied in efficiency. How about quality of work—does it matter? Probably. Interestingly, multitasking may seem to be the only solution for satisfying disparate bodies of work but if by multitasking you never put full attention on a single task, the quality and creativity of work will suffer.

It is okay to multitask as long as you recognize that the tasks are not going on simultaneously. A mindful approach to work is to put full attention to each task as you take it up. It does not mean you cannot have multiple tasks but that when working on one (unless of course there is apparent need for crossover) you keep your attention to that task. If you switch to another task, as you will, switch your full attention to that task. If you switch back, then again take your attention with you.

If you are a very busy person with a number of tasks that need to be completed, you probably find yourself thinking about other tasks as you work on your current one. So here is something to try. Break your work into ten minute increments and for those ten minutes make it your intent to only focus on the task you have decided to work on for that time period. When thoughts of other tasks come to mind, consciously push them aside and continue to work on the present task. In the beginning you may want to use a timer for this. Once you have practiced this technique for a while, you will find that you are able to focus more clearly on issues and tasks. As a side affect you may find that stress is reduced and the quality of your work will increase.

There are other approaches you can take to awakening your personal mindfulness within your workspace and the building. The intent is to make yourself conscious of the movement and awareness of your current experience and your movement to and awareness of the next. In this way the continuity of the day is never completely broken but flowing from one moment to the next.

CONCLUSION

Most of us move through life spending an incredible amount of time within built environments that we either actively dislike or, at best, ignore. If this statement rings true for you, then you may want to bring these feelings to the top of your consciousness and begin to question how buildings could become better environments in which to work. If buildings and the spaces they surround and the environments that surround them have the power to affect our senses, and thus shape our moods, perceptions, and productivity then should we not care enough about ourselves to see that the effects are positive ones?

You do not have to move into a new building to find a space that supports mindfulness. In fact, it seems evident that very few of our new buildings have considered the mindful aspects of human responsive design during their design. It only takes a few simple changes to the built environment—paint colors, floor coverings, cubicle layout, the addition of a few plants to set up a green space—to make a big difference in how a space affects your senses. These changes can occur over time; all buildings get a new coat of paint now and then; what is to stop us from choosing colors that bring a sense of delight? It does not require much physical space to set up a small green area with a bench or two. How about oiling the hinges of a squeaky door or fixing the closure device on a door that continually bangs shut? What effort or cost is required to buy one nice large table for the break or lunch room and to then designate it as the "community table" where workers come to intentionally engage in community?

Even if none of these changes happens tomorrow, or even next year, there is still a way to make a difference. Though you may not have the power to make changes to your building, you and only you have the power to create change for yourself. When you adopt mindfulness practices you are taking steps that will inevitably make you a better building occupant, people manager, and overall employee and human being. Your perceptions and your ability to stay focused and positive within the environment are ultimately your responsibility. You can make new choices on your own and thereby change your building and your community. Go ahead. No one can stop you.

6 / The Productivity
Variables of Buildings and People

WHAT IS THE impact of the shape and configuration of the building on the workforce and how does it directly influence work and learning styles? Now that you can picture what a productive, environmentally friendly, and people friendly building looks like it is time to merge the building and people discussions into the HRD^2 discussion. The human responsive design and the human resources development models do correlate creating a single model for building community, productivity, and creativity in buildings. An engaged and motivated workforce is more productive and creative and makes money. This chapter discusses six basic building blocks of creativity, productivity and morale, and how they are affected by building design: security, community, responsibility, reward, health, and comfort. Examples include organizations such as Herman Miller in Holland, Michigan, who have measured significant increases in productivity and efficiency that is directly attributable to their building design.

THE HRD^2 PRODUCTIVITY VARIABLES

Human responsive design and human resources development have six productivity variables[1] in common. Interestingly, these variables match up quite nicely with the approach to organizing behaviors that Maslow described in the 1940s and that was described in Chapter 1. Here are the HRD^2 productivity variables and how they relate to Maslow's Hierarchy.

1. Healthy buildings and healthy people—Maslow's 1. Physiological needs
2. Safety and security—Maslow's 2. Safety
3. Comfort and control—Maslow's 1., 2., and 5. interact here.
4. Community—Maslow's 3. Belonging
5. Rewards—Maslow's 4. Esteem, recognition
6. Creativity and morale—Maslow's 5. Self-actualization

The HRD[2] productivity variables begin with individual concerns because until personal needs get met, an individual cannot be productive, cannot be creative, and cannot interact effectively with others. The first three of the six productivity variables fall into the domain of individual concerns. First is the variable of healthy buildings and healthy people. As presented in Chapter 1, sick buildings lead to sick employees. Sick employees are not as productive as they can be. The goal is healthy buildings and healthy people. Living a healthy life is one of the basic needs of human beings. Second is the variable of safety and security. Human beings also need a sense and an experience of physical safety, mental and emotional safety, and of personal security. Third is the variable of comfort and control. Once the first two variables have been addressed, human beings begin desiring comfort in their environment and control of their environment. The "Adaptive Comfort Standard" developed by G.S. Brager and R.J. de Dear[2] recognizes this and provides an expanded interior temperature range (a few degrees cooler or warmer) based on data that shows people are willing to experience slightly warmer or cooler spaces when they have an element of control.

The next two variables, community and rewards, fit into the domain of others and interacting with others. Everyone has some form of interaction with others. Everyone who goes to work in a building and via virtual technology has a need to interact with others in a way that leads to productivity, morale, and creativity. The fourth variable is community. Coming together for a common purpose helps community form. Community implies a sense of connection to other human beings and a place where interactions can occur in the process of living in a community. As presented in the forward, community is formed by a group of people in one workplace, or working for one organization in multiple locations. A community is also made up of people who have shared interests within their organization of employment and may include people who work in like professions yet work for different companies. The community definition phrase "A group linked by a common policy," by definition makes everyone working for the same company or organization a part of a community whether or not it is acknowledged, recognized, appreciated or, in Maslow's terms, actualized. The fifth variable is rewards. Both individuals and teams want to be thanked and recognized for their work and contributions. Organizations can reward individual and team contributions. People can experience a sense of reward when able to interact with and in the space in which they work so that the resulting response is "I enjoy going to work."

The final variable falls into the domain of peak productivity in which the psychological and the physiological come together to produce buildings and people who can be highly creative and can enjoy a great sense of morale in the workspace provided by the organization. This sixth and final productivity variable is embodied by creativity and morale. The experience of high creativity and high morale comes from the self-actualizing behavior that happens best when the preceding five variables have been addressed. Creativity and morale involve both thinking and feeling in the natural and built environments, and when all things are working together greater achievements can be realized.

The creativity component of this variable is best recognized by three criterion; (1) the timeliness and quality of work produced by the individual, team, or company/organization. It is important to move into production or action as quickly as possible but only quickly enough to ensure that product quality, viability, and usefulness for the intended function remain high. Quality includes a measurement of the satisfaction of the end user when applying the product to its intended function; (2) the functionality of the work product, how useful it is to intended users, or how relevant it is to the intended market; and, (3) by the level of satisfaction the product that is experienced by both the workforce that produced the work and the end users.

The morale component of this variable is best recognized by the meaningful interactions people have with each other in a safe, well-equipped, responsively designed, and mindful work environment. When morale is high, things work well and work gets done with enthusiasm and creativity. As a result, high morale is often less concentrated on and less reinforced than it should be. When morale is low, creativity and productivity drop causing alarm in organizations and causing concentrated focus on making improvements. Of course creativity and morale flow both ways as creativity creates confidence —one of the key indicators of morale. Negative or low morale is typically easily recognized because more interpersonal conflict arises, productivity drops, and absenteeism tends to rise. Dozens of firms can measure, record, and report on creativity and morale. The key in this book's discussion is that people and buildings interact and have influence on each other in ways that can enhance or can limit creativity and morale.

DETAILS OF THE VARIABLES

Variable 1: Healthy Buildings and Healthy People

In Chapters 1 and 2, we referenced the cause and effects of sick buildings on the workforce. If you look back over the past 50 years, you will notice that there is a definite correlation between time spent in buildings and personal health. Healthy buildings can help employees, customers, and visitors feel and stay healthy. Healthy people are more productive and more likely to remain at a job and not look for something better elsewhere. Businesses and organizations can help employees be healthy by integrating human needs for kinesthetic input with the human responsive design elements of office buildings and workspaces. Employee benefit programs such as medical, dental, and eye care insurance plans can help. As can employee assistance programs that include counseling for individual employees and their families.

The C.K Choi building, a case study included later in this chapter,[3] was designed and constructed to be a healthy building. Occupants are continuously provided 100 percent outside air[4] at a rate of 20 cubic feet per minute per person. In addition to this continuous washing of the interior space with fresh air, indoor materials were selected to minimize volatile organic compounds. As we mentioned in Chapter 2, VOCs have been shown to have unhealthy effects on humans and include industrial solvents, paint and paint thinners, glues and adhesives used in carpeting, tiles, and cabinetry, and so on.

Another good example of health considerations comes from the Herman Miller company. Their 1995 Greenhouse Factory (see Photo 6.1) was designed to provide better airflow rates than prescribed by the then building codes, with large fans in the manufacturing area to provide high capacity airflow to the factory work floor and natural cross-flow ventilation throughout the building. In addition, indoor materials and finishes were selected for their low off-gassing qualities. More on this landmark building for worker productivity is provided later in this chapter.

Variable 2: Safety and Security

Safety is both physical and psychological. Safety exists when people are free from being bodily harmed and when people are free from being berated or criticized in ways that create a lack of emotional safety. Security is being free from danger and free from fear or anxiety. Security is also something given in order to offer protection from danger or harm. A sense of safety and security must exist before people will interact with each other and work as productively and creatively as possible.

Safety and security includes attending to inventory safety, building security, employee safety, and visitor safety. However, the way in which security measures are implemented can destroy a sense of community if not implemented in a manner appropriate for the existing culture. In one example in which Ken is familiar, a government agency moved from an older 1960s building to a modern structure that was built with many of the green features presented throughout this book: high efficiency electric lighting integrated with good daylighting and view strategies; underfloor air distribution with occupant control of airflow into individual spaces; and well designed community space on each floor. The old building provided none of these high performance features and yet, upon moving into the new building, worker morale took an unexpected downward turn. Why? The old building's security system was centralized, allowing workers, once they were in the building, to freely move from floor to floor and space to space interacting with personnel along the way in other departments. In such a space, friendships were made across work groups. The new building's security system was not centralized requiring the use of a magnetic badge each time a new workspace was entered. In a real sense, workers became segregated from one another. When Ken interviewed one employee she stated with sadness that, "I've been in the new building for three months and haven't run into any of my old friends who I used to visit with a couple of times a week." If you are thinking, "Well so what, how hard can it be for these people to schedule breaks together," or "Since they aren't in the same workgroup anyway, won't not seeing each other give them more time to focus on forging better relationships within their team?" Consider this: though two people may not be in the same workgroup, or even work from the same skill sets, interaction between what may first seem to be disparate work groups can lead to idea sharing and innovations that can benefit the business as a whole, just as presented in Chapter 3 in the Pfizer building discussion. So in this case, security actually led to a reduction in morale and the potential for cross-team creativity.

Signs and wayfinding indicators (see Chapter 5) aid in the safe and secure experiences of people in a building. Entrance, exit, rest room, directional, fire escape, clean-room directions, emergency eyewash stations, and first-aid kits are all signed and all relate to the safety of people, processes, and products. During the end of the twentieth century and in the beginning of the twenty-first century, office buildings began posting "No firearms allowed on these premises" signs so that people entering were clear about the rules for carrying weapons and concealed weapons into the building. While people carrying weapons may feel a greater security carrying them, the people not carrying weapons typically grow concerned for their own safety.

Pathways and traffic patterns—the foot traffic and vehicle traffic on your site—need careful attention so that people are both safe and productive. For instance, does your site have a guard station that people are expected to stop at when driving onto the site? Is it clearly marked? Once in the building, are people clearly directed to check in and to wait for an escort into the building or can they move about freely once on-site or in buildings? Do certain parts of the building have restricted access so that people, processes, and information can be protected?

Furthermore, when using written signage or instruction it is also important to consider the end user of the information. For example, packaging labels contribute to safety—can everyone who works for you read and understand the labels and directions on the products, maps, and programs used in the company? For instance, one company with over 10,000 employees is comprised of people speaking more than 72 languages. The fluent speaking and comprehension of the language used in any place of business is critical to everyone's safety and productivity.

Corporations work diligently to help employees and customers feel safe on their properties. Take for instance Target Corporation's parking lot security cameras. The cameras are there to help deter crime, to help employees and customers feel safe, and to capture on film any crimes that may occur in the parking lot. With 1,400 stores, Target formed a forensic lab team to help with the video research that needed to be done from time to time to help solve crimes. From 2004 to 2006, Target's forensic lab work helped more than 125 U.S. police departments solve a variety of crimes. Because the store's parking lot cameras record some of the crimes, and because of the lab specialties in surveillance equipment and digital images, Target has determined that a part of its community contributions and corporate citizenship will include helping to solve crimes. Target has determined that helping communities be safe is a part of keeping its employees safe too.

Washington Group International has "Safety Tips for Our Visitors" guide sheets (which are localized to each site) at their lobby reception desks. The guide-sheet information includes a request that you check in and out of the building, and register your vehicle. The hours of the building are listed. The safety commitment is stated along with phone numbers for safety assistance or for reporting safety hazards. Steps for providing accident assistance and calling for 911 help are listed. A printed reminder that no alcohol, drugs, or firearms are permitted on the "premises, including parking lots" is included. "Smoking is prohibited inside of Washington Group International facilities and vehicles." Tips on using the telephone system are included. A phone number is listed for assistance in moving furniture or heavy items and for lighting or HVAC concerns. Fire emergency procedures are detailed and end with a reminder not to use the elevators in such an instance. As a visitor to the building, Jana felt safe knowing that the corporation had thought through these details and communicated them clearly upon her entry to the facility.

Additionally, at the Washington Group there are designated employees who serve as emergency/fire wardens. There are at least two wardens per floor. They all receive first aid, CPR, and AED (automated electronic defibrillator) training. Each warden also serves on the safety committee to be the go-to person for employees regarding health, safety, and ergonomic issues; facilitates employee exit procedures during emergency drills and actual emergency events including checking the floor to assure that everyone has exited and then conducting a head count at the muster-point to assure everyone has made it out safely, including any visitors to the building. Safety is so important at the company that at any meeting with five or more people, a safety message is the first item on the agenda. This reinforces the commitment to safety for the visitors and employees and keeps them focused on daily safety.

While working for a privately held company in Minnesota, Jana experienced a scare when a woman in the company cafeteria fell out of her chair and began having a seizure. Several people rose to clear the area while others went to be with her. One person went to the cafeteria phone and kept dialing 911. The phone system would not allow the call to get out of the building. In the collective panic and concern for the woman in danger, no one remembered that what should have been dialed was 9-911 to get out of the building's phone system and into the emergency dialing area. Marking all telephones in your company with emergency calling procedures and security phone numbers will help everyone be and feel more safe.

Are you surviving in an unsafe building and work environment because you love your job? Here are some things you can do to increase your own and others' safety. Park in well-lit areas. Be aware of the hazardous or potentially dangerous areas in your office and work environment. For instance, manufacturing floors, lab research areas, and warehouses may appear more dangerous than an office cubicle; however, each workspace has potential dangers. Office and cubicle oriented environments include file drawer hazards, heavy boxes and equipment being moved, and more everyday types of hazards that could occur in a break room where cooking is allowed. Another safety tip for moving around the office complex or business campus is to keep your cell phone well charged and available. If something happens you can call 911 and you may need all the charge your phone battery has to offer. Additionally, when going to and from a vehicle, being able to ask for security escorts can provide both a sense of security and real protection that may be needed by employees.

Building security systems can help employees feel safer. Entire books have been written on electronic surveillance systems, access codes, cards, and scanners; security scanners that people walk through; and guards, guard stations, and security checkpoints. Look around your complex or building, do the safety features make employees feel secure, or do they create a disconnection among the community? The balance between security and community can be difficult to achieve, as security many times is dependent on the nature of the work performed, and not specifically on the needs of the workers. Providing for differing levels and zones of security within a building or facility can help to facilitate the sense of security among workers and visitors while maintaining a feeling of openness and access in the workspace. In this way, people can feel safe without feeling unduly scrutinized. A good example of spaces that provide both security and access are airports. It is relatively easy for anyone to gain access to the outer spaces, such as check-in counters and public areas. The security at this level generally manifests in the form of the visible presence of security staff at parking and drop off areas and nonobtrusive walkthroughs of the space, and you are free to go about your business. Access to the terminals requires a more direct interaction with security systems; you must have a ticket and identification and be willing to pass through a screening device. But once you have been accepted into the terminal, you are again free to go about your business.

There is safety in numbers—when large groups of people work or gather, the need for clear evacuation plans becomes clear. Recall one of the stories that prompted the research that has resulted in this book: the story of the New York City World Trade Center towers coming down. After this disaster, the Centers for Disease Control conducted a variety of interviews and discovered that only 45 percent of the interviewed 445 Trade Center workers knew that the buildings had three stairwells. This proves that annual or semiannual building evacuation drills are a good idea, not just for schools but also for offices and workplaces of all kinds.

In many cities, the threat of terrorism and of flu pandemics affects the way that security measures and policies are established. In other cities, security is less regulated, and employees come and go freely without any notice of security policies, cameras, or systems. Joel Kotkin in his book *The City: A Global History* (Modern Library Chronicles, 2005) suggests that "There are three elements that contribute to great urban experience: economic power, personal security, and sacredness." We suggest these same three elements contribute to successful workplace experiences. For instance Kotkin's economic power ties to the ability to earn a living which relates to productivity variable number 1 in which individuals focus on getting their physiology needs met. Next, Kotkin's mention of the need for personal security ties to productivity variable number 2. Finally, Kotkin's inclusion of sacredness relates to the Chapter 5 discussion in *Building Community in Buildings* and ties to productivity variables 5 and 6 in which individuals feel respected and valued and act in ways that demonstrate high creativity and morale.

The key for organizations when addressing this productivity variable is to create a sense of safety and security without creating paranoia and without creating a sense of danger both of which contribute to low employee productivity. And, of course, keep in mind how security can be accomplished while allowing personnel the freedom to act as a community.

Variable 3: Comfort and Control

This variable describes the level of ability for personal control over an environment in order to create personal comfort. Control and comfort generate productivity because they engage a person's sense of contribution to and ability to affect his or her environment.

The U.S. Census Bureau has indicated that noise now ranks as Americans' number one neighborhood complaint. People want quiet sanctuaries at home. At work, people want enough quiet to be able to concentrate on productive work and creative problem solving. As discussed in Chapter 4, people have even begun purchasing white noise machines for their cubicles to block out distractions. Alice Domar, PhD, founder and director of the Mind/Body Center for Women's Health at Boston IVF says, "Turning off the noise around you gives your brain a chance to rest. If you are constantly listening, you never really relax." Historically, when human beings heard bugs and birds, people knew they were safe. When the bugs and birds stopped singing, human beings knew that a predator, and therefore danger, was nearby. We need more quiet and attentive listening and less noise in our lives to feel both safe and comfortable.

Comfort factors in our homes have been discussed for the last century. Ranging from "be able to do your own work with our appliances" to "decorate your house in your colors and style," the messages about comfort have proliferated our thoughts and have established expectations that come into the workplace. For instance, by-in-large everyone has a personal computer or laptop which creates a sense of personal control and ability to get work done. Office furnishings have changed significantly over the past half century not only in response to personal comfort but also as a means to reduce fatigue in the workforce. Sitting in a comfortable and supportive chair can help to keep employees at their workstations thus increasing output and productivity. Furniture maker Herman Miller looks at furniture design as a combination of science and art. The design of an office chair, for example, is based on behavioral variables that look at tasks performed, torso postures and upper extremity postures, and the percentage of time one occupies a position, posture, or spends performing certain tasks.[5]

Having an ability to make individual choices rather than having choices made by someone else on your behalf is a part of experiencing control and comfort, enjoyment and satisfaction. Office building developers have increasingly exercised control over what kinds of businesses can occupy and co-occupy buildings and office campuses. Peter Drucker, world recognized management and business productivity consultant and prolific author, commented during his lifetime that when workers are allowed to participate in decisions (control—productivity variable 3), they become happier (higher morale—productivity variable 6) and more productive—even providing more valuable insights to their organizations and companies (greater creativity—productivity variable 6). Increasingly employees who will be using office, research lab, medical room and warehouse space are being asked for their input and space design ideas. This makes sense because they typically know more about the productivity of their space than outside designers and architects.

The U.S. government and its various departments, including the military, has been one of the most strident advocates of office spaces that provide good sensory interaction (see the discussion on sensory design in Chapter 5), comfort, and control. In their *Design Guide for Interiors* the U.S. Army Corps of Engineers also recognizes that differing functions require differing human responsive attributes. On the value of interior design, the guide states that, "We all expect a facility to be functional and maintainable. Achieving co-ordination of the building interior and furnishings, meeting human ergonomic and psychological needs, and providing optimum aesthetic effect are identifiable and attainable goals for every interior design project."[6] They go on to state that, "People's reactions to interior environments is critical to the success of every facility type." It is interesting to note that the main criterion or reasons they list for design facilities in this manner is to positively affect comfort, productivity, creativity, morale, and health.

In order to meet the comfort and control needs of individuals, it is also critical to recognize that everyone learns, works, and processes information differently. (The discussion in Chapter 4 explored this more fully.) Consider the people you know who prefer piles of paper over file drawers of paper. Look around for tell-tale signs that communicate whether someone is an introvert (people who have no personal information in their cubes) or an extrovert (people who have family photos, vacation pictures, and kids' drawings in their cubes or offices). People who like to talk through problems need community gathering spaces in order to solve their problems without interrupting those people who need quiet to work. These are social people who derive creative energy through dialogue and discourse with others. People who are perfectionists want to have all the right equipment and resources available at their fingertips in order to work productively. Visual thinkers are people who generally need some sort of visual aids to get their ideas expressed: the aids may be as simple as a flip chart and marker upon which they can make lists or produce sketches or draw relationships between ideas and thoughts. Reflective thinkers may like to have intervals of and spaces for information input, the opportunity to discourse regarding the information, and then private time for reflection. Hands-on thinkers need tools, equipment, modeling tools, and space to solve problems, create, and work productively. Without their individual needs being met, each person in the organization is less likely to experience a sense of comfort and control.

Recognize that different cultures, genders, and age groups have different needs and definitions of comfort and control too. Men generally like cooler conditions than women. Older people whose capillaries no longer bring blood flow to the skin's surface with the efficiency they did in youth need warmer air and surface temperatures to feel comfort. Of course, a lot of comfort lies in the individual's choice to dress appropriately for conditions which includes dressing for seasonal conditions and for the conditions typical in the work environment.

Variable 4: Community

Community requires a sense of inclusion—events that include men and women equally. Both indoors and outdoors a sense of work-site community can be created by the ways in which group space, walking space, reflective space, and meeting space is protected and appointed. Consider the building structure, the décor, and the activities made available to employees as a part of the community-building work for which an organization is responsible.

Flexibility in employee schedules can contribute to a greater sense of community. Allowing people to work from 7 to 3, 8 to 4, 9 to 5, 10 to 6, noon to 8, or splitting the eight hours with a break of an hour, two, or three in the middle can raise the level of commitment to your company and decrease the rate of burnout because people work during the hours that best meet their needs. The flexibility in scheduling also can create a sense of community within the groups that work the same hours. Sue Shellenbarger reporting for the November 17, 2005, edition of The Wall Street Journal summarized her story on fair workplace flextime (page D1) by saying that "Some employers are allowing all employees to apply for flexible schedules, requiring proposals that outline how the plan will work, evaluating flexible setups regularly, making scheduling a team responsibility, and training people to back up co-workers."

During the 1990s, some financial institutions began closing for a day so that employees could spend that day volunteering in the community, at schools, retirement homes, nursing homes, libraries, and wherever they chose to volunteer. Some companies allow two paid work-hours a month to be spent volunteering in the community. This encouragement of volunteerism increases the sense of community within the organization and in the city-community at large.

Chapters 3 and 4 more extensively explored some examples of the ways that companies and organizations pursue to foster community on-site and in built work environments.

Variable 5: Rewards

Rewards should be used to accomplish organizational goals rather than to punish people. Use rewards and incentives to inspire interaction and achievement of goals. Be consistent with what is rewarded and how rewards are given. For example, set up some objective measures so that employees know what specific actions they need to take to receive an award and then make sure that the presentation for same-level awards are consistent.

Protecting time for volunteerism both creates a sense of community (variable 3) and serves as a form of an individual reward. Treating people with dignity and respect is a form of reward. As is training and coaching employees how to treat guests, customers, and vendors with dignity and respect. Luxury Attitude, a Paris, France consulting firm, suggests that an experience that is luxurious is one in which individuals feel recognized and that human interactions define luxury experience more than products do. In fact, Luxury Attitude has defined more than 450 interactions with hotel guests that contribute to a sense of experiencing luxury. Asking for employee ideas and then actually using those ideas is a form of reward, as is giving people a vote or a say in what happens in the organization when it comes to suggesting how a new building gets built (as Pfizer did in preparation for their Building 220). HP's employee councils are an ongoing form of employee recognition and serve as implementation forces for change that create rewards for all employees. Having a variety of food offerings in the cafeteria also can be rewarding.

Variable 6: Creativity and Morale

Creativity and morale happen when people feel healthy, safe, and comfortable, and have a sense of community and identified pathways to reward. Creativity and morale are expected to be visible in the workspaces of certain industries, such as marketing, advertising, design, and architecture. As you have been reading, some companies have built basketball courts and fitness centers right into the office space to inspire creativity. Other companies grant employees cube-decorating allowances of several hundred dollars so that workspace can reflect the creativity of those at work.

Take this story from a space-crowded workplace: Because both the men's and women's rest rooms had large sitting areas and the firm was out of storage space, filing cabinets are located in both rest rooms. This use of space dampens morale because now information and files are not equally accessible to all employees of the building, and because people seeking a respite while meeting their physiological needs are visually assaulted with reminders of the work they just walked away from. Seek ways to inspire creativity and morale in every space within the building.

HOW THE PRODUCTIVITY VARIABLES INTERRELATE FOR PEOPLE IN BUILDINGS: BUILDINGS THAT MAKE THE CASE

The following stories are about some pretty incredible buildings that make the case for the productivity variables and human responsive design. As a group, they certainly address all of the six productivity variables. Individually, they address most. Because the design teams were not designing to the productivity variables described in *Building Community in Buildings*, documentation of the variables is not always readily available. This was most apparent for the safety and security variable that is not presented in any of the upcoming case studies. The building designs do, however, very succinctly reflect the broader aspects of human responsive design, responsiveness to the site, climate, and people. All of the buildings are in North America. Three of the buildings, the Herman Miller Greenhouse, Lockheed 157, and C.K. Choi were designed previous to accessible green building programs. Two of the buildings, constructed after 1999, are certified Platinum, the highest level of the U.S. Green Building Council's Leadership in Energy and Environmental Design program.

Let us consider a building that meets the USGBC LEED standard. A LEED building has four certification levels that building designers can target. From highest to lowest they are Platinum, Gold, Silver, and Certified. The strategies and technologies and construction methodologies utilized in a LEED building can harvest points and achieve a designated rating, but it is important to note that the level of certification, even if at the Platinum level, does not guarantee any measure of human productivity in the building. LEED is a good measure of sustainability, resource, and energy efficiency; and most LEED buildings can be said to utilize the elements of human responsive design if not also human resource development strategies; even so, a LEED building is only predictive of end use human efficiency in a general sense. That is why it is important to consider the variables that are the building blocks of productivity.

The buildings profiled here differ in their approach to the breadth and depth of human responsive design and human resource development, and the productivity variables. Each building was designed and constructed with intent to provide space that their end users would value. All have been designed and constructed with worker productivity as a main goal. Most of the data from the following building productivity profiles was taken from a database of the U.S. Department of Energy's Building Technology Program, High Performance Buildings.[7] Though this information is in the public domain, many individual researchers, architectural, landscape, and engineer teams, and other professional organizations, individuals, and agencies were responsible for the human responsive features expressed in the buildings and in the creation and compilation of this information. Jana and Ken are grateful for the foresight of these building professionals and their dedication to human resource development, what we call HRD^2.

Because of space considerations, not every productivity variable has been fully described in each case. Instead, we have attempted to provide you with good representations of the strategies and technologies as they are used effectively in select cases. In this way you can get a feel for the broad range of design ideas that make work spaces creative and productive. For more information on a particular building, visit the web site BuildingGreen.com to peruse these and other studies. In each case presented, the productivity variables are commented upon and some case-specific productivity information is provided.

C.K. Choi Building for the Institute of Asian Research

Completed in 1996, this three-story Vancouver, British Columbia, building is an Asian research center housing research offices and seminar rooms. It beautifully embodies the full elements of human responsive design and human resource development. HRD^2 goals for the project included use of natural ventilation, daylighting, salvaged materials, water wise landscaping, and human health and productivity.

Both local Canadian and Asian cultural elements are reflected in the site through the interior and exterior expressions of the building. Especially noteworthy was the intent to preserve existing ecosystems. Many existing trees were maintained on the site and new trees were planted with the intent to remove carbon dioxide from the air while providing shade for the building and people. Natural marshes are part of the site, extending the range of available biology to wetland creatures. The landscape plantings need little water beyond what is brought through natural rainfall and they require little maintenance and care. The irrigation that is provided is harvested rainwater and gray water recycled from the building's sinks. Pervious pavers are used in areas of the site to allow natural water percolation into the soil.

- Healthy buildings and healthy people
  - ○ This variable was a major goal of the building and site's architectural program. It was met through natural ventilation strategies that supply occupants with 100 percent outside air, good daylighting and views, exterior garden spaces, the use of individual control systems for heating and cooling, the use of occupant controlled operable windows, and the use of formaldehyde- and solvent-free building products and adhesives.
- Safety and security
  - ○ No data was provided on this variable.
- Comfort and control
  - ○ Occupant control is provided through operable windows, individual heating and cooling controls, and task lighting. Comfort is provided through daylighting, views to the exterior, and natural ventilation.
- Community
  - ○ The community aspect of the building is satisfied through cultural design elements that blend Asian culture within a campus setting. An exterior stone garden set with benches and large stones engraved with Chinese characters extolling Confucian virtues provides the building user and visitor an opportunity to socialize while surrounded by Asian symbols and space. Asian artwork and styling are also apparent throughout the space.
- Rewards
  - ○ The site in itself provides good rewards for visitors and occupants to the campus and building. The multiple Asian-themed gardens and beautiful landscape provides good space for walking or contemplation, conversations, and work-oriented discussions.
- Creativity and morale
  - ○ No data specific to creativity and morale were found. A post occupancy evaluation, now underway, should shed light on this variable. The building and site is quite beautiful and very accessible making it easy to expect high scores in this area.

Herman Miller Greenhouse

Herman Miller has long been noted as a "green" or environmentally sensitive and aware company. An international furniture design and manufacturing company, they utilize recycled materials and environmentally friendly processes in their manufacturing. In the early 1990s, they hired architect William McDonough, noted then for his ecological design work and later for the groundbreaking *Cradle to Cradle*, coauthored with Michael Braungart, to design a new 290,000-square-foot manufacturing facility, office, and distribution center.[8] The Greenhouse Factory and Offices, located in Holland, Michigan, were completed in 1995, about four years before the LEED program appeared in the United States. Human responsive design strategies were abundant in the facility's design. The site features protection of wildlife habitat, use of indigenous vegetation, and good storm water management. The design was climate responsive utilizing natural ventilation and photo-sensor control of electric lighting to take advantage of natural daylighting and sophisticated HVAC control systems. But the standout HDR[2] strategy was to provide a healthy and productive space for people. The design invites communication between the interior and exterior landscapes as well as interaction among employees.

- Healthy buildings and healthy people
  - As with the C.K. Choi building, addressing this variable was a major goal, and because of the manufacturing nature of the facility, pre- and post-productivity were measured. Design elements for health included natural ventilation, daylighting, garden spaces, and views of greenery and wildlife.
- Safety and security
  - No data was provided on this variable.
- Comfort and control
  - Occupant comfort and health was the first of three primary goals set for the facility. A post-occupancy survey showed high scores for windows and daylighting, health, and attractiveness of the overall environment. Interestingly, originally temperature and noise received low marks for occupants and have subsequently been addressed. The clear message here is that post-occupancy evaluations are important, but only if acted upon.
- Community
  - Communication within the facility was a key consideration of the company. A daylit interior thoroughfare provides occupants visual communication with the site and co-workers. A fitness center provides a means to both stay healthy and socialize with fellow workers.
- Rewards
  - Good lighting, view corridors, outdoor wildlife habitat areas, and positive post occupancy evaluations are good indicators of reward in the space.

- Creativity and morale
  - No data was provided on this variable but employees were involved with the design from the beginning of the design process, helping to make decisions about the space. The productivity gains as noted below may also be an indicator of higher than average creativity and morale.

As stated earlier, productivity gain was a goal for the building. According to the Department of Energy case study, in the Greenhouse "worker effectiveness rose from 98.54% to 99.53% and work quality rose from 98.97% to 99.23%." This was considered to be a significant increase for the company and easily offset any additional cost for constructing a sustainable building.

Genzyme Center

One of two LEED buildings profiled, the Genzyme building was completed in 2003 in Cambridge, Massachusetts. It is a large, 344,000-square-foot building, serving as corporate headquarters for a biotechnology company and designed to be the company's signature building. Human responsive design strategies for the building's heating and cooling system are very unique. The exterior façade is a double wall which blocks summer heat and is used as a preheater for incoming air in the winter.

- Healthy buildings and healthy people
  - Natural daylighting, views, outdoor patios, and 18 interior gardens were designed into the building to provide occupants comfortable and interactive space in which to work.
- Safety and security
  - No data was provided on this variable.
- Comfort and control
  - Though it is a 12-story high-rise, operable windows were designed into the building to give occupants some control of personal airflow. The 18 gardens, natural daylighting used throughout the building, a library, and multiple coffee bars were provided to allow for comfortable, relaxed communication and collaboration opportunities for workers.
- Community
  - The Department of Energy's Genzyme Center case study suggests a strong focus on community for the building, including an extension into the adjacent neighborhoods. Access to the riverfront has been extended to the community through the Genzyme Center.

- Rewards
  - ○ Coffee bars, gardens, and views provide a good level of reward for building occupants.
- Creativity and morale
  - ○ Many spaces throughout the building were built with the employee in mind. Coffee bars, cafes, and interior gardens and seating areas were placed throughout the facility to encourage employee interaction.

Though specific productivity numbers were not given for the Genzyme Center, the individual was of primary consideration in the building design. During early architectural design programming the project team decided to design for the individual—as a strategy for creating healthy space for the whole. Productivity was given as a goal in the building program. The building is described as being "comfortable, beautiful, unusual, and joyful."

Philip Merrill Environmental Center

Noted as the first LEED Platinum building, the Philip Merrill Environmental Center, a 32,000-square-foot building located on Chesapeake Bay in Annapolis, Maryland, is one of the most profiled green building case studies in the world.[9] It is also noted for a very thorough and professional post-production occupancy evaluation that was prepared by Judith Heerwagen, PhD, a much noted and accredited productivity expert.[10]

- Healthy buildings and healthy people
  - ○ This building's open design features great daylighting and views. Extensive natural habitat on the site creates a strong occupant-environment connection. Interior and exterior finishes used were nontoxic or low toxic. Natural interior finishes such as cork and bamboo flooring were used throughout the interior. Natural ventilation is tied to a carbon dioxide meter so that the interior space is always filled with fresh air.
- Safety and security
  - ○ No data was provided on this variable.
- Comfort and control
  - ○ In the post occupancy evaluation performed by Judith Heerwagen and Leah Zagreus,[11] acoustical conditions in the building were rated lower than other rated areas for the building; although it is noted in the building case study that these ratings were still above average marks when compared to other buildings. The reason given for

Photo 6.1 Herman Miller Greenhouse, Interior Street, William McDonough + Partners. The interior street became a key design element for increasing workplace satisfaction among occupants. This plant-filled walkway allows employees to access different areas of the factory and provides both natural light and views for the workers, as well as a pleasant space in which to socialize in a summer-like environment during the cold Michigan winters (The Herman Miller Company).

acoustical discomfort was the openness of the space and subsequent noises from other occupants.

- ○ Access to views and good daylighting were rated high by occupants as was air quality, esthetics of the building, openness of the space and the connection to the natural environment.
- Community
  - ○ The open office space and access to video conferencing to telecommuters provides good opportunity for work and interpersonal communication, although the noise level from the open design elicited some negative response from staff. Since the Chesapeake Bay Foundation exists as an environmental advocacy and educational organization, there is a very strong connection to the community at large. Restoration of the natural environment on a formerly developed site allowed the Foundation to make a clear statement about values that the local community holds close.
- Rewards
  - ○ The Chesapeake Bay Foundation implemented incentives for employees to bike or carpool to work. Shower and dressing rooms are provided for bikers, runners, and walkers. Employees are given options to telecommute and video conferencing can be used for telecommuter communication with office staff.
- Creativity and morale
  - ○ A post occupancy survey reported that 80 percent of building occupants experienced a high level of morale, well-being, and sense of belonging at work.

Lockheed Building 157

Built in 1983, this large and modern style five-story office building is located in mild Sunnydale, California. In a climate where heating is not necessary, the major goal for the building was to reduce cooling loads and associated energy costs. The major strategy used for reducing loads was use of daylighting and an automatic dimmable electric lighting system.

- Healthy buildings and healthy people
  - ○ Daylighting provides up to 75 percent of workspace lighting in this large modern structure. Trees and plants add greenery throughout the building. Special care was taken to reduce sound and noise in the building.
- Safety and security
  - ○ No data was provided on this variable.

Photo 6.2 Philip Merill building, exterior deck. This deck and structure serves several functions. It provides shade for the interior building and for people using the deck, serves as a support structure for photovoltaic panels that supply power to the building, and adds to the architectural and aesthetic interest of the building (Dr. Joel Loveland).

- Comfort and control
  - Built in 1983, automatic control systems dominated buildings of this magnitude. The electric lighting system was tied into a control system to automatically dim lights when daylighting was available. Workstation task lighting gives occupants some control of light. Visual comfort was also considered so windows were selected for their ability to reduce heat gain and glare into the interior.
- Community
  - An open layout and a large cafeteria were designed with the intent to provide space for interaction and communication among employees.
- Rewards
  - No data was provided on this variable.
- Creativity and morale
  - No data was provided on this variable.

In the case study on this building it is noted that productivity and decreased absenteeism were an unexpected offshoot of daylight use and other interior human responsive design strategies such as green spaces, view windows, and a central atrium skylight measuring 60 feet by 300 feet. After moving into the building, these results were obtained: absenteeism dropped by 15 percent and productivity increased by 15 percent. The case study also reports that Lockheed management believes that their increased productivity was responsible for winning a large defense contract with enough profit to pay for the entire cost of the project.

Zion National Park Visitors Center

The National Park Service has been a leader in the development of buildings that reflect the best aspects of HRD^2. This would seem to be an obvious charter for a national park but even if good design were the rule, the Zion Visitors Center, located in Springdale, Utah, would be a notable exception. It is a living example of the positive outcome of integrated design. All of the strategies for HRD^2, daylighting, natural cooling, state-of-the-art electric lighting, aesthetically pleasing natural finishes, solar heat, and a photovoltaic electrical system were built for a cost 30 percent less than comparable national park buildings.

- Healthy buildings and healthy people
  - Healthy features include daylighting, natural wood beams and finish materials throughout the building's interior, and passive cooling

towers that exchange the building's air volume five times each hour. Outdoor rooms and views of the surrounding vegetation and rich colored mountain peaks and clean air create a delightful healing experience for visitors and occupants alike.

* Safety and security
  * No data was provided on this variable.
* Comfort and control
  * The airflow from the passive (nonmechanical) cooling towers is controlled through a louver system that building occupants control. Controls for the electric lighting allow occupants to increase or decrease lighting based on the current contribution of daylight. Many windows are operable allowing for occupant control of cross ventilation through the building. Shading is provided by orientation of the building, placement of vegetation, and overhangs on the one-story visitors center. Wintertime conditioning of the space relies on direct sun penetration into the space and utilization of an interior trombe (thermal storage) wall to collect direct solar energy.
* Community
  * For those who have opportunity to visit this space, the elements of community are readily apparent. Extensive exterior pathways lead to shaded and protected exterior learning rooms where visitors share experiences with each other and park staff. Sitting areas are frequent throughout the native vegetated grounds. With grandeur and simplicity, this visitor center communicates the natural features and elements of the park. The center's entry allows a transition from a simple outdoor patio area into a large central daylit atrium complete with concrete floors stained the color of the surrounding mountains and high ceilings framed with massive timbers. The Park's staff is friendly, helpful, and happy to talk about both the Park and the building's pleasant features.
* Rewards
  * No data was provided on this variable.
* Creativity and morale
  * No data was provided on this variable; however, Ken has been to this facility several times and finds that Park staff always seems genuinely engaged in their work and have always enjoyed talking about the building and their work.

Photo 6.3 Zion Park Visitors Center. Rarely can a building blend in with the beauty of surroundings such as in Zion National Park. The use of stone and wood, natural landscaping and light makes this a landmark Park building. During warmer months the large towers (chimneys) that rise above the roofline are used to create a natural downdraft of air that flows across water-soaked media in the top of the towers, cooling the air and the building's occupants. The inset photo of the building's retail space shows the contribution of natural light within the building's interior (Ken Baker).

VeriFone

VeriFone in Costa Mesa, California, was not among the BuildingGreen case studies, so data for many of the productivity variables as shown for the preceding building profiles was not available. However, the remodel of this call center is a great story of measured productivity gains. The remodel of the 76,000-square-foot building, utilizing strategies like skylights for daylighting, improved cooling and ventilation, better windows and vastly improved aesthetics, realized a one-year return on the investment. After the building remodel, measured productivity increased by 5 percent and absenteeism dropped by a whopping 40 percent due to improved comfort and daylighting in the space.

More Stories on the Productivity Variables

In order to protect the entity that built a structure with some problems, here is a modified version of a how-not-to-do-it case study. In a geography of mostly clay soil and periodic rainfall that allows the soil to be dry much of the year and yet saturated at certain times of the year, a building has been built that floats. That is right—"floats" because when the ground gets wet, the clay soil expands causing the foundation and floor of the building to shift, causing loud noises in the structure and corresponding cracks in the walls of the building. Hard to believe, but true because Jana has toured the building and even asked in disbelief "Why hasn't the architect and the contracting team fixed it?" This floating of the building ties to the productivity variables because it creates a lack of a sense of security (variable 2) and a lack of a sense of control (variable 3). Yet the story of this building continues on the interior with three more examples of the productivity variables having been violated.

As the interior of this same building was completed, three more problem areas surfaced. First: The office building's reception area was designed for desk space, filing cabinets, and windows to create a daylight space that would be both nice to work in and productive. The filing cabinets were to be built into a wall alcove of sorts to hide the cabinets from visitors and to create a half-wall along a walking corridor. The alcove got built, the carpet got laid, and the filing cabinets would not fit into the alcove, which was now too short for the height of the file cabinets. That is right, the thickness of the carpet had not been taken into account when the sheetrock alcove was built. So a frustrating rework of the space had to occur. This mistake is an example of violating productivity variable 3—comfort and control—because the receptionist and office team needing to use this space were inconvenienced for several months waiting for the rebuild. Productivity was negatively affected because the receptionist did not have easy access to and control of the files that needed to be used every day to accomplish work.

Second problem: The dock doors to the warehouse space in the building ended up being too short for the driveway and truck door openings meant to align with the doors to the warehouse. Again, a loss of a sense of control (variable 2) was felt by employees because their work was now impeded by having to create makeshift unloading accommodations with each truck that arrived until new doorways were constructed and new doors hung.

Third problem: One of the building's elevators was meant to be used for the movement of materials, inventory, and equipment. However, upon completion, the elevator turned out not to be big enough to accommodate the standard-sized carts already owned by the business and already in use to haul materials from floor to floor. Rather than reinstalling an elevator that actually met the needs of the business, the business had to accommodate to the elevator. So, a duplicate set of carts was purchased and a modified system of loading the carts, unloading the carts, and reloading the carts was created so that the elevator could still be used to help move items between floors. Hard to believe but it is true. This error violates variable 1 because the mental health of employees was impinged upon. This error also violates variable 4 because the ability to interact with the building in a productive way was clearly prevented. Furthermore, this error violates a sense of safety (variable 2) because of all of the extra loading, unloading, and reloading now required by employees as they handled the building's contents.

These three faults in the building process also demonstrate a lack of reward (variable 5) because employees feel unrewarded by having communicated the needs for the building, and yet not having a building that met the needs for easy access, easy unloading of trucks, and easy access to materials needed on a daily basis. Yes, all of the problems described really did occur in one building. And each of the problems created a violation of the productivity variables. The brand new building turned out to not be appropriately functional after all. How many buildings in your community have had similarly poor experiences? Do not let it be your experience. Use this chapter and Chapter 7 to ensure that your results are what your company, organization, and employees need to be productive, healthy, and creative in your workspaces.

HRD² PRODUCTIVITY VARIABLE QUESTIONNAIRE

Use the following questions as a starting place for applying the productivity variables to your workspace and employee community design, rebuild, remodel, and culture changing and supporting activities.

Individual concerns and domains—personal needs getting met:

1. Healthy buildings and people
   - What airflow and ventilation issues need to be considered for your workspace?
   - Can new furnishings, desks, partitions, and carpeting, be specified as VOC free?
   - Are photocopy machines placed in separate and ventilated rooms?
   - Are plants brought into the interior landscape healthy for those with allergies?
   - Are exercise facilities and safe walking areas part of the facility?

2. Safety and security
   - What safety and security features are needed for employees to feel physically safe?

- What security features are needed to protect the intellectual property created in the building?
- What security features are needed to protect intellectual and physical property from outsiders who visit the building, who might hack into your computer network, or who might ask an employee or contractor to steal information?
- How can your building simultaneously provide personal security and a sense of personal freedom?

3. Comfort and control

- What sense of and actual control can employees be given to influence their workspace?
- What office and human resources policies do you have in place that allow employees to express their individuality in their attire, workspace, and community space?
- Is there intent to use colors and textures appropriate for the workspace activities but supportive of human needs?
- Do employees understand that their clothing decisions affect personal comfort? How will you help them understand?
- Are operable windows integrated into HVAC system use?

Others and interacting with others:

4. Community

- What amenities does the building offer to employees?
- What team gathering places does the building provide?
- What events and activities are held to encourage team building, group interaction, and esprit de corps?
- What policies are in place that allow and encourage or discourage employee interactions?

5. Rewards

- What incentive plans for individuals and for teams does the company have in place?
- What has been included in the building design to ensure that employees and users of the building can productively and creatively interact with the building and each other?
- Are their elements in your space that bring a sense of delight or wonder to occupants?
- Do occupants have opportunity to contribute to and participate in the decisions regarding changes to the building space?

Peak productivity occurs with the marriage of the psychological and physical as people work alone and interact with others in buildings:

6. Creativity and morale
   - How has your company adequately addressed the five preceding productivity variables?
   - How will your organization address creativity and morale in the built environment?
   - What rewards for creativity and innovation does your organization offer to employees, vendors, and contractors?
   - When was the last time you conducted an employee survey to learn how people feel about working for your company? What did you do as a result of the survey?

CONCLUSION: THE SHAPE AND CONFIGURATION OF BUILDINGS AFFECT PRODUCTIVITY

During the interviews for this book, we heard repeatedly that office locations and office building environments play a role in recruiting and retaining employees. The city chosen or the community created on the worksite can affect who will take a job. Human resources managers can play a bigger role in the construction of buildings by recognizing that the fluff and stuff of amenities that tend to get cut when financial times are tough are not the only ways in which to ensure that buildings are built and maintained to be productive and responsive to human beings and the environment. There are good low-cost strategies for creating more effective workspace; the use of color and light, low or nonemitting carpets and furnishings, cubicle layout, access to views, and designated community space are all choices to be made by the HRD^2 team (more on this is discussed in Chapter 7). Facilities managers, architects, engineers, and occupants can play a more effective role in the construction of workplace buildings by participating in an integrated design process where human needs are effectively communicated. It is only through early communication that design teams can fully consider HRD^2 strategies and creatively deliver them at little to no cost.

Designing and building consciously for building occupants is not another trend that will be placed by the wayside a few years from now. We are only now on the cusp of learning the strategies and technologies that will ensure workplaces of the future follow a continuous cycle of evaluation and implementation in response to human need. In 1964, U.S. President John F. Kennedy gave a forward-looking speech that included this sentence: "I look forward to an America which will not be afraid of grace and beauty, which will protect the beauty of our natural environment, which will preserve the great old American houses and squares and parks of our national past, and which will build handsome and balanced cities for our future." The buildings and organizational cultures you have read about in the first five chapters of this book depict this approach toward creating and protecting spaces that contribute to the building and existence of a bright future. Chapter 7 introduces the tools and processes that can be used to plan for, design, implement, build, and maintaining HRD² productive buildings and workplace communities.

7 / How to Build Buildings for Productive People

PRIOR TO THE twenty-first century, the world of work could be best characterized as a marketplace that was filled by forest, mine, and field products. By the end of the twenty-first century and into the foreseeable future, marketplaces were also and will continue to be increasingly filled with mind and data-driven products. This change in the sources of goods and services changes the needs to be filled by our buildings.

Historically, tree plantings have symbolized everything from marriages to deaths in our social lives. In our business lives, tree plantings to commemorate a co-worker or to celebrate a store opening are an activity designed to foster community in the moment of pause around the celebration. The beauty of tree planting ceremonies is that both the human and the built environments benefit because of the promise of growth, the delivery of air purification and oxygen, the shared moments of memory about the event and the tree. During the 1980s a new conversation about corporate citizenship and responsibility, beyond tree plantings and commemorative events, began. Today, discussions of and implementation around green building, human responsive design, and human resources development as it relates to the built environment and overall business productivity come together in an expanded conversation about corporate responsibility. For instance, the corporate community's responsibility includes building structures that both fit the needs of employees and the site upon which the building is built; health of workers; productivity of workers; profitability of the company; community giving, philanthropy, and volunteerism; and sustainability into the future. As a part of corporate citizenship and of daily business conduct, HRD^2 is just good business. Understanding what your goals and objectives for the building and workplace community are really is the place to begin. Then, understanding what you are paying for in the design and construction of the building and in the development of workplace community is the next discussion. For instance, an environmentally built and safe building (as discussed in Chapter 6) does not necessarily in and of itself create space that is conducive to working. As this book has explored, workplaces conducive to work include the six productivity variables: healthy buildings and people; safety and security; comfort and control; community; reward; and creativity and morale.

When Jana and Ken began discussing the human responsive and human resource concepts this book would explore, they were struck with the idea that the relationship between the office worker and the building space is somewhat like a marriage, certainly akin to a contract. When we commit to a job are we not also committing some part of ourselves to joining the community that exists within the building space? Are we not giving a silent commitment to accepting the condition of the built space, for better or for worse? Perhaps we have not taken any vows to the space itself, but surely we have commitments to our management, the shareholders, or to each other to produce a work product of value.

A marriage is most functional when both partners bring something to the relationship—not just one time, but again and again. Since the building and physical space also play a role in this relationship, why do we not expect them to give something back to us? What can we do to ensure that there is ongoing growth and satisfaction for the work force from the workspace? Clearly the building and physical space play a role in the interactions of people in the building. If we are to spend a third of our working lives in union with space and people then what can we do to ensure that there is ongoing growth and satisfaction for employees in the spaces in which they work? This chapter explores the roles, processes and discussion starters, and occupant survey tools that business owners, leaders, and managers can implement to create positive, productive, creative, and profitable workplaces that promote both individual and organizational well-being and offer practical solutions to the issues highlighted in Chapter 6—HRD^2—human responsive design and human resource development.

This chapter brings together the ideas presented throughout the book so that no matter what your role in the design and construction of a new workspace, you can actively and effectively contribute to the conversation and the creation of community and productivity in buildings. This chapter explores the roles that business owners, leaders, and managers can employ to create positive, productive—and profitable—workplaces that promote both individual and organizational well-being. In this chapter you will find ways to start workplace community and built-environment productivity conversations; an occupant survey; a presentation of the process and project management approach additions that can help ensure meaningful conversations during the design process that lead to successful implementation; implementation ideas; and in the chapter closing, a Top 10 Ideas for Building Community in Buildings.

BUILDING COMMUNITY IN YOUR BUILDING

The discussion on building community, productivity, and creativity within workers and workplaces includes a continuous process of idea development, implementation, and improvement. Spaces that support productivity and creativity are evolutionary in nature, they evolve with time due to many factors such as change in the workforce, change in work type, and with the change in our philosophy regarding the larger community that surrounds us. Remember, nothing ever remains in stasis; changes will occur in the everyday work environment whether through good intent or through no perceived intent. Recognizing this evolutionary nature of the people-to-building relationship reminds us to consider our past work structures (hopefully productivity measurements were in place), identify where we are now (more measurement) and where we want to be, and to then implement what we believe are the good ideas that will affect positive change. Then we measure again and adjust those HRD^2 strategies to move closer to our goals.

Some of the ideas that have been presented throughout this book and in this chapter will work well for you. Some, you may have already tried with good result, while others may not have had strong results. The mistake many of us make is to consider failure as failure, when in fact we should see it as part of our evolution. If failure teaches us to do something differently, and by doing so we find success, have we really failed? The biggest obstacle to success is apathy toward ourselves and our work. True failure manifests only when we have broken or less-than-optimal systems in place and we either do not recognize the need or do not have the courage to change.

True success manifests when we keep learning, adapting, improving, and evolving. Hopefully, the stories and case studies presented throughout this book have given you and your firm or organization knowledge of some proven approaches for building community and productivity in your built environment and your immediate work building.

BUILDING COMMUNITY IDEAS

Occupant Surveys

One of the most beneficial actions any employer can take is to ask for workforce feedback on workspace and employees' sense of community. An annual survey of worker needs within the environment and built space, when acted upon, creates a pathway for organizational success. An occupant survey need not be an expensive, complex, or time-consuming process. Though there are professionally developed post occupant surveys (more on this later), and though these surveys will give you valid input on which to build change in your organization and building, too few organizations are currently using them. Thus the potential good effect of post occupant surveys is minimized. If you are not surveying your building occupants on an annual basis, how can you truly understand the environmental and human issues within your organization as the organization evolves?

Consider this observation and see if you know it to be true. Typically, soon after a new building is occupied, remodeling and building system changes begin—HVAC, controls, space design, and lighting. Just because a building is new does not mean it functions as it should or as occupants most desire. This scenario is typical; in order to become more efficient and productive, a new space is remodeled. For example, one newer building that we are familiar with that was LEED Silver certified was partially remodeled just two years after occupancy to redesign existing space for better serving the public and to redesign employee space to provide for better daylighting, electric lighting, views, and team communication. If integrated design, design that seeks to open communication and receive input from a broader group of stakeholders, is the driving directive of the first design, costly remodels can be avoided altogether. Then, after a new building has been occupied for at least five to ten years, new design elements that satisfy evolving needs can be considered. A good question for a design team to ask is, "How will the building and building systems satisfy owners' and occupants' needs to be creative and productive and ensure that the building supports the business and surrounding community for the next ten years?"

So, do not make changes in an existing building or build a new one without first surveying your people. Each of the stories of success in earlier chapters included employee input. All of the HRD^2 ideas presented in this book have been tried and implemented with success, which may or may not mean they will work for you. The key is to have productivity discussions about the building with the people who will work in it. If you are designing a new building, it is going to be cheaper or at least more cost effective for you to build in HRD^2 strategies from the beginning of the design process. Do not wait until your design is almost finished or your building is under construction to begin implementing HRD^2 ideas. Once you have moved into the new building, implement your first post-occupancy survey to establish a baseline of responses to the space that can be used to measure changes in future surveys. If you are in an existing building, previous to making facility changes, implement an occupant survey to see what building occupants want; pick the top one to three strategies, implement, measure, and resurvey.

Perhaps the best reason for a survey is to find out what workers most value within the space and the organization. This book offers you a simple survey that can be used to determine what HRD^2 strategies may be appropriate for your organization. Why are we offering this survey when other professional surveys exist? Because we think there is a chance that the simplicity of the survey will make it attractive enough to implement, and the information you harvest will provide benefits that will be obvious—a few ideas, that when initiated, will grow community and increase the productivity in your organization.

The questions below form the basis for a simple survey you can give to your occupants to begin to determine where they place value within the built environment, office, and community at large. Consider it an interactive feedback tool and use it to benchmark the first year in a new building or the current year in an existing space. We suggest you create a database out of these questions and others you may feel are appropriate, and then survey your staff online each year. If you are planning to build a new building, remodel an existing structure, or explore with employees what they value most in their built work environments, the answers to this survey could serve as a guide to the design team for building strategies. This instrument is only useful when you apply what is learned. If you make changes to the built environment based on this survey and you do not have in place other assessments for productivity and creativity, it will be difficult to attribute value to your efforts and you will have no assurances, other than anecdotes, that implemented changes provide a return on investment.

The HRD² Survey Directions

Part 1: Employee Values

How important are each of the following built environment and workplace community elements to you personally? Please indicate your rating of each element with a number 1 through 5.

1 = Very important for me to have at work
2 = Important for me to have at work
3 = It does not matter to me
4 = Not important to me to have at work
5 = Do not spend any money or effort on this element

The Survey Part 1   **EMPLOYEE Ratings**

Productivity Variable 1. Healthy Buildings and People
  1. Natural light that reaches my workspace   _____
  2. The ability to see out of a window while sitting at my desk   _____
  3. Large quantities of outside air are brought into the workspace   _____
  4. Good filtration of workspace air   _____
  5. Plants or green space both inside and outside the building   _____

Productivity Variable 2. Safety and Security
  6. Security personnel that regularly patrol the buildings and grounds   _____
  7. Good lighting in the parking area   _____
  8. A central, secure access into the building or complex   _____
  9. A safe place to take walks on campus or in the neighborhood   _____
 10. A company policy on safety and security   _____

Productivity Variable 3. Comfort and Control
 11. Moderate to high light levels throughout the workspace and individual task lighting in my workspace   _____
 12. Low light levels throughout the workspace and individual task lighting in my workspace   _____
 13. Comfortable and ergonomic furniture including my desk and chairs   _____
 14. A more quiet space surrounding my personal workspace and meeting rooms   _____
 15. An ability to organize and accessorize or decorate my workspace the way I want to   _____

Productivity Variable 4. Community
 16. Quiet spaces where I can meet with my team   _____
 17. Access to good foods, a nice cafeteria on site   _____
 18. The opportunity to help others in my community   _____
 19. The opportunity to help others in my office   _____
 20. Well-appointed meeting areas that have the equipment needed to accomplish group work   _____

Productivity Variable 5. Rewards
 21. An exercise facility at work   _____
 22. A child care facility at work   _____
 23. A choice of how I am rewarded   _____
 24. Reward for work performance that meets key organizational objectives   _____
 25. A nice area outside the building where I can take walks   _____

Productivity Variable 6. Creativity and Morale
 26. A vote on the colors and patterns for office floors and walls   _____
 27. Ability to bring a quiet child to work once a week   _____
 28. Ability to bring a well-trained and quiet pet to work   _____
 29. Ability to choose my office furniture and décor   _____
 30. Ability to telecommute at least one day per week   _____

Further Comments:
What else do you feel is important in your workspace?

Part 2: Measuring the Building's Delivery on Employee HRD^2 Values

How well are each of the following built environment and workplace community elements (the same ones you just rated) being delivered upon in your company and in your workspaces? In other words, how well is the company doing to meet these needs?

Please indicate your rating of each element with a number 1 through 5. This time the numbers mean:

1 = Building/Company is providing for this very well
2 = Building/Company is providing for this somewhat
3 = Hard to tell what is being done
4 = Building/Company talks about doing things but does not appear to be doing anything
5 = Building/Company is not spending any money or effort on this element

The Survey Part 2	BUILDING Ratings
Productivity Variable 1. Healthy Buildings and People	
1. Natural light that reaches my workspace	_____
2. The ability to see out of a window while sitting at my desk	_____
3. Large quantities of outside air are brought into the workspace	_____
4. Good filtration of workspace air	_____
5. Plants or green space both inside and outside the building	_____
Productivity Variable 2. Safety and Security	
6. Security personnel that regularly patrol the buildings and grounds	_____
7. Good lighting in the parking area	_____
8. A central, secure access into the building or complex	_____
9. A safe place to take walks on campus or in the neighborhood	_____
10. A company policy on safety and security	_____
Productivity Variable 3. Comfort and Control	
11. Moderate to high light levels throughout the workspace and individual task lighting in my workspace	_____
12. Low light levels throughout the workspace and individual task lighting in my workspace	_____
13. Comfortable and ergonomic furniture including my desk and chairs	_____
14. A more quiet space surrounding my personal workspace and meeting rooms	_____
15. An ability to organize and accessorize or decorate my workspace the way I want to	_____

Productivity Variable 4. Community
16. Quiet spaces where I can meet with my team
17. Access to good foods, a nice cafeteria on site   _____
18. The opportunity to help others in my community   _____
19. The opportunity to help others in my office   _____
20. Well-appointed meeting areas that have the equipment needed to   _____
    accomplish group work   _____

Productivity Variable 5. Rewards
21. An exercise facility at work   _____
22. A child care facility at work   _____
23. A choice of how I am rewarded   _____
24. Reward for work performance that meets key organizational   _____
    objectives
25. A nice area outside the building where I can take walks   _____

Productivity Variable 6. Creativity and Morale
26. A vote on the colors and patterns for office floors and walls   _____
27. Ability to bring a quiet child to work once a week   _____
28. Ability to bring a well-trained and quiet pet to work   _____
29. Ability to choose my office furniture and décor   _____
30. Ability to telecommute at least one day per week   _____

Further Comments:
What do you see that the company can be doing to improve the building and the sense of community in the workplace?

Scoring the HRD² Survey

Whether one, one hundred, or one thousand or more employees respond to the HRD² Survey, the resulting scores and employee written comments will provide guidance on how to proceed with the design, remodel, ongoing improvements and maintenance of your building, and ongoing community building in buildings. The survey is scored and interpreted in three parts.

Part 1: Scoring the HRD² Survey—Employee Values

Determine what employees feel is important.

1.a. *Total* Employee Values Score _____

Add up the rating points for all 30 questions for all of the participants who took the survey, then divide that total by the number of participants who took the Survey. (For example, 575 total points divided by 6 for the number of people who took the survey equals 95.8 as the *total* score.) Then, enter the resulting total on the line above. Remember that the total potential range of scores is 30 to 150.

1.b. What the *Total* Employee Values Score means:

30–40 Human responsive design is very important to employees.—Do something based on what you have discovered in this book.

41–75 Human responsive design is important to employees.—Do something based on what you have discovered in this book.

76–115 Human responsive design is perceived as a neutral or nonissue by employees.—Keep exploring what needs to be done.

116–134 Human responsive design is not important to employees.—Survey again in 6 to 12 months.

135–150 Employees are suggesting that you do not spend any money or effort on human responsive design.—Survey again in 6 to 12 months.

2.a. Individual Productivity Variable Scores

In order to take relevant steps to address employee concerns, the key is to study the responses to each one of the productivity variables. Add up the rating points for the *five* questions under each productivity variable. Remember, the possible point totals for each productivity variable ranges from 5 to 25 points.

Productivity Variable 1: _____
Productivity Variable 2: _____
Productivity Variable 3: _____
Productivity Variable 4: _____
Productivity Variable 5: _____
Productivity Variable 6: _____

2.b. What each Productivity Variable Score means:

5 to 16 points means that this productivity variable and the elements described in the five questions are of *high* importance to employees. Address the productivity variables with these point totals by conducting focus groups, stakeholder conversations, or further surveying in order to determine what employees would like to see done to make improvements in the workplace.

17 to 25 points means that this productivity variable and the elements described in the five questions are of *low* importance to employees. Productivity variables with these point totals can be addressed last, or not addressed at all.

Part 2: Scoring the HRD^2 Survey—Building's Delivery on Employee Values

Determine how well the company is doing to deliver on and to meet employee expectations and values regarding their workplaces and spaces and their sense of community at work.

1.a. *Total* Building Delivery Score _____

Add up the rating points for all 30 questions for all of the participants who took the survey, then divide that total by the number of participants who took the survey. (For example, 975 total points divided by 8 for the number of people who took the survey equals 121.9 as the *Total* Building Delivery Score.) Then, enter the resulting total on the line above. Remember that the total potential range of scores is 30 to 150.

1.b. What the *Total* Building Delivery Score means:

30–40 The building and company are providing for the needs and HRD^2 values of employees very well.—Celebrate and keep doing what you are doing.
41–75 The building and company are somewhat providing for the needs and HRD^2 values of employees.—Celebrate and keep looking for ways to improve.
76–115 The building and company are not providing clear responses to HRD^2.—Keep exploring what needs to be done.
116–134 The building and the company appear to be talking about HRD^2 values but not living up to or delivering on them.—There is a disconnect going on. Keep exploring what needs to be done.
135–150 The building and company do not appear to be spending any money or effort on meeting the human responsive design needs of employees.—Keep exploring what needs to be done.

2.a. Individual Productivity Variable Scores

In order to take relevant steps to address employee concerns as it relates to making changes in the building, building design, and creation of community and productivity, the key is to study the responses to each one of the productivity variables. Add up the rating points for the *five* questions for each productivity variable. Remember, the possible point totals for each productivity variable ranges from 5 to 25 points.

Productivity Variable 1: _____
Productivity Variable 2: _____
Productivity Variable 3: _____
Productivity Variable 4: _____
Productivity Variable 5: _____
Productivity Variable 6: _____

2.b. What each Productivity Variable Building Delivery Score means:

5 to 12 points means that this productivity variable and the elements described in the five questions are being well addressed by the building and the company. Keep doing what you are doing and continue to periodically conduct focus groups, stakeholder conversations, or further surveying in order to determine what employees would like to see done to continually make improvements in the workplace.

13 to 25 points means that this productivity variable and the elements described in the five questions are *not* being addressed well by the building and the company. Action needs to be taken to improve the company's and the building approach to HRD[2]. Conduct focus groups, stakeholder conversations, or further surveying in order to determine what employees would like to see done to make improvements in the workplace.

Part 3: Matching Employee Values to Building Delivery Scores

When the total scores are within 10 points of each other, the employee values and the building/company's delivery on those values is a good match. Keep doing what you are doing and keep asking where ongoing improvements can be made.

When the total scores are more than 10 points apart, there is a disconnect between what employees are saying is important and what employees feel they are seeing, experiencing, and receiving from the company and/or in the building. A spread of more than 10 points between the total scores suggests that more exploration of what is wanted, what is needed, and how employees want to see changes is needed. Again, conduct focus groups, stakeholder conversations, or further surveying in order to determine what employees would like to see done to make improvements in the workplace. Or consider hiring an outside firm to conduct the discussions and assist in the facilitation and implementation of the human responsive design process.

SURVEY USE OVER TIME

In the first year of implementing the HRD[2] Survey, you will discover what is important to employees and how well your company is doing to meet their expectations for HRD and community. In the second year, you will learn about what employees feel that the company has done toward making improvements in what they said was important. By the third year of implementing the HRD[2] Survey, based on the improvements reported, you will want to modify the questions under the six productivity variables in order to make continuous improvements. In the fourth year, you will again be measuring improvements based on the year-three new version of the HRD[2] Survey. By the fifth year, the company has likely grown, and you will be using the survey for additions to the building, for significant remodels, or for new buildings.

A SURVEY PROCESS WOULD HAVE HELPED

Here is an employee account from a public community hospital undergoing ongoing remodels.

> Shortly after I started at a local hospital as an x-ray technologist, the hospital opened a new emergency room. While the new emergency room looked nice, it really was not as functional and conducive to patient care as it could have been. Not one employee that I talked to had been asked about the design or set up of the x-ray rooms. In my naiveté, I thought that it had been constructed without any consultation from the radiology department. I now know that probably was not a true assessment. The department administration was probably in on the design, but the people using the room and equipment did not have much input into the room design. Things such as turning the fixed x-ray table a different direction or shortening the wall where the controls are located could have made the new room much better.
>
> Having now been through several remodels of different departments or subdepartments, I know that there is a committee of architects, department chairmen, etc. who come up with the eventual design for the remodel. The hospital has also opened a new surgery wing and still has several new surgery suites to construct. We are facing a shortage of equipment storage for the rooms we already have; however, we have been told that increasing the storage area is a waste of real estate and we will not be getting any more. It will be interesting to see where all the beds, c-arms, tables, and other equipment for the new construction are kept. Simple things in the new surgery suite could have made our lives much easier, but someone wasn't thinking when the plans were drawn up. Things like locations of video plug-ins. To send images from an x-ray machine to the archive in most of the surgery rooms requires one to get down on their hands and knees and plug into an outlet underneath a desk. These plug-ins could just as easily have been put up on the wall in a more accessible location.

TAKING THE SURVEY TO ANOTHER LEVEL

Several organizations offer a standardized post occupant survey with integrated data management and reporting tools. These services offer some important advantages to post-occupancy evaluation (POE) initiatives, including

- tried and true questionnaires developed by researchers with experience in the field and tested over time;
- the ability to provide highly processed and graphically displayed survey results measured against benchmarks created from the pool of other projects on which the same survey has been used;
- the contribution of the POE results to the pool of data, which, if it becomes large enough, can be used by researchers to draw widely applicable conclusions for the benefit of the industry as a whole.

The Center for the Built Environment (CBE) at the University of California, Berkeley, offers one such standardized survey in the form of a web-based questionnaire (http://www.cbe.berkeley.edu/). CBE's industry partners get to see how their survey results compare against the background data set, which currently includes about 45 projects. CBE researchers frequently work with POE users to develop custom modules to address specific questions of interest. CBE research specialist Charlie Huizenga reports that it typically takes 5 to 12 minutes for a user to complete the core survey, and up to 20 minutes if additional modules are included. Their typical response rate is 45 to 65 percent—though it varies greatly depending on how the building occupants learn about the survey. Typically, building staff receive an e-mail asking them to participate in the survey. "If the e-mail comes directly from someone people are accountable to, we can get a 70 or 80 percent response rate," says Huizenga.

The Usable Buildings Trust in the United Kingdom (http://www.usable-buildings.co.uk/) has performed post-occupancy evaluations around the world. For close to 30 years their goal has been to supply building owners with feedback on getting better value—through people productivity—in their buildings.

BALANCING BUILDINGS, PROCESS, AND PEOPLE

Mark Olsen, a business consultant in organizational development, says, "Buildings are about people, process, and people being empowered to do what the organization or company's mission is so that prosperity for all is achieved. Buildings should not be about just the bucks and the basic structure of the box." What follows further states Mark's premise.

> I'm often struck with how buildings and structures are designed and engineered. It often seems that the architect or designer had some idea in mind that did not either "come across" effectively or lacked any real passion or purpose in its result. An example can be seen in institutions designed to serve many people and multiple purposes. So often the buildings lack the very core of the purpose for which they were ostensibly constructed. Ever been inside a large theater auditorium that lacked good acoustics? Couldn't hear anyone on the stage for all the noise around you? Or, how about any school? Was the impression one of cold, over-stated metallic hallways and high, empty ceilings? Design and functionality are critically important. When serving on boards and committees for church designs and fellowship halls, I have emphasized the practical and serviceable needs of people. It's more important that the construction remains flexible, takes into account many uses, and lends itself to openness and warmth. The key elements of design and construction should always be about these three things:
>
> - people (meeting their needs and providing comfort and ease);
> - process (of service and making it serviceable—that includes color, light, sound, and even where the "plug-ins" are located); and,

- prosperity of the future (where can this grow, be added to, and help serve needs in the future).

To fulfill these elements and get effective results, we ought to guard against the human tendency to *only* control the "things" surrounding the construction. These things can, and often do, dictate ineffective results. There seems to be three controlling issues in construction and design, and I think they are

- the building (often translated as someone's idea of an ego trip or cheapness gone very wrong);
- the box (translated: "let's just get it done quickly and start using *something— anything*"); and,
- the bucks (read that, "we have to have another fund raiser"; or, "we've got to get a better interest rate"; or, pick another detail about the finances). Building, box, and bucks are important, yet, sticking only to these points brings us to missed fulfillment of people's expectations and the building's purpose.

Olsen continues:

The greater the vision, the broader the thinking, and the bolder the purpose, the more we want and seek a greater purpose of the utility and mission of building and design. When we do that, we have reached for a standard of excellence that brings chills of excitement to people, sends out messages of greatness to the heart and soul, and invites everyone in to share places of safety. When we strive for excellence, we then live in a process of change and evolution.

THE PROCESS: WORKING WITH PEOPLE AND THE PROJECT

In *Building Community in Buildings*, both the beginning point and an end point are the conversations to be had about physical buildings and about the people in them as they work together, create a sense of community together, and enjoy creativity and productivity together. Chapter 6 presented the six productivity variables and the questions to begin asking in order to ensure that buildings get built with human responsive design that contributes to human resource development and overall productivity. The HRD^2 Survey, described earlier in this chapter, also provides a series of questions to ask in order to discover what is important to building occupants, no matter who owns the building. Now the question becomes, who needs to be involved in the discussions and conversations? When the right people are not involved from the beginning, the end-product building misses the mark and fails to deliver what is needed from the building and the workplace community in order to create productivity and morale.

So, who is responsible, who is a good person to include in the conversation, and who will want to be a part of the discussion about how to improve built space and workplace communities? Throughout the book, we have introduced cases and interviews that demonstrate how people can work together to ensure that a human responsive designed building is built and that workplace community is grown and maintained. One or more dozen people may be appropriate to bring to the discussion. Depending on the nature and scope of your building community project, any and all of the following people, often referred to as stakeholders, make sense to bring together to give input, share ideas, respond to questions, and provide ongoing guidance. In all cases, we suggest including the end users of the building.

Whom to Invite and Why

From the start, invite each of the following people to the HRD^2 process because they bring different expertise, talents, insights, experience, concerns, and needs to the discussion and the implementation strategy.

- Architects—building design
- Contractors—implementers of the design
- Engineers—integrate systems with design
- Building owners—funding, vision
- Owners of the company/companies to occupy the building—vision, long-term needs, expectations
- Building users/end users—daily use, needs and expectations, things wanted for productivity and success
- Building and facility managers—maintenance and operations
- Human resource managers—employee counts, expected growth, amenity and productivity considerations
- Safety specialists—workplace designed for safety, traffic patterns
- Government code/permitting people—compliance issues of all kinds, including the Americans with Disabilities Act
- Executive team representative—long-term vision and budgets
- Management team representative—midterm vision and budgets, implementation expectations
- Team leader representative—daily workplace needs
- Customers/clients—images and impressions of the company, things they want in the building environment
- Vendors—images and impressions of the company, things they want in the building environment
- Someone from the community—images and impressions of the company, things they want in the building environment

Project Process

Every project is dependent on people. Once you have gathered the people you will bring into the conversation and have working on your project, be sure to use sound meeting and project management strategies. Dozens of approaches can be used to manage conversations, people, the building construction project, and the ongoing building of community. What follows is one architect's discovery of how to most effectively work with teams of people in order to achieve sound building design, and most importantly its maximum utilization.

Ernest J. Lombard, a retired architect, real estate developer, avid traveler, and chairman of a state parks and recreation board offers terrific insight to working successfully with groups. Lombard starts his comments with, "Architects often come up with ideas that do not necessarily consider human productivity. Take the open offices—less expensive, simplifies mechanical systems, efficient use of space—but no one really asked whether it makes for improved worker efficiency and productivity. Typically people still want window space—getting an office means you have arrived and if you do not have an office, you are still swimming upstream."

So, to get good buildings built, start with good people process. Lombard shared the seven-step following approach that he has assimilated during his architectural career from a variety of sources and actual work with clients, community groups, and stakeholder groups.

1. Clearly define your goals—answer the questions: "What do you want to create?" and "Why?"
2. Collect and organize factual information, including what others have done, what the facts are about the type of building you want to build.
3. Uncover and test concepts—what are the real and successful concepts? Do your homework.
4. Determine real needs—what is really needed for this project? What needs to be included? What else is in the market? What makes the building yours? What makes it competitive and a recruiting-tool space for great employees? Also consider the function of the space—how does it really work? Who needs to be next to whom? What about public access? What forms do you really need to supply the functionality you are looking for? Remember the guide: form follows function. Look into the economy—what are the costs and opportunities and markets? Consider too the element of time—in the context of history of the area, what are the best types of buildings to be constructing? Another element of time: what is on the horizon, what does the future hold?
5. State the real problem—distill all the gathered information and state what the real problem is, what the opportunities are and what some of the limitations of the finished building might be. Include the priority of the people in the community. Include all the uses the building will realistically be called upon for use. Can you make a space that works and does all of the things needed to be done? Do the functions and forms balance and achieve the goals of the building? *Really do* this— take the time to do it so the project is successful and the buy-in is

complete, and the sense of ownership, involvement and ongoing maintenance is high. (The University of Idaho case presented in Chapter 3 indicated that the team took one and a half years to distill and get to stating the real problem and begin making choices.) Let people participate in the whole process and own the contributed ideas so that a better finished building comes together! It takes time to mature this process. Figure out how to sell the benefits—no matter what building is being built. Every building that involves a large group of people uses a similar process—the process is transportable to any project. In this, the goal is to end up with 10 or fewer really concise statements of what the problem is; what the *real* needs are. For instance, "We need..." statements. Lombard emphatically says, "Never take your eye off of these statements—make it happen. It really does work when you work the process with the right people involved. It really is phenomenal how the answers seem better coming out of the process than they often seem going in."

6. Make choices and decisions—who has responsibility for carrying out what parts of the project? What really will get built? What bid processes will be used? What project documents, diagrams, budgets, and so on will be needed? It is important that the design architects are privy to all of the discussions so they know what they are expected to do and what the project vision is—so that when the building gets built and when people enter they can say, "We got the building we wanted." A paper plan does not necessarily translate into the desired building unless the conversations and process participation has involved the design architects! There cannot be a disconnect between the visionaries, the designers, and the builders—when there is, things get lost in translation. There is a big difference between reading a regurgitation of discussions and *really* understanding the desired vision and the actual needs of the people who will be in and using the building. This is the stage for creativity, of which Lombard says, "Creativity is the highest form of human endeavor—it is the essence of what makes the world go round."

7. Act—get it done. Be sure that everyone has a document to follow and *knows* what needs to be done. Once you get the plan done and defined, the momentum is in place to get the building done. Quality is sometimes a question. If you have the right team in place and you know what is to be produced and who will use it when it is finished, then the users/maintainers will know how to use and maintain the building after its completion. Know the building's strengths and weaknesses when you get ready to use it, to sell it, to office in it, to lease it, and so on. Also, you need people who know how to use the building, its systems, and who can implement productivity within the space!

Problem solving, project planning, and people participating are all key to the process of engaging discussions that lead to productive and healthy workplaces. Of course, sometimes the conversations can get sidetracked, and even derailed. So, stay the course, keep the conversations and input flowing so that truly useful and human responsively designed buildings do get built.

The Project and Project Technology

Project management software can help get the project done, on time and on budget. For example, Autodesk Buzzsaw is a web-based collaboration service that allows building owners, designers, architects, and contractors to share information and processes related to the life cycle of a building. The service starts at $10,000 a year and appears to focus on building details and not necessarily HRD^2 components. So, the key is to use the productivity variable questions in Chapter 6, and the HRD^2 Survey and people/building process approaches from this chapter to ensure a truly human responsive design for your building.

Implementation Ideas to Explore

Once you have held the HRD^2 conversations, gathered input to shape the design of the building, and planned the building and workplace community approaches, it is time to implement the ongoing human and built environment care approaches that will ensure ongoing maintenance and positive evolutions of community, productivity, and creativity in your workspaces. Here is a starting list of some ongoing community building implementation ideas that your company or organization may choose to pursue. Add to this list the things that are already working for your organization. And, of course, keep adding new, workable, and innovative implementation ideas.

Office Layout

How many of us can say we really like cubicles? Probably most of us would rather have the corner office. But cubicles can work well for community interaction and certainly play a role in good office design. They can be laid out to allow good visual privacy; can be personalized with plants, furnishings, and other homey items; offer views to the skyline and sometimes direct line of sight to outdoor spaces. What they generally lack is acoustical privacy and appropriate and controllable workspace lighting. Provide several quieter spaces where small groups can meet or make business calls utilizing a speakerphone.

Green Space and Exercise

Ask for volunteers to develop a garden space/quiet space within your office. Many buildings already have plants inside and outside the building that are taken care of by specialists from within or without the organization. The garden space is a separate space unto itself that team members build and maintain. Once established, use this space as a reward and allow interested teams or team members who have achieved at designated levels to spend an hour a day (not lunch time) for a week or a month tending the company garden. Of course this only works as a reward for those who want to spend time in a garden. As an alternative to working in the garden, let the reward be an hour of quiet time (for an individual) or group time within the garden. Another alternative is to reward people by giving them time for a walk. Depending on the security of your facility and the surrounding area, the walk could be off campus. Try giving the team a problem to solve and send them for a walk in a nearby safe park. You may be surprised at the creative outcome. Plus, team members will come back to the office invigorated from the exercise.

Telecommuting

If you are a private consultant and work from home, you get to choose your work team. Generally speaking, your team might be your clients, other consultants and specialists such as accountants, lawyers, web designers, graphic artists, and marketing specialists. If you are part of a larger organization and have opportunity to telecommute, you encounter a special set of issues. When you are working from home, even if only one to two days per week, it means you do not have day-to-day face time with fellow team members. How then can you build a productive community system when the community is virtual? The answers are similar to what you would need to do if you were physically in the office:

- Use your e-mail to communicate on a daily basis with key players in your team.
- If you have a computer with broadband digital access, you can easily access web services that allow you to interact and share files visually over the internet.
- Depending on team size, members can agree to call each other once per day, or every other day. If your team has video streaming capabilities, a camera mounted to your computer and software will allow your team to make visual contact, via the interenet, with each other while on the phone.

- It is also important to have some face time. Effective team members meet in person at least once a week. Meet in a space that allows you to do your work and that provides for social interaction. Building spaces that make it comfortable for two or more to gather to work do more for you than smaller, more intimate spaces. If your office has nice meeting rooms adjacent to a cafeteria, take advantage of the opportunity to lunch together.
- If you find you cannot meet in person, make a plan with team members to meet virtually for a cup of tea or coffee once a week. Agree to a time, pour yourself a cup of tea and focus on taking time to relax and chat with your team member or members much like you would if you were in the break room at the office.

Whether you are telecommuting or sit among co-workers in an office environment, remember to be inclusive. Sometimes a community is small. It only takes two of us to make a community. But there is danger in small communities within large work forces. The danger is that of segregation or separation from others that could or should be part of your community. In other words, others can feel left out when communities "team up" without them.

Ongoing HRD^2 Education and Input

Place an interactive kiosk (computer) in a quiet space and use it to educate office workers on the company's values, mission, and goals. Set it up so they can take a quiz and earn rewards for correct answers. Use it to get feedback in specific areas such as an ongoing occupant survey for HRD^2 strategies.

Color, Light, Texture, and Furnishings

For ambient space electric lighting, try to use a direct/indirect lighting source. Generally these sources direct 60 to 70 percent of available light down and reflect 30 to 40 percent onto the ceiling where it reflects providing the space with a feeling of brightness. Provide workers with choices in and controls for their personal task lighting. If not a choice in the fixture itself, then give them a range of choices in the type of lamp that the fixture uses. Different lamp temperatures will produce differing light colors from warm yellows to cool blues.

If possible, allow workers to select the color and type of furniture in their space. Allow for options in desk and shelving modules in cubicles. Use paint colors for walls that a majority of workers find acceptable. Ceilings need to be painted with brighter or reflective colors.

Accessibility and Inclusion

Most if not all organizations are aware of the requirements to provide their workers space that is safe and accessible. The Americans with Disabilities Act requires that state and local building codes in the United States provide minimum levels of access and protection to physically and mentally disabled persons. Like any code or standard, it sets a minimum level for compliance. There is nothing to stop your organization from going beyond minimum standards and implementing building changes that will enhance the work environment to disabled employees.

It is also important to consider implementing changes that are inclusive of all employees. The occupant survey can provide input on building changes that will positively affect the majority of workers. Look also to meet some of the needs of the minority.

Celebrating Milestones

An important part of building community is celebrating the milestones of innovation, creativity, community contributions, and overall company successes. Ways to celebrate include newsletter items, newspaper stories, press releases and press conferences, anniversary parties, new product rollout events for employees, all company meetings, and dozens of other creative celebrations.

Choosing Building Materials

Choose building materials that are made from recycled materials and produced locally or within your geographic region. This action supports local business and encourages new startups and associated economic development within the area you live. Also choose materials that are volatile organic compound free, that are not produced with processes that harm the natural environment, and that help to keep the building's interior environment healthy.

Ongoing Maintenance

Finally, here are some directions for increasing the life of your built building and ongoing creation of the workplace community. Add the following items to your implementation strategy to ensure ongoing success:

- Maintenance—maintain all parts of the building on a daily, weekly, monthly, quarterly, and annual basis, based on the requirements of the parts and systems in the building.
- Healthy and productive workers—use the many ideas from this book, keep exploring and implement new approaches, and keep celebrating successes along the way.

- Productive managers and leaders—Encourage ongoing education, activities, and performance reviews that support community building, productivity, creativity, and morale.
- Emergency plans—storm watches, natural disasters, and emergency evacuation procedures all need to be planned for, practiced, implemented when needed, and debriefed after having been implemented.
- Security systems—define, install, continually improve, and maintain the security plans, systems, monitoring services, personnel, and any needed bodyguard services for your building and employees.

LOOKING TO THE FUTURE

As each day draws the future toward us, reflecting on where community and productivity has and will come from in our workplace buildings can lead to powerful implementations of human responsive design. For instance, drawing from the last century and the stories in the beginning chapters of this book, it becomes clear that conversations about buildings, people, and now people in buildings will continue. Frank Gehry, Founder, Gehry Partners, LLP, Los Angeles, California, and architect of such buildings as The Walt Disney Concert Hall, when interviewed in FastCompany magazine, in June 2003, said, "Every great building pushes boundaries, which also means pushing the client." That sometimes means drawing from other disciplines to accomplish the building project at hand. For instance, Gehry's team turned to airplane building software to aid the design of the curved walls in the Disney Concert Hall. What this means to our closing discussion is that the status quo for buildings, for people working in buildings, and even for green building, is not enough. *Building Community in Buildings* suggests how the merged conversations of building buildings and human productivity or human responsive design, can make a difference for people, productivity, and morale. The cases shared throughout the book and the cases that you will soon gather support this.

Look around our built spaces. In 1908 Sears Roebuck introduced kit homes that could be ordered from a catalog and shipped to the building location by rail, and today this continues with prefabricated building parts being used in a variety of fashions for both homes and businesses. Whether people are in a home, a workplace, a single- or multi-story tower, community can be built, fostered, and maintained for everyone's health, well-being, productivity, creativity, and morale.

By 2004, architectural reviewers and museums of art were commenting upon and showcasing a new form of multistory towers called "super skyscrapers" and suggesting that these more than 1,400-foot-high towers are destined to be an ongoing part of twenty-first-century architecture. Super skyscrapers can be found in cities such as London, Paris, Vienna, Tokyo,

Hong Kong, Beijing, Mexico City, Kuala Lumpur, Shanghai, and Taipei. Many of the tallest structures are found in Asia with Malaysia (1998) and Taiwan (2004) holding world record height status. This being the case, that tall buildings are here to stay, human beings need to actively engage in the building process, the building occupation, and the building's use for greatest productivity and creativity. In fact, in April 2006, the Seattle, Washington, City Council began seeing the future and repealed a 1989 voter initiative that limited new building construction to 540 feet in height. The goal: open up for growth and increasing mixed use of buildings in the downtown core. The projected results include buildings that stay in the 40 to 50 story range because available lots will not support taller buildings. Potential results include buildings that are energy efficient as well as people friendly to include things like awnings to keep pedestrian traffic dry and showers for people commuting by bicycle to work in office towers.

Ada Louise Huxtable, reporting for *The Wall Street Journal* in a January 2003 story about architectural plans for the World Trade Center site wrote,

> An expert on the subject, the architect David Childs of Skidmore Owings and Merrill, is quoted as saying that above 65 or 70 stories a building is increasingly expensive and inefficient and must be heavily subsidized. It becomes an act of vanity, or greed, or both. When that gives us a Woolworth or Chrysler Building, we can be nonjudgmentally grateful. But should those subsidies go into the emotional rush of flinging something defiantly into the sky, or should they go to the parks and housing and cultural institutions that will make downtown a viable and desirable community?...The skyscraper is not dead: these marvels of our time will be built as long as egos, demand, art and greed, and the sheer, vertical exhilaration of the city exist.

Watch for buildings projected to be completed in 2010—such as the London Bridge Tower in London, England, projected to be the tallest building in Europe at 1,016 feet high and which will include office, hotel, and conference space. And in Vancouver, Canada, site of the 2010 Winter Olympic Games, the Vancouver International Airport expansion creates new workspace, travel space, and incentives for tourism. Countries, Olympic venues, and World Cup Soccer/Football challenges all focus on creating a community culture for the event so that athletes, teams, coaches, and spectators all are and feel safe, have a sense of wonder, and experience entertainment and fun while eating good food. The built space for these events is just as much a part of the event experience as is the sporting events themselves.

Speaking of tourism, lessons in community building also come from the meetings event industry. Meeting planners work with clients to develop themes that create a learning and living community for the period of a few days up to ten days. Themes, room décor, educational sessions tied to the theme or the location of the event, all of these elements work together to create a temporary community of thought and interaction that can lead to new ideas, new collaborations, and new business opportunities. Convention centers around the world have taken note. From the 1980s and on, convention centers have worked to create a sense of place and uniqueness in their buildings while maintaining total functionality of meeting and convention, education and exhibit spaces. The mountain backdrop of Salt Lake City is complimented by the Salt Palace in Salt Lake City, Utah. The Hawaii Convention Center nestles sleekly into the landscape of Honolulu. And the Navy Pier built in 1914–1916 is now a convention space in Chicago, Illinois, which incorporates pier, navy, city, and U.S. history with amazing exhibits including the Smith Museum of Stained Glass which opened in 2000 and displays Tiffany glass and illustrates glass making in the United States.

The human responsive design discussion began with building design; it can expand to include pursuits such as those being made by car manufacturers who now design cars with pregnant women in mind and companies who produce building products from recycled materials such as plastics, wood, and tires. HRD also includes making observations about how well our buildings are serving us—the people who work in them. Consider too that when a building becomes too big, it becomes impersonal and human behavior can become inhuman. Witness the changes in high school students' behavior as the buildings got bigger and graduating class sizes went from a few dozen to several hundred more than a thousand. What happened? More cliques, more school shootings, and more dropouts.

Applying human responsive design and the six productivity variables leads to different results. Expanding the HRD approach from within the boundaries of one company to include the building of community between companies working in the same office complex or tower is important too. Many of the same building and community-creation ideas shared in this book can be used when working as a building owner with multiple tenants or as a company with co-tenants in your building. A sense of community among companies and organizations sharing the same physical space can again enhance community, creativity, and productivity for all employees in the building. The enlarged experience of community can help everyone be safe in times when safety and security are needed.

The Fragility of Community

The fragility of our communities demands we pay more attention to the building of community in buildings. Take for instance this firsthand account of September 11, 2001, in New York City from a man named Kevin, then in his late twenties, working and living in New York. (Note, very little editing has been done on this story, so that the September 12, 2001, journaled rawness of the September 11th experience of communities lost and community extended via technology is maintained.)

September 11, 2001

It was a beautiful Tuesday morning. I woke up early in Battery Park City. At 8:00 a.m., I went to World Financial Center in Battery Park City. Today was the day of the Primary in New York and I got up early to vote. I fidgeted in line as the volunteers took too way long to let me vote. I finally voted and then rushed past the World Trade Center Towers (WTC) around 8:20 a.m. and got to the Multex office about 200 yards past the towers at 100 William Street. Around 8:50 a.m. a co-worker and I were finishing up a great meeting. We were concerned with our trip the next week to London. Everything I was doing seemed so important. I was efficient and had started early and now before 9 a.m. we had had already accomplished a lot. We had meetings scheduled all day. At the end of the meeting, my co-worker says to me, "it looks like it is snowing, there are a ton of papers flying around the street." Looks like a ticker tape parade. What the heck? Someone runs in the office and says a plane has crashed into the World Trade Center. Someone checks CNN.com and there is a picture of the hole in the WTC. From the window, we can't see the World Trade Center towers. Wow, another New York spectacle. This should be an interesting morning. A bit of a distraction for a nice day. I plan to go outside and show up a few minutes late for a meeting with the Fidelity reps at 9 a.m.. We are changing our 401K provider and things are looking good today. So my plan is to go outside and report to my Mom that I saw this interesting thing today. I expect a minor crash with a bit of a problem. We get down to the plaza in front of 59 Maiden Lane. I look up at Tower One. "Holy s...., that thing is really on fire." I am about 200 yards (maybe more maybe less) from the Tower. It is about three city blocks. "How are they going to put it out?" the crowd debates. It is a well-dressed, well-informed, Blackberry-ed, cell-phoned crowd of very self-important, smart people, and we all have recommendations and analyses about how the fire department should best put out this fire. Sirens are blaring but the level of tension is not too high.

Oh my god. A guy just fell out of the window. Wow another five, ten people seem to be jumping out. This is about the most interesting thing that New Yorkers have seen but the crowd still watches. People are falling out left and right of the building. We are getting scared as this thing is becoming too real. You know what, it is bordering on almost too scary but it is still something that the crowd all waits to see. We all declare that this is something that you will never forget. Things are sad but New York is sure it will be able to cope.

9.03 a.m. BOOOOOOOOOOOOOOOOOOOOOOOOM. I distinctly remember the moment when the event went from spectacle to sheer terror. The sky lights up with a beautiful orange cloud that turns dark. The sound reverberates between the buildings and New York begins to run. The morning coffee diversion is definitely over. We scatter in the plaza. I am with five friends. "Stay together," I yell. "Stay together." I grab someone's arm. I hug my friend whose apartment we are heading towards. "Let's get away from these buildings. We need to get away from the Federal Reserve Bank" (across the street). We head down Dey Street a small street next to William. Looking back over our shoulder. Walking and running. Walking and running. What the hell was that? A bomb? People are trying cell phones which are not working. Head out to Water Street. Traffic is out of hand. People are pissed.

Someone flew a plane into the f—ing World Trade Center. Was it an accident? Definitely a terrorist, a goddamm terrorist? Get out away from the buildings. Cross over Water Street. Get out to a pier on South Street Seaport. Hot day to be wearing a suit. We have gotten pretty far way. Can't see the WTC. I am unable to use my cell phone for phone calls. I can send e-mail. I write my mom and dad, "world trade center bombed i am ok" Tons of smoke over the city. We are wandering around the pier. I just want to sit down. This has already been a tough morning. (President) George Bush is on TV in a bar. Two planes have crashed into the World Trade Center. He gives his condolences to the victims and their families. Yikes, there are victims and this is the first time I have heard them talked about directly. We wait. One of the guys who was with us when we went to the Seaport is not dealing well. He is angry, "This is BS," he says, "I am heading back to the office at 100 William. This is BS, I am going home." He goes back into the city towards the office. I pray he is ok but I don't know his name. We begin to walk up the East River. Five Wall Street guys are now walking under the FDR Drive through the Fulton Fish Market. It is an incredible visual clash of the classes. The fish workers are staring at guys in suits coming through their market. Tons of traffic. I wonder if the fish workers think we are a bit crazy.

I now have a good view of the towers and I get above the Fulton Street Fish Market. Both towers are still standing fiery and burning. People are jumping out of the building left and right. Both towers. God damn this is horrible. People still jump to their death. No idea how this is all going to stop. My group of four guys is walking up the East River but I get a bit dazed and fall behind watching the towers of death. Is this really happening, holy smokes. How can we walk away? Isn't there something we should be doing. Helpless. We head into the projects of the Lower East Side. Neighborhoods that we would never go into on a normal day. The residents are very sympathetic. People are gathered around car radios playing them loudly. 1010 WINS says we have other attacks with other planes. Too much stuff to keep track of. This is getting too complicated. I am getting e-mails from friends. Are you ok? Please respond, we are praying for you. On my phone, I tap the messages "OK." "Safe." And get back "thank god you are alive." I get to a corner and look back. The front of the first tower falls off. I begin to weep. It looked like a sandcastle coming down. I walk arm in arm with my friends to the North. We are crushed. We turn a corner. We are met by phalanx of police officers, some in riot gear and who are preparing to head into the WTC. They look scared. The tough police officers that you know look frightened. "Good luck fellas" Their reply: "Thanks we will need it." Someone tells us that the other building has fallen. We did not see that one fall. We need to get north to the West Village, north and away from the smoke. More e-mails pour in, are you still alive? "OK" "Safe" are my responses. People I grew up with, more people than I can imagine. Friends, family. It is even more emotional. They are all praying for us. If only they knew how much those messages meant. Tears stream down my face. My friends are crying, "Please tell us that you are ok." On this day, God said I would be ok. We are hot. Our suits have been folded up into backpacks. Ties are off. I need some water. We have been walking for a while. We walk by NYU Stern. It is weird. As I walk through the city, I feel as if I have never been there before. I am in a daze. We take out cash from the ATMs. By noon or 1pm, we get to 135 Charles Street in the West Village. Looking down Greenwich Avenue the WTC towers are gone in a midst of smoke. We sit in my friend's apartment, watch TV and eat fruit. In shock, I wonder when I will ever get home to my apartment in Battery Park City and I thank God that the wind is blowing the other way. I think of the people who have been killed and hope to God no one I know is dead.

Community is fragile. Community thrives on human connections—whether they are face-to-face or via technology. In a way, this is confirmed by the phrase, "Relationships are measured in years rather than dollars" as premised by a Bremer Bank advertisement. The building of community over a period of time is the human part of HRD^2—relationships, human needs, and interactions being met with human provisions for health, safety, comfort and control, community time, rewards for work done and contributions made, and for creative and productive workdays.

CONCLUSION

Christine King, President and CEO of AMI Semiconductor, Inc., says that their key "to pioneering technology and to an entrepreneurial and innovative spirit is defining what you are good at, having a winning plan, getting the skills needed to implement the plan, having a will to win, and following through to get things done." Applied to the discussion of *Building Community in Buildings*, this means that the key to sound human responsive design and human resources development is defining what your company wants to accomplish with its building and for people; creating a plan of action that achieves your goals; building a building that allows you to implement your plan; putting your money, resources, and will into building the right building; and actually building community in buildings because both the built space and human community speaks to all six productivity variables and moves the company toward high productivity, creativity, and morale.

This book is a call for expanded conversation and work teams so that built projects reflect and incorporate meeting the productivity needs of human beings. Ken and Jana invite you to incorporate human responsive design and human resources development into the building of community in your workplace and offer these ideas for getting started today!

Top 10 Ideas for Building Community in Buildings That Have Human Responsive Design

1. Make a commitment to increase the productivity and creativity in your organization through implementation of human responsive design strategies.
2. Involve a broad cross section of building stakeholders and design professionals at the beginning.

3. Seek to understand. Previous to making change or designing new space, survey the entire workforce and incorporate responses to each of the six productivity variables as found in the HRD^2 Survey into your discussions on building change.

4. Use the input gathered as discussion points when designing your human responsive building. Ask yourselves what variables or ideas hold the most value for creating productive community in your organization. Ask why these variables will show value. Ask how they can best be implemented throughout the environment and organization.

5. Think green or sustainable—in the building's design, materials selection, construction, and in the live-planted areas in and outside of the building. Ask yourselves what ideas and expressions in building will create the most value for the surrounding community.

6. To maintain productive workspace, maintain the building. For instance, keep HVAC and control systems functioning to design standards.

7. Maintain people processes and people interaction space that encourage human community.

8. Measure worker productivity yearly.

9. Institute an annual process for occupants to evaluate their workspace. Use the HRD^2 Survey.

10. Drawing from the words of others, Ken and Jana again urge you forward in your conversations about community and productivity. Human responsive design effectively mirrors what author Wallace Stegner writes: "Create a society that matches the scenery." Finally, HRD is really only successfully driven and accomplished when remembering architect I.M. Pei's words: "It is not an individual act, architecture. You have to consider your client. Only out of that can you produce great architecture."

Notes

CHAPTER 1

1. Carnegie Mellon's BIDS, Building Investment Decision Support, is a case-based decision-making tool that calculates the economic value added of investing in high performance building systems based on the findings of building owners and researchers around the world. The framework of multiple life-cycle variables to cost justify key design innovations within a rich data base of international case studies, and the EVA/NPV calculator that incorporates a range of financial assumptions linked to international organizations, is fully patented by U.S. and Pennsylvania law as well as legally adopted by all Advanced Building Systems Integration Consortium members.

2. The National Building Museum, http://www.nbm.org.

3. Linda Brody Lyons, *Building a Landmark: A Guide to the Historic Home of the National Building Museum* (Washington, DC: the National Building Museum, 1999), 17.

4. CSHQA Architects/Engineers/Planners, Boise, Idaho, and Isthmus Architecture, Inc., Madison, Wisconsin, *The Idaho State Capitol Master Plan* (Boise: Idaho Division of Public Works, July 19, 2000).

5. U.S. Department of Health and Human Services, National Institutes of Health, http://www.nih.gov/.

6. U.S. Government Energy Information Administration, http://www.eia.doe.gov/cneaf/electricity/epa/epat7p4.html.

7. International Energy Outlook 2005, Report No. DOE/EIA-0484(2005) (July 2005), http://www.eia.doe.gov/oiaf/ieo/pdf/ieoreftab_9.pdf.

8. Worldwatch Institute, *State of the World Trends and Facts, Making Better Energy Choices*, http://www.worldwatch.org/features/consumption/sow/trendsfacts/2004/07/07/.

9. The emission data was taken from the U.S. Energy Information Administration web site http://www.eia.doe.gov/cneaf/electricity/epa/epat5p1.html. The ways that buildings contribute to occupant health is explored more fully in Chapter 2. It is important to note here that buildings have an impact on both our indoor and outdoor air quality.

10. R.H. Blackwell, "Development and Use of a Quantitative Method for Specification of Interior Illumination Levels on the Basis of Performance Data," *Journal of the Illuminating Engineering Society* 54 (June 1959): 317.

11. Judith Heerwagen and Gordon Orians, "Adaptations to Windowless: A Study of the Use of Visual Décor in Windowed and Windowless Offices," *Environment and Behavior* 18, no. 5 (1986): 623-38.

12. Heschong Mahone Group, *Daylighting in Schools: An Investigation into the Relationship Between Daylighting and Human Performance—Condensed Report* (San Francisco, CA: California Board for Energy Efficiency Third Party Program, August 1999), 2.

CHAPTER 2

1. For current information, access the USGBC web site at http://www.usgbc.org/.

2. U.S. Department of Energy, *Buildings Energy Data Book* (Washington, DC: August 2005), Table 3.4.1.

3. Edward O. Wilson, *Biophilia: The Human Bond with Other Species* (Cambridge: Harvard University Press, 1984).

4. Paul Hawkins, *The Next Economy* (New York: Holt, Rinehart and Winston, 1983), 17.

5. U.S. Department of Energy web site, http://www.eia.doe.gov/emeu/aer/eh/frame.html.

6. U.S. DOE, *Buildings Energy Data Book,* Table 1.3.9.

7. Alvin Toffler, *The Third Wave,* (New York: Bantam Books, 1991).

8. Hawkins, *The Next Economy,* 17.

9. Beverly E. Thomas and John P. Baron, *Evaluating Knowledge Worker Productivity: Literature Review* (Champaign, IL: U.S. Army Construction Engineering Research Lab Interim Report No. FF-94/27, 1994).

10. Sandy Smith, "Office Workers Blast Indoor Air Quality Conditions," *Occupational Hazards* (March 16, 2005), http://occupationalhazards.com/articles/13108.

11. Good information on productivity can be found by subscribing to the Carnegie Mellon University Center for Building Performance and Diagnostics BIDS tool at http://cbpd.arc.cmu.edu/bids/.

12. R.J. de Dear and G.S. Brager, "Developing an Adaptive Model of Thermal Comfort and Preference," *ASHRAE Transactions* 104, no. 1 (American Society of Heating, Refrigerating and Air-Conditioning Engineers, 1998): 27-49.

13. The Center for Building Performance and Diagnostics, Carnegie Mellon University, Pittsburgh, PA.

14. Richard Hyde, *Climate Responsive Design* (London: E&FN Spon, 2000).

15. See Gail Lindsey, Joel Ann Todd, and Sheila Hayter, *A Handbook for Planning and Conducting Charrettes for High-Performance Projects* (Golden, CO: National Renewable Energy Laboratory, August 2003) for more on this design tool. The term charrette comes from France and, by one definition, refers to a collaborative and creative effort by a design team.

16. Sarah Susanka, *Creating the Not So Big House* (Newtown, CT: Taunton Press, 2000).

17. Heschnog Mahone Group, *Daylighting in Schools. An Investigation into the Relationship Between Daylighting and Human Performance* (San Francisco, CA: Pacific Gas and Electric, 1999).

18. Heschong Mahone Group, *Windows and Offices. A Study of Office Worker Performance and the Indoor Environment* (Sacramento, CA: California Energy Commission Technical Report No. P500-03-082-A-9, October 2003).

19. R.H. Blackwell, "Development and Use of a Quantitative Method for Specification of Interior Illumination Levels on the Basis of Performance Data," *Journal of the Illuminating Engineering Society* 54 (June 1959): 317.

20. G.Z. Brown, Jeff Kline, Gina Livingston, Dale Northcutt, and Emily Wright, *Natural Ventilation in Northwest Buildings,* prepared for the Northwest Energy Efficiency Alliance and Seattle City Light (Eugene: University of Oregon, 2004).

21. Better Bricks Case Study, *Hood River County Library* (Portland, OR: Northwest Energy Efficiency Alliance, 2002).

22. Nathan Good, "Learning from a Library," *Environmental Design and Construction* (October 2001).

23. See more photos on architect Tom Bender's web site, http://www.tombender.org/BOA.pdf.

CHAPTER 3

1. Reid Ewing, Tom Schmid, Richard Killingsworth, Amy Zlot, and Stephen Raudenbush, "Relationship Between Sprawl and Physical Activity, Obesity and Morbidity," the Science of Health Promotion, *American Journal of Health* (September 2003).

CHAPTER 5

1. *Encarta World English Dictionary* (Microsoft Corporation, 1999). Developed for Microsoft by Bloomsbury Publishing Plc.

2. For more reading on stress reduction through mindfulness practice refer to Jon Kabat-Zin, *Wherever You Go There You Are* (New York: Hyperion, 1994).

3. http://www.webterrace.com/fengshui/history.htm.

4. Tom Bender, *Song Silence and Shadows* (Manzanita, OR: Fire River Press, 2000).

5. For current U.S. Green Building Council conference information go to http://www.usgbc.org/

6. The word *elegance* as used here to describe integrated design is borrowed from Mark Frankel, New Buildings Institute, White Salmon, Washington; formerly with Paladino & Company, Inc.

7. Information on integrated design can be found in literature and on the internet. A good place to begin is at the Northwest Energy Efficiency Alliance's Better Bricks web site, http://www.betterbricks.com/.

8. A good source of information on the Anasazi or Ancient Pueblo People is the web site http://www.crystalinks.com/anasazi.html.

9. *Northwest Public Health* 22, no. 1 (Spring/Summer 2005).

10. Daniel Winterbottom, "The Healing Nature of Landscapes," *Northwest Public Health* 22, no. 1 (Spring/Summer 2005): 18.

11. Louis Henri Sullivan was born in Boston on September 3, 1856, in Boston, Massachusetts, and became a major force in American architecture.

12. You can find out more about LEED at the U.S. Green Building Council's web site, http://www.usgbc.org/DisplayPage.aspx?CategoryID=19.

CHAPTER 6

1. Productivity variables for buildings have been identified and discussed by several building researchers. Perhaps most notably by Adrian Leaman and Bill Bordass of the Usable Building Trust, U.K.

2. R.J. de Dear and G.S. Brager, "Thermal Comfort in Naturally Ventilated Buildings: Revisions to ASHRAE Standard 55," *Energy and Buildings* 34, no. 6 (2002): 549-61.

3. Unless otherwise noted, this database and others in this chapter were provided by the U.S. Department of Energy Building Technology Program in High Performance Buildings. The work was prepared for the U.S. Department of Energy, Office of Energy Efficiency and Renewable Energy by BuildingGreen, Inc., and its subcontractors under subcontract no. AAX-1-31423-01 from the National Renewable Energy Laboratory (NREL) Division of the Midwest Research Institute, available at http://www.buildinggreen.com.

4. Whether or not people perceive that outside air is fresher than air inside of a building, it generally is because of the dilution factor, i.e., the outside container that encapsulates air is infinitely larger than the air volume of the building.

5. Herman Miller Company, "Everybody Deserves a Good Chair" (2002): 4, http://www.hermanmiller.com/hm/content/research_summaries/wp_Deserves_a_Good_Chair.pdf.

6. U.S. Army Corps of Engineers, *Design Guide for Interiors,* publication no. DG 110-3-122 (September 1997).

7. U.S. DOE Building Technology Program (see chap. 6, n. 3).

8. William McDonough and Michael Braungart, *Cradle to Cradle, Remaking the Way We Make Things* (New York: North Point Press, 2002). The book strongly makes the case for changing our manufacturing processes to develop products that continue to nourish the environment after their useful lives.

9. Judith Heerwagen and Leah Zagreus, *The Human Factors of Sustainable Building Design: Post Occupancy Evaluation of the Merrill Environmental Center, Annapolis, MD* (U.S. Department of Energy Building Technology Program, April 2005).

10. Judith Heerwagen holds a PhD in psychology from the University of Washington. Her research and writing have focused on workplace ecology, the psycho-social value of space, and the human factors of sustainable design. She has been a staff scientist at the Pacific Northwest National Laboratory since 1994, with a year off in 1999 when she worked as a principal and co-director of research for Space, LLC, a planning and design firm. She currently has her own consulting and research business in Seattle.

11. Heerwagen and Zagreus, *The Human Factors of Sustainable Building Design: Post Occupancy Evaluation of the Merrill Environmental Center, Annapolis, MD,* 13.

Index

About the Authors

JANA M. KEMP, founder and owner of Meeting & Management Essentials, is a management trainer, facilitator, and speaker, specializing in improving individual and organizational productivity and performance and working with clients in the private, public, and nonprofit sectors. In 2004 she was elected to the Idaho House of Representatives. Recipient of several small business ownership awards, and a regular commentator in newspapers, radio, and television, she is the author of *Moving Meetings* and *No! How One Simple Word Can Transform Your Life.*

KEN BAKER is owner of K energy Consulting, a Boise-based research and consulting company that works with communities, building owners, and building design teams to develop environmentally sustainable and human responsive buildings. In 1982 he opened a residential design and construction business, Integrated Living Designs, specializing in energy and environmentally efficient housing design, and from 1985 to 2000 he worked for the State of Idaho Energy Division as a building energy specialist.